PALESTINE: PROFILE OF AN OCCUPATION

PALESTINE: PROFILE OF AN OCCUPATION

• CONTRIBUTORS •

Adel Samara   Toby Shelley   Ben Cashdan
Richard Thomas   Ehud-'Ein-Gil
Haim Bresheeth   Rosemary Sayigh
Laila Al-Hamdani

KHAMSIN

Zed Books Ltd.
London and New Jersey

2001983

Palestine: Profile of an Occupation was first published by
Zed Books Ltd., 57 Caledonian Road, London N1
9BU, UK and 171 First Avenue, Atlantic Highlands,
New Jersey 07716, USA, in 1989

Copyright © Khamsin 1989

Typeset by Boldface, 17a Clerkenwell Road,
London EC1M 5RD
Cover design Adrian Yeeles (Artworkers)
Cover photograph Chris M. Lane
Printed and bound in the United Kingdom at Bookcraft
(Bath) Ltd. Midsomer Norton

British Library Cataloguing in Publication Data

Palestine: profile of an occupation – (Khamsin)
1. Israel. Palestinian Arabs. Social conditions
I. Title II. Series
305.8'9275694

ISBN 0-86232-888-8
ISBN 0-86232-889-6 Pbk

Library of Congress Cataloging-in-Publication Data

Palestine: profile of an occupation.
       p.   cm. — (Khamsin)
    ISBN 0-86232-888-8. — ISBN 0-86232-889-6 (pbk.)
    1. Palestinian Arabs—Israel.   2. Palestinian Arabs—
West Bank. 3. Israel—Ethnic relations. 4. Jewish-Arab
relations—1973-
    I. Series: Khamsin (London, England)
DS113.7.P33   1989
956.94'0049274—dc20   89-35868
                                               CIP

CONTENTS

Introduction

This book goes to print around the time when the *Intifada* celebrates a year of its momentum. The *Intifada* – the Palestinian popular uprising in the Occupied Territories of the West Bank and Gaza Strip, has engaged the whole population – women and men, adults and children, rural and urban people, the more well-to-do and the poor, those who have to continue to work in Israel and those who are developing an alternative Palestinian economy in the territories. Israel has responded to the *Intifada* ineffectively, but with increasingly oppressive measures: random killings, limb breaking, beatings, detentions without trials, round-ups and deportations.

The Israeli-Palestinian conflict, and probably the Middle East as a whole, are at what we consider to be a historical watershed. The *Intifada* and the Israeli reaction to it have started to transform the situation in the Middle East. A Palestinian state was declared by the Palestine National Council in Algeria in November 1988 in order to consolidate the national achievements of the *Intifada*, and there has been a growing sense of international urgency about the Palestinian situation. In Israel itself, the internal contradictions between growing fascism on the Right, both secular and religious, including an emphasis on plans for the mass transfer of Palestinians from the Occupied Territories on the one hand, and the growing resistance and dissociation of the Left from the reality of Zionism on the other hand, have started to intensify Israel's internal crisis of legitimation and national coherence.

The endurance, ingenuity and national unity of the *Intifada*, and the callousness, open brutality and ineffectiveness of the Israeli reaction have astounded many outside observers. What is important to emphasize is that the *Intifada* did not break out in a vacuum, but has emerged in the very specific economic, political and cultural historical context of twenty years of occupation. Nor are the modes of organization and behaviour used by both sides during the *Intifada* new; rather they are an intensification of what has been there all along.

This book, then, is NOT about the *Intifada*. We shall dedicate the next book in the *Khamsin* series to its analysis. In this book we present a series of articles which analyse various aspects of the CONTEXT in which the *Intifada* has developed.

The first article is by 'Adel Samara, on the political economy of the West Bank 1967-1987. The paper, based on a chapter from Samara's PhD and book of the same name (published by *Khamsin*), discusses the general features of the political economy of the West Bank and the ways in which the Israeli occupation has destroyed and transformed it. It has confiscated lands and recruited its workforce as cheap migrant labour in Israel, while tempting into collaboration some parts of the local bourgeoisie. The project is one of economic dislocation with an ultimate political aim: to destroy the Palestinians as a viable national entity.

The second article by Toby Shelley discusses a particular feature of the West Bank political economy–Palestinian migrant workers in Israel. The article describes the conditions and the types of work carried out by Palestinian migrant workers and the ways they have been affected by the general political and economic climate. The article points out that among many employers, the Histadrut is a large exploiter of Palestinian labour, demonstrating that Zionist Labour relies heavily on the Palestinian workforce. Bantustan-like conditions have created a situation where class and national demands reinforce each other, enhancing the Palestinian migrant workers' sense of group identity.

The next article, by Ben Cashdan, investigates the ways in which the law has been used by the Israeli state to create an ideological legitimation of land expropriation and a demise of Palestinian civil liberties. Cashdan shows how traditional ideologies and 'security' arguments justify a legal system which excludes Palestinian interests from the domain of 'public interests' and criminalizes their resistance to the occupation.

The following article by Richard Thomas illuminates some of the issues discussed in a more general way in Cashdan's article. Thomas concentrates on the settler politics in the Old City of Jerusalem. His article shows how government and settler policies collude in the city, as well as some of the constraints, especially the demographic one, within which such policies operate.

Ehud Ein-Gil's article discusses new programmes for the solution of the Palestinian-Israeli conflict that have recently been proposed by some maverick Zionists. These programmes, based on the principle of federalism, are shown to be heavily weighted against the Palestinians. Nevertheless, Ein-Gil points out that the federalist idea itself can also be used by socialists to propose a form of state in which Israelis and Palestinians, as well as other Arab peoples, can live together on equal terms.

Haim Bresheeth analyses wider and more basic perceptions of the relationship between Israelis and Palestinians. By looking at Zionist Hebrew literature, especially the recent work of left-Zionist authors, he points out the deep roots of Zionist racism and neo-colonial attitudes towards the Palestinians. He examines the central role played by myths in the constitution of the Zionist Self–the ideological backbone of the Israeli state.

The last two articles in this collection relate to the specific roles and organizing of Palestinian women. The first article, by Rosemary Sayigh (published in French in *Peuples Mediteraneens*, 1988), gives an overview of Palestinian women since 1948 and contextualizes the *Intifada*. Sayigh reminds us that no full understanding of the Palestinians in the Occupied Territories is possible without examining the general historical and social processes which have influenced the Palestinian people in its entirety, including the Palestinian Diaspora. Of particular importance in this respect are the refugee camps, from which the first impetus of the Palestinian national resistance movement emerged.

The last article, an interview with Laila al-Hamdani, concentrates on the specific role of Palestinian women in the Occupied Territories, describing the *Intifada* itself and the central role women have been playing in it. Thus it brings us to the stage to which we shall return in our next *Khamsin* book, to be wholly dedicated to the *Intifada*.

Adel Samara

THE POLITICAL ECONOMY OF THE WEST BANK 1967-1987
from peripheralization to development

THE ECONOMIC RELATIONS between countries are relations of exchange, rather than of production. The exchange relations between Israel and the West Bank are not standard 'centre-periphery' relations despite the fact that both are integrated into the world order. Since 1967, when the Israeli authorities assumed political control, the West Bank has been peripheralized to a settler-colonial capitalist economy. Israel has not annexed the West Bank politically but adopted another alternative – the uprooting and destruction of the West Bank's economic production structure, characterised by the expropriation of land and the expulsion of large numbers of indigenous inhabitants.

The unique relations between Israeli settler colonialism and the West Bank cannot be described as internal colonialism despite features common to both. Neither does it fit with Wolpe's model of internal colonialism in South Africa[1] which describes the articulation between modes of production as an extension of the capitalist mode of production at the expense of non-capitalist modes of production. The 'articulation approach' asserts that peripheral social formations are constituted by the articulated combination of the dominant capitalist mode of production and subordinate, non-capitalist modes of production.

But the relation between the Israeli economy and the West Bank is a relation between two separate economies, between a developed capitalist

mode of production dominant in one and a controlled peripheral capitalist mode in the other. In this case, the relation is an external and settler
colonial one.

The social formation of the West Bank has been a peripheral capitalist
one since the Jordanian era when the capitalist transformation was
implanted. The arbitrary peripheralization of the West Bank economy to
Jordan's and the orientation of its production towards export, which
drained it of its surplus and hindered internal accumulation, has stunted
the home market and, in the end, blocked its economic development.

Wolpe conceives of articulation as an expression of the coexistence or
combination of two modes of production (an expanded dominant mode
and a restricted subordinate mode. The 'expanded mode' comprises
relations of production, forces of production and a general law of motion,
whereas the 'restricted mode' comprises relations of production and
forces of production only. Wolpe maintains that within articulation literature in general the reference is to the 'expanded' capitalist mode of production only. This mode is characterised as being dynamic and capable of
reproducing itself on an expanded scale. For the 'restricted mode' to be
capable of reproducing itself, Wolpe argues that, 'concepts like "circula-
tion" or the "state" have to be introduced. Without these concepts the
restricted cannot be changed to be expanded.'[2]

Wolpe conceptualizes the peasantry as 'individual and isolated enterprises'. These individual and isolated enterprises are passive and resis-
tant to any capitalist transition. Any capitalist transition must be imposed
from outside. This imposition is the only way to break the peasantry's
passiveness and resistance. Cardoso notes that:

'Contemporary "dependent capitalist development" in certain Latin
American countries, notably Argentina, Brazil and Mexico, produces an
'internal structural fragmentation' in which the "advanced" sectors are
internalized and hence integrated with the new forms of monopolistic
expansion of capitalist world economy. Other, more "backward" sectors
producing essential urban wage-goods, such as urban petty commodity
production but especially staple agricultural products, are character-
ized as "internal colonies", in their relations with the internationalized
sectors. Thus a "new structural dualling" is the counterpart of the structural dynamism of "associated-dependent-development"; it results
directly . . . from capitalist expansion and is functional to that expansion,
insofar as it helps to keep wages at a low level and diminishes political
pressure inside the "modern sector".'[3]

In the case of the West Bank, the advanced sector is 'agricultural' and is not freely integrated with the capitalist world economy. It is controlled by the Israeli economy which directs the West Bank's externally oriented production to fit Israeli needs and contracts with the world market, and has adapted it to provide Israel with comparative advantages in terms of exchange with the world market.[4] Thus the West Bank's externally and internally oriented sectors are colonized by the external Israeli economy. What should be noted here is that the Israeli settler capitalist mode of production works in two integrated phases in respect of the West Bank:

Firstly: It is extended at the cost of the peripheral capitalist mode of production and other non-capitalist modes in the West Bank through a process which could be described as a peripheralization through incorporation. In its early years, the capitalist mode of production of Israeli settler colonialism, enforced by the Israeli military governorate, incorporated the West Bank economy so as to disarticulate its sectors internally. With this policy, the occupation precluded the possibility of independent capitalist development. This was carried out alongside land expropriation which precluded even limited 'fair' agricultural and industrial competition. As Kahan notes: 'In both the regions no support was provided for capital investment directed to the processing of produce in competition with products of Israel (e.g. dairy processing).'[5]

Secondly: The Israeli settler capitalist mode of production entered a new phase in 1976, one which continues to date: uprooting the productive factors in the West Bank economy–for example larger scale expropriation of land, competing with local industries, arbitrarily increasing taxes and forcing the inhabitants abroad. Briefly, the second phase is peripheralization without articulation or further incorporation of the West Bank's productive economic sectors but rather the beginning of their total destruction as an independent economy. In parallel with the continued weakening of the West Bank's productive sectors, the produce of Israel's big companies has flooded into the West Bank's market. Foodstuff and textile companies involved include Tnuva, Osem, Ketan, Ladizia and others.[6]

The deliberate Israeli policy of making the West Bank economy dependent is paralleled by another Israeli policy which keeps Israel independent of the West Bank for any vital produce. Any form of dependence would represent a security risk for Israel and it is considered preferable to ensure continuous supply from Israeli sources, even at the cost of possible seasonal excess supply. This was one of the reasons given for subsidies and minimum prices granted to farmers in Israel.[7]

In both cases, the role of Israeli military force is still the main tool of the two phases of the peripheralization (through military orders for example, which cover all aspects of life). It is not the only tool in the process. Besides the military power of the Israeli authorities, there is unequal exchange imposed through Israeli merchants and capitalists on the one hand, and West Bank merchants on the other. It is the latter mechanism which is discussed in detail here.

Early class collaboration in the West Bank

ISRAELI ECONOMIC ANNEXATION of the West Bank started in the early days of the occupation. The West Bank was denoted a military area at the advent of the occupation in June 1967 and since then Israel has issued well over 2000 military orders and regulations, governing all aspects of life. In particular, the military governorate has promulgated various economic regulations such as the imposition of Israeli currency (military order no 27) and the banning of exports and imports except through Israel (military order no 24). This latter ban, however, is not strictly applied to all produce. Those goods which might compete with Israeli produce are often exempted. Such produce may still be exported across the 'open bridges' into Jordan.

During the first year of the occupation, Israel paved the way to peripheralization of the West Bank; this is clear from the military orders, strategic plans and resulting developments. Following the application of military rule to the West Bank, hundreds of thousands of inhabitants migrated to Jordan, either as emigrants or because of expulsion. This affected the productivity of the economy. Israel outlawed the West Bank's existing import-export relations (orders nos 10-12) during the first few months of the occupation. Since then, local merchants have started marketing Israeli goods or goods imported through Israel. Thus the merchants can be seen as the first social class to become linked to the Israeli economy. Some of these merchants have imported raw materials from Israel – wood, metal, cement – so as to supply the local factories. The result is the dependence of local manufacturers on Israel. Manufacturers, as a result, have become the second class to be linked with the Israeli economy.

Israel's economic structure is constantly changing in accordance with the needs of the world division of labour. These continual changes affect the economy of the West Bank as an occupied and peripheralized adjunct to the Israeli economy. In the mid 1960s, Israel started to transform its industries toward specialization in electronics and sophisticated armaments industries so as to accommodate the world division of labour which has pushed the developed countries towards technological specialization. This is why Israel has decreased emphasis on many of its traditional industries such as textiles, footwear and chemicals. The West Bank and Gaza Strip face a process of re-allocation of industries to their detriment. While Israel concentrates on industries with a future, the West Bank and Gaza Strip are left with branches of production at a lower technological level and with fewer prospects of growth, a situation which perpetuates the economic gap between them. Much of the re-allocation has taken the form of transfering textile production to the West Bank and Gaza Strip.

Despite the 150-200 thousand strong wave of emigration in the wake of the 1967 war and the mass expulsions which followed it (such as the ten thousand persons of the three villages of Immwas, Yalo and Beit Nuba in the Ramallah district which were destroyed in the week following the 1967 war), the unemployment rate actually increased. The reason for this was a sharp decline in the demand for labour in the West Bank.

The effects of the war paralysed various spheres of manufacturing and agriculture. Moreover, the public services sector which had been a major employer under Jordan was cut to the minimum by the Israeli occupation authorities. As a result, many Palestinian workers were faced with the choice of emigrating or of working in Israel. The first step in the latter case was work with Israeli contractors inside the West Bank itself as Israel started to enlarge roads there and appointed local foremen who, in turn, recruited local workers.

Ten thousand workers were hired daily for road construction whether paving new roads or widening and maintaining those which existed. This marked the beginning of the creation of the stratum of sub-contractor and mediator which stands between the Israeli entrepreneurs and capitalists on the one hand and the West Bank workforce on the other. Even before the large scale expropriation of land and the accelerated development of capitalist relations of production, Palestinian workers came primarily not from the cities and refugee camps but from rural areas.

The peasant family was compelled to increase its cash income by sending members to seek hired employment and, as a result, the West Bank consumers and producers (the whole society) began to depend on the Israeli economy. This was not, of course, a voluntary dependence, (except for the traders and compradors) since it was shaped and formed by the policies of the Israeli state. The political factor (the role of the state) worked relatively autonomously in the peripheralization of the West Bank. Nevertheless, the economic factor was and remains the determining one, crystalized in land expropriation, collecting taxes, employing cheap labour and accumulating profits through unequal exchange and the obstruction of the West Bank's internal accumulation process.

Alongside limitations on external trade, Israel has maintained the West Bank agricultural trade with Jordan. This policy can be described as an open offer for Jordan to participate in the peripheralization of the West Bank and be a partner in a political compromise in the Arab-Israeli conflict. However, the 'open bridges' policy has also created a channel for financial remittances from Palestinians abroad to their families in the West Bank and from the Palestinian-Jordanian Joint Committee and other Arab countries. Indeed, 'The percentage of the disposable income derived from external sources may have reached over 40%, and it is growing'.[8]

Local classes as mechanisms of peripheralization

ALTHOUGH THE POLICIES of peripheralization by integration were created by the occupation authorities, a significant portion of the peripheral bourgeoisie of the West Bank has acted as local bearers and agents of these policies. This portion consists of three main strata:

(1) The merchant bourgeoisie (city merchants) which has existed since the period of Jordanian rule and has intensively exploited local farmers.

(2) The large agricultural landowners who orient their production towards exchange with Israeli and foreign centres.

(3) The new comprador capitalists created directly and intentionally by the occupation authorities.

These three strata provide a good example of the structural dependence (economic, social, political and cultural) of peripheral capitalism.

Just as Israeli capitalists engage in relations of production with Jewish workers and agricultural wage earners in Israel, so the West Bank agricultural capitalists have a relationship with West Bank workers and poor peasants. The merchants in the two geographic areas are mediators. This is especially true of the West Bank merchants who are primarily importers from Israel. In this role, their interests have become totally dependent on Israeli-produced goods and the marketing of those goods in the West Bank. The mediating role of the merchants is not a new phenomenon developed during the period of occupation, nor is it purely economic.

The comprador capitalists, merchants and traders have existed since Jordanian rule over the West Bank. Some changes have taken place in terms of individuals but not in the role of the stratum. In addition to these old classes, the Israeli occupation has backed a new group of local collaborators who have acquired franchises to market the produce of Israeli companies in the West Bank. This new comprador class has made a quick profit mainly because it alone was granted the right to import to and export from the West Bank by the military government. In other words, these merchants have been created by the occupation. When it is considered that 90 per cent of the West Bank's imports come from and 50 per cent of its exports go to Israel, the importance of this class can be seen. Moreover, in 1984 the West Bank balance of trade showed a deficit of $220 million with the Israeli economy. This demonstrates the role of the merchants as a channel draining the surplus from the local economy into that of Israel, importing luxury goods and leading to the inability of the West Bank to maintain its surplus.

The contribution of such merchants to the local market is deformed. Whilst expropriating the majority of the surplus, Israel's colonialism leaves a certain amount of surplus value and surplus labour to its allied classes in the West Bank and this is distributed among the comprador-capitalist, financier, and land-owning strata. 'This distribution provides the basis for an internal demand, larger for luxury (department IIa) goods'.[9]

The larger demand for luxury goods does not enlarge popular demand but rather increases the demand for import goods to satisfy the desires of the self-same strata. Moreover, the strata in the West Bank which have allied themselves with Israeli colonialism have not maintained their share of the surplus inside the country. Much of this is exported to Arab and foreign banks as credits, invested there or consumed by luxury imports.

As a result of the expropriation of the West Bank surplus by Israeli colonialism and some local strata, West Bank agricultural producers are unable to accumulate or to enlarge the home market. All these producers can do is to reproduce themselves and their families on a limited scale.

The aforementioned alliance is inevitable continuing the analysis from the level of production to the level of relations of production existing between labourers and non-labourers.

Despite the national struggle of the Palestinian masses for liberation and self determination in their homeland, the comprador-capitalist, financier, and land-owning strata have allied themselves with settler colonialism, revealing their double role, as economic collaborators with colonialism and thus, as collaborators in the political sphere.

The following extract from an interview fully represents the political position of this strata: Ian Black, a journalist from *The Guardian* interviewed Abdul Rahman Abu Sninah who was appointed by the Israelis after they dismissed Haj Tawfiq Abu Al-Nasser, the elected mayor of Qalqiliah:

'How can I not be worried? A stone or a molotov cocktail thrown at an Israeli vehicle destroys the good relation between the Jews and us. We are very close to Israel and 80-90% of all our produce goes to the Jews. Now they do not come here to do their shopping any more'.

If Abu Sninah is trying to guarantee that West Bank produce is marketed inside Israel without taking into consideration the question of dependency, his position towards settlements is the same:

'We have no problems at all with "Alfe-Menashe" [the closest Israeli settlement to his town]. The people who bring trouble come from other settlements. There are extremists here too, maybe small children, maybe sent by PLO.'[10]

It is in the interests of the merchants, compradors, and big landowners to have a quiet political situation in the West Bank in order to maintain their profits. They have failed to concert their interests with those of Palestinian nationalism. Thus, Abu Sninah talks amicably about an Israeli settlement which is built up on his own town's land.

A merchant of Bethlehem attributes the market depression to the political situation. The store manager said:

'Politics is the reason. We had a demonstration here two weeks ago and there's been virtually nothing since. We haven't had a single customer all day'.[11]

What this strata wants is a quiet political situation, no political resistance to the occupation.

Peripheralization through the production process

The effects of peripheralization are not limited to the level of exchange but continue down to the level of production, from the external factor to the dialectic between the external and internal factors and social forces.

Under Jordanian rule, most West Bank peasants and farmers produced for the market. Their surplus production was exported to the East Bank and to several Arab countries, like Kuwait, Syria and Iraq.[12] Peasant production under Israeli settler colonialism has been drastically reoriented towards several markets, in the first place the Israeli but also the Jordanian and the East and West European markets. This rapid reorientation was achieved during the first phase of Israeli policies in the West Bank (peripheralization through integration).

It is not only the production of the large landowners which is oriented mainly towards foreign markets but also that of the small peasants. This is an assertion of the domination of capitalist relations of production over the peasantry. The orientation of the peasants' production towards external markets was achieved through (a) *al-Mushahada* policy: Israeli incentives and bonuses paid to farmers planting certain crops which Israel requires to satisfy its exports, (b) the low price of the peasant's traditional crops when compared to the *al-Mushahada* crops and (c) because the West Bank market is small and unprotected, Israeli-subsidised products succeed in competition with peasant produce.

As long as Israeli producers freely market their subsidised produce in the West Bank's open market, the local peasant farmer cannot compete. He has two alternatives, either to produce the crops demanded by Israel or be beaten by Israeli competition. In the second case, he abandons his small plot of land and becomes a wage earner inside the Green Line.[13]

Since the peasant's farm is no longer the major source of income, land ceases to be of value in itself. The farmer begins to rely on employment as a migrant worker and not on ownership of land to acquire material security. After several years of abandonment, in addition to the passive effects of the Israeli economic crisis which has resulted in the redundancy of thousands of the West Bankers working in Israel, the peasant/worker faces the problem of lack of liquidity to reclaim the land (if it has not been expropriated by the Israelis in the meantime).

Various forms of peripheralization
Rural surplus workforce

BESIDE THE ORIENTATION of the agricultural capitalists and the small (independent) peasants towards producing for the foreign markets, the surplus rural workforce has also been directed towards the Israeli and the Arab markets. The reason why this surplus workforce has become externally oriented is that the local cities are unable to provide extra employment.[14] Rather, this surplus West Bank workforce flows into the Israeli economy as a cheap labour force. The forms of exploitation of migrant (commuter) labour are complex and require analysis.

The employment of West Bank migrant workers takes several forms. Since these workers gain jobs in the Israeli economic sectors, they are exploited on the level of class relations of production despite the fact that the worker and the capitalist originate from different economic systems. Moreover, the worker is exploited as a Palestinian. It is this nationality which permits lower wages, lack of job protection and of social security. Tsur emphasizes this when he notes:

'The Israeli investor prefers the intensive cheap manual labour over the intensive capital and technology which contains the future of Israel.'[15]

On the contrary, Jewish workers are not employed in West Bank farms or enterprises and so are not exploited by West Bank capitalists in any sense.

The process of labour migration is facilitated by West Bank subcontractors. Such people form another West Bank mediator stratum, one which has developed on the margins of the migrant labour phenomenon. The role of this stratum is to recruit migrant labour to work in Israeli enterprises. These mediators deduct part of the migrant worker's wage for themselves. Their role is facilitated and protected by the occupation authorities.

Seventy per cent of migrant labour is rural in origin, and most of the 'illegal' workers are from rural areas close to the Green Line.[16]. The Israeli daily, *'Jerusalem Post'*, mentioned that: 'a checkpoint between Bethlehem and Jerusalem registered the number of workers passing the point was 7,780, of whom 2,000 were illegal, that is about 26 per cent.' Moreover, most of the women migrant workers inside the Green Line are illegal.[17] The peasant majority among migrant labourers is demonstrated by the fact that: 'A further 162,000 had been driven or locked out of their land during or following the Israeli occupation in 1967'.[18]

Another form of exploitation of West Bank workers is the employment of the workforce inside the West Bank itself, but in projects or workshops which are entirely devoted to satisfying Israeli needs, such as brickworks and quarries. The workers in these enterprises are mostly villagers. Although the places of work are in the West Bank and the local bosses are West Bankers, they are sub-contractors of an Israeli company. In other instances the entire operation is locally owned but production is entirely geared towards Israeli demand. In the first case the Israeli capitalist and the subcontractor divide the surplus produced by the workers. Here the Israeli capitalist is not a mere merchant but also a direct exploiter. An extreme example of this mixed case is that of some of the sewing work-shops that exist in most West Bank villages. The workshops operate as follows: the Israeli entrepreneur provides the cloth and the capital and distributes the cloth through and/or with a local sub-contractor to the village women. The Israeli capitalist pays the sub-contractor a sum as commission. This sum is a marginal amount of the surplus which goes directly to the Israeli capitalist. Such cases evidently represent direct class exploitation, particularly the exploitation of West Bank women as cheap labour whose production is sold in Europe.

The joint-ownership of companies between Israelis and a few West Bank capitalists provides another example of direct Israeli exploitation of both West Bank workers and economy.[19]

By far the most striking example is the employment of Palestinian villagers as wage earners in the settlements built on their expropriated land. Those who have thus lost their only plot of land, transfer totally to wage labour while those who still own land become peasant-workers.[20] These workers and peasant-workers labour inside their country but in purely Jewish-owned projects and communities. These projects are not Israeli projects in the Palestinian economy but projects inside Jewish communities in the Israeli settlements which are directly articulated to the Israeli economy and which simultaneously exploit local labour along both class and national lines.

The effects of migrant labour on the local economy can be summarized as follows:
- Increasing abandonment of land.
- Increasing money liquidity which encourages consumerism that is satisfied through imports from Israel.
- The export of labour power to the Israeli economy which extracts surplus value.
- Surplus value is extracted from these labourers at a higher rate than from Israeli workers. This is expressed not least in terms of wage rates.
- The conversion of the village from unit of production to workers' dormitory.
- Physical and psychological separation of the peasant from the land.
- The greater the separation, the greater the deterioration of the land and the amount of money necessary for its reclamation.
- Israeli capitalism doubly exploits the migrant worker whose wage is repayed by buying Israeli commodities to satisfy daily needs. Thus, unwittingly, the migrant worker hinders internal accumulation in the West Bank.

– Finally, that part of the rural surplus labour which is not absorbed in the West Bank cities or inside the Green Line must emigrate to Jordan or other Arab countries.

The destination of the surplus labour of migrant workers

EVEN IF WEST BANK MIGRANT WORKERS return to their villages after work, they are nevertheless exploited through the capitalist relations of production in the place of work inside the Green Line. That is to say, this exploitation is a class exploitation despite the fact that the two classes in the exploitation process are from two separate economies. At the same time, there are the emigrant workers working and residing outside the West Bank, in Jordan and the oil states who are also exploited on a class basis.[21] What is interesting to note here is how the class exploitation of the two groups of workers, both created by peripheralization, contributes to the yet further peripheralization of the West Bank.

From those employed inside the Green Line Israel extracts the highest possible surplus value. Their wages are 50-60 per cent of those of Israeli workers. In addition to this, their work rights are either non-existent (in the case of 'illegal' migrants) or very limited (in the case of registered workers). The West Bank is a pool of cheap labour for Israel and for the Arab oil states and other countries, and is the source of a mobile workforce. West Bank migrant workers in Israel contribute to Israeli accumulation through their extracted surplus labour. On the surface the Israeli economy temporarily loses the wages which migrant workers take back to the West Bank, but in the third step of the process, these wages are returned to Israel through the merchants who import consumer goods either directly or through middlemen. It is as if the wages were loans from Israel to these workers. This circle of labour, wages and prices of commodities primarily expands the Israeli home market, not that of the West Bank. The labour power of migrant workers is exported to Israel through the sub-contractors and their wages are returned or channelled back to Israel through the merchants. Both sub-contractors and mediators are agents of the peripheralization of the West Bank economy.

Those workers employed outside the West Bank also comprise a pool of cheap labour but the surplus of these workers is extracted outside both parts of their homeland. Their wages are divided into two categories: (a) part of it saved in banks or in investments outside; (b) part sent back home as remittances to their families. These remittances find their way to

Israeli home market in the form of payment for the goods consumed by their families. [22] Neither the wages of the migrant in Israel nor of those outside contribute to internal accumulation. Quite the opposite, they contribute to the deepening of peripheralization.

The increasing consumption of West Bankers [23] increases the outflow of money to the Israeli market. Another factor contributing to the outflow of money is the decreased production of field crops and subsistence production and the increased production of externally oriented crops by West Bank farms. In the end, most of the income of West Bankers flows out to the Israeli economy.

Migrant labour without a solution to the agrarian question

DURING JORDANIAN RULE, the agrarian question remained unsolved. Jordan's peripheralization within the world system lies behind this. West Bank agriculture during the period failed to achieve the two conditions necessary to solve the agrarian question. These conditions are: firstly, agriculture has to generate a surplus to make industrial development possible; secondly, it must contribute towards the development of a home market for the goods produced by the industrial sector. [24]

Because of its deformed structure, the surplus of the West Bank agricultural sector was not devoted to industrial development even though production was for the market. As the surplus did not stay in the West Bank itself, it did not contribute towards the development of the home market. Moreover, the West Bank's deformed economic structure did not absorb the peasantry's surplus workforce into industry. So the differentiation of the peasantry did not help to enlarge the 'home market' since the peasantry's surplus workforce emigrated to Arab oil states and North and South America. In other words, the Jordanian state channelled the surplus labour power towards emigration in order to avoid the tasks of solving the agrarian question and starting industrialisation of the West Bank.

The Israeli occupation opened several channels for absorbing the surplus peasant workforce, employment in the Israeli economic sectors or emigration to Jordan, Arab countries and elsewhere. As a settler colonial occupation, the Israeli occupation is not interested in resolving the agrarian question or in enlarging the 'home market' of the West Bank. As Cardoso noted:

'. . . it is possible in some 'peripheral' economies, that capitalist development is progressive, raising the level of productive forces and widening the domestic market'. [25]

It is clear that in the West Bank, under Israeli occupation, this is not the case. The productive forces have been deformed as follows: firstly, traditional subsistence agriculture has declined to the minimum in accordance with the Israeli policy of 'improvement and commercialization'; Secondly, all fertile land has been oriented to production for foreign markets. In both cases, production is diverted from the local market. Thirdly, industrial production has stagnated since 1967. [26]

A marginal widening of the home market comes from another direction but this too deepens the deformation. This is the money liquidity from outside in the form of remittances and transfers, 'which comprises 40 per cent of the GNP', that is the Steadfastness Aid. This money liquidity is part of the cycle of deformity and only boosts the consumption of the population without increasing their productivity. It is not invested in productive enterprises and increases the foreign currency entering the Israeli economy through trade. So, the real expansion here is the expansion of the Israeli home market. In the West Bank the means of consumption, not the means of production, have developed, partially financed by remittances and transfers.

The West Bank's political peripheralization to Jordan

AS MENTIONED ABOVE , the West Bank was a periphery of the Jordanian economy. This peripheralization was created under Jordanian rule through policies which kept the West Bank economy weak and dependent on Jordan, aiming to block any Palestinian attempt to re-create Palestinian national identity. This is demonstrated by Jordan's policy of concentrating all industrial and agricultural projects in the East Bank. In the period 1950-1967, Jordan played the leading role in the West Bank's economic peripheralization.

Through its peripheralization to the backward Jordanian economy, the development of the West Bank's economy was prevented. After 1967, the West Bank economy became primarily and easily a periphery to the Israeli economy.

Beside the West Bank's peripheralization to the Israeli economy, Israel maintains a continued and controlled relationship between the West Bank and Jordan through the 'open bridges policy' and through political contacts. The 1984-85 Israeli annual report on the West Bank notes that: 'increasing division within the PLO ranks caused a continuous decline in the PLO's support and influence in the area.' [27]

While attributing a decline in support for the PLO to the latter's internal division, the report emphasizes that Jordan's influence has increased considerably. The report notes that Jordan has intensified efforts to strengthen its influence by intervening in various aspects of life, thus exploiting the decline in the PLO's support in the area.

The report does not mention what made it possible for Jordan to intervene freely in the West Bank nor does it discuss the reasons for the supposed decline in PLO influence. The Israeli occupation, which controls all aspects of life on the West Bank, has facilitated Jordanian activities on the West Bank while harshly repressing those of the PLO.

Israel's aim in pursuing this policy is to keep the door open for a political compromise with Jordan. The content of this compromise can be described in the words of Moshe Dayan, ex-Israeli defence minister who said in the early days of the occupation:

'If King Hussain cannot accept our conditions for peace, let the Jordanians find another King. And if the Jordanians do not accept our conditions for peace, they have to find another homeland for themselves'. [28]

The 'open bridges policy' also aims to facilitate the emigration of West Bankers to Jordan and beyond. The Israeli aim meshes with Jordanian political ambitions to restore even a minimum of control over the West Bank, such as security administration. This ambition connects with Dayan's theory of the 'functional division' of the West Bank. What should be noted here is that Israel's policy on West Bank exports to Jordan is much more flexible than its policies towards its imports. This facilitates emigration or future eviction. Moreover, the 'open bridges policy' has become a channel for foreign currency to enter the Israeli economy through Arab transfers and Palestinian remittances.

Concerning political contacts; in 1967 Israel proposed 'self rule' for the West Bank and Gaza Strip. This same project was revived by Israeli Prime Minister Shimon Peres in 1985. This project suggests that: 'Israel is going to hold the responsibility for security in the Occupied Territories, Jordan is going to take responsibility for policing. Water resources should be under common administration.' [29]

Due to many considerations, Jordan has accepted the offer in order to confirm its role as a marginal centre for the West Bank and to block (if possible) Sharon's plan which aims to evacuate half a million West Bankers to Jordan.

The agricultural peripheralization relationship of the West Bank to Jordan must be emphasized. The West Bank merchant-capitalist stratum mediates between Jordanian, Israeli and West Bank producers to facilitate the export of West Bank agricultural crops through Jordan. This stratum has remained a part of the fabric of the Jordanian economy since the pre-1967 period through its farms and factories in the East and West Bank. This stratum enjoys Jordanian facilities for marketing its agricultural crops and industrial production. 'One third of the industrial export to Jordan is Samna (plant-based margarine produced in Nablus), forty per cent is olive oil and soap'. [30] The Samna and soap factories are owned by the agricultural-merchant capitalist stratum.

At the same time the Arab regimes also facilitate the exporting of West Bank crops through Jordan in accordance with decisions of various Arab summit meetings. The Arab decision allowed the West Bank to export 50 per cent of its total agricultural production to the Arab countries through Jordan. The exportation is conditional on a document called *'Shahadit Mansha'*, a certificate to prove that the crop is of West Bank origin. [31]

At this level, Jordan is still free to buy West Bank exports or not, whereas West Bankers are prohibited from marketing freely in Jordan. Their crops are supposed to be transported to the central Amman market and thus they cannot compete with foreign products such as Spanish olive oil or Turkish grapes. [32] In fact, it is the other Arab states which purchase the bulk of West Bank agricultural exports. Kahan notes:

'Approximately 95 per cent of the volume of agricultural exports tend to be exported between January and June. Only a small proportion of the exports remain in Jordan. The majority are forwarded to Saudi Arabia and the Gulf states'. [33]

At the same time, Jordan imposes taxes on agricultural exports from the West Bank and Gaza, but for political reasons these taxes are waived on occasion. [34] But the story is not as simple as that. The West Bank's exports have also been over-burdened with problems ensuing from the protectionist policies of several importing Arab countries. In addition, the fate of the West Bank's exports depends on Jordan's political relations with the PLO and the Palestinians inside the Occupied Territories. The following is a striking example of Jordan's politically-oriented policy towards the West Bank:

'Twenty trucks carrying melons from the West Bank were not allowed to cross the bridge to Jordan. The Jordanian authorities claimed that the period of melon export had expired. Israel radio reported that Israeli authorities tried to interfere and convince the Jordanians to give access to the twenty trucks but the Jordanians refused.'[35]

Moreover, some Arab countries are competing with the West Bank crops in the Jordanian market as is the case with melons of Saudi Arabian origin.

Conclusion

THE MASS UPRISING which began in December 1987 can hardly have come as a surprise to anyone. However, the dramatic events which have unfolded in the streets of every town, village, and refugee camp in the occupied territories and which have found support among the Palestinians inside the Green Line, constitute a new phase in the ongoing Palestinian struggle for justice, dignity and independence. For the first time, the masses are expressing their resistance to occupation through sustained demonstrations, strikes by traders and migrant workers, and street fighting. The people have developed and employed their own weapons of struggle and an air of popular democracy has pervaded the atmosphere. Everyone lends support, everyone has become a militant and a leader. Villages under siege by the occupation forces and their paramilitary settlers have been relieved by the people of neighbouring villages who have infiltrated through Israeli lines to bring milk for children, food for adults, and reinforcements for the defenders. The aspiration for independence has been expressed not only by the stone throwers but also by popular decisions to boycott Israeli goods and to stop working for Israeli enterprises. Depending on themselves alone, the Palestinian masses have taken their struggle onto the political, national, and economic planes and in so doing have taught the occupation authorities a bitter lesson, revealing the deficiency of the orientalism and militarism of their theoreticians and planners.

The uprising has brought the mechanisms of peripheralization to the brink of collapse: the compradors have seen bankruptcy looming and despite the threat of hunger, workers have maintained strike action month after month, rejecting combined class and national exploitation but ready to accept work within their own economy so long as it is geared toward the common good. The Palestinian masses have proved day after day, month after month, that they are searching for (and finding) ways to break the dependence and peripheralization which has been forced upon the occupied territories. For its part, the Israeli state continues its policies of military, economic and social repression, maintains its refusal to negotiate with the PLO, preferring to attempt backroom deals with Arab regimes. In so doing, it not only prolongs the ongoing Palestinian tragedy, it also deepens Palestinian determination to be rid of peripheralization and to create their own economy and their own state.

Notes

1 Wolpe, H. *The Articulation of Modes of Production*, University of Sussex, 1980, p 38.
2 Ibid, p 36.
3 Cardoso, F. H. Dependent capitalist development in Latin America, *New Left Review*, 1972, no 74, p 90.
4 Kahan, David. Agriculture and water in the West Bank and Gaza, *West Bank Data Project*, Jerusalem, 1983, p 62.
5 Ibid, p 51.
6 Tsur, *Davar*, 22.8.1986.
7 Kahan, David, op cit, p 109.
8 Benvenisti, Meron. *The West Bank Data Project*, Jerusalem, 1986.
9 Taylor, John. *From Modernisation to Modes of Production*, Macmillan Press, London 1983.
10 *The Guardian*, London, 13.5.1987.
11 *The Guardian*, London, 24.12.1986.
12 Before 1967, most of the West Bank's grapes, tomatoes, olives, olive oil, fruits and grain crops were exported from the West Bank through the East Bank to several Arab countries. The export of these crops was governed by the political relationship between Jordan and those countries. In 1954, '58, '61, '63 and '65, West Bank farmers were unable to export their produce to Syria because of deteriorated political relations between Jordan and Syria, resulting in the latter's closing of its borders. Thus, farm produce was not marketed.
13 Landowners and merchants facilitate the bankruptcy of the independent farmers by controlling the resources. In addition to the extracted surplus from the farmers, they make substantial profits through marketing seeds and fertilisers at high prices. The most striking example is the Arab Jerusalem Cigarette Company whose board of directors decided to buy raw materials from South Africa through an Israeli third party in an attempt to force West Bank farmers to sell their crops solely to the company at a 'minimum' price. (Jarar, *Samed*, no 60, 1986, p 31).
14 The number of those employed in industry inside the West Bank was 14.6 thousand in 1970, 15.7 in 1980 and 15.9 in 1984 (*Israeli Statistical Abstract*, 1985, p 725). This reflects the stagnant situation of industry on the West Bank and invalidates Israeli claims that 'the decrease in agricultural employment and the increase in industrial employment are usually linked with internal migration from the villages to the towns' (*Coordinator of Government Operations in Judea, Samaria, Gaza Strip and Sinai*, 1967-1981, April 1982, p 5).
15 Tsur, op cit.

16 Interview with Faisal Hindi, General Secretary of Tulkarm Trade Union, 20 September, 1984.

17 In 1984, legal workers inside the Green Line numbered about 47,000. Illegal workers numbered 30,000 and those working in Israeli workshops inside the West Bank about 20,000. Those 20,000 must not be included in the total of 104,000 who were working inside the West Bank itself.

18 Jordanian Development Plan, 4.8.1986.

19 Samara, Adel. *Iqtisad al-Jou fi al-Diffa wal-Qita'a (The Economics of Hunger in the West Bank and Gaza Strip)*. Dar al-Amel, Ramallah, West Bank.

20 Migrant labour in the West Bank is still unstable. As a result of Israeli expropriation of the farmers' land, those who became landless have lost their livelihood and therefore have to work for several years as wage earners inside the Green Line. Having lost their ownership of the means of production, they became proletarianised.

21 The Ministry of Labour in Jordan estimates that of the 350,000 'Jordanians' (40% of the labour force) working abroad, one third are from the West Bank (see *Associated Press*, 14.4.1985).

22 The remittances of West Bank workers in the oil-producing countries are estimated at $350 million per annum. (Ibid).

23 For more analysis on the increase of 'consumerism' in the West Bank, see Samara 1979, pp 188-208 op cit.

24 Lenin, V.I. *Collected Works, Vol. 3*, Lawrence and Wishart, London, 1972.

25 Goodman D and Redclift M. *From Peasant to Proletarian, Capitalist Development and Agrarian Transition*, Camelot Press, Southampton, 1981, p 51.

26 Benvenisti, Meron. *The West Bank Data Project*, Jerusalem 1986, p 10.

27 Introduction to the Civil Administration, *Judea and Samaria Annual Report*, 1984.

28 *Yediot Ahronot* 17.7.1967.

29 *Al-Hadaf*, no 824, 14.7.1986.

30 Benvenisti, Meron. A Survey of Israeli policies, *The West Bank Data Project*, Jerusalem, 1984, p 10.

31 *Al-Awdeh*, no 70, 10.7.1985.

32 Ibid.

33 Kahan, David, op cit, p 110.

34 *Al-Arab*, 16.6.1986.

35 *Al-Fajr*, 27.6.1986.

Bibliography
Books
—Abdulkhaiiq, Juda. 1985. *Man Yusa'aed Israel ('Who Assists Israel?')*, Dar Al-Mustakbal Al-Arabi, Cairo, (Arabic).

—Abu-Alnamil H. (Shu'n Filistiniah), nos 63/64 Feb/March 1977. *Ma'zaq Al-Iktisad Al-Israeli (The Crises of the Israeli Economy)*.

—Abu-Lughod, Ibrahim. 1982. (ed.) *Palestinian Rights, Affirmation and Denial*. Media Press Washington.

—Al-Faiez, I. 1975. *Al-Nitham Al-Hashimi Wa-Alhoqoq Al-Mashroa'a Lil-Shab Al-Filistini (The Hashimite Regime and the Legitimate rights of the Palestinian people)*, Al-Fajr publications, Jerusalem. Quoted from *MERIP Reports*. Feb. 1972.

—Alawi Hamza & Teodor Shanin. 1982, ed. *Sociology of Developing Countries*, Macmillan Press Ltd, London.
—Allon, Yega'l. 1970. *The Making of the Israeli Army*. Banton Books (NY).
—Amin, Samir. 1974. *Accumulation on the World Scale*. Monthly Review Press (NY).
—Amin Samir. 1976. *Unequal Development*, Monthly Review Press (NY).
—Amin, Samir. 1980. *Class and Nation: Historically and in the Current Crisis*, Monthly Review Press (NY).
—Amin, Samir. 1982. *Dynamics of Global Crisis*, with Giovani Arrighi, André Gunder Frank and Immanuel Wallerstein. Monthly Review Press (NY).
—Aruri, N. 1972. *Jordan: A Study in Political Development 1921-1965*, Martin Nijhoff, The Hague.
—Aruri, N. 1984. ed. *Occupation: Israel over Palestine*. Zed Books, London.
—Assad, Talal. 1976. *Class Transformation under the Mandate*, in *MERIP Reports* no 53.
—Awartani H. 1986. *Samed Al-Iktisadi*, no 61. Amman and Beirut. (Arabic).
—Back, Howard. 1971. *Structural and Economic Policy in Israel*. Yale Univ. Press, New Haven.
—Barour, N, Warringer. 1969. (D, Nisi Dominus): *A Study of the Palestine Controversy*. Institute of Palestine Studies, Beirut.
—Benvenisti, Meron. 1984. *The West Bank Data Project. A Survey of Israeli Policies*, Jerusalem.
—Benvenisti, M. 1986. *The West Bank Data Project*. Jerusalem.
—Bober, Arie. 1972. (ed.) *The Other Israel*. Anchor Books. New York.
—Bashir, Sulaiman. 1980. *Gothour Al Wisaiah Al Urdoniiah*. ('*The Roots of the Jordanian Mandate*') (A Study of the Documents of the Zionist Archives). Abu Arafah Publications. Jerusalem.
—Byres, T. (1979), 'Of neo-populist pipe dreams', *Journal of Peasant Studies*. 6, 2. pp. 210-244.
—Dajani, S. 1986. *Samed Al-Iktisadi*. no 61. Amman and Beirut.
—Delwin, A. Roy. 1978. *Journal of Palestine Studies*. vol. VII, no 3, Spring 1978.
—Fahd Al-Fanek. 1972. *Altafkir alIktisadi fe AlUrdun* (*Economic Thought in Jordan*). Amman.
—Emmanuel, Arghiri. 1972. *Unequal Exchange. A Study of the Imperialism of Trade*. Monthly Review Press, New York and London. English edition.
—Emmanuel, Arghiri. 1972. 'White settler colonialism and the myth of investment imperialism', *N.L.R.* no 73.
—EUROPA. 1984-1985. Thirty-first edition of an annual survey containing detailed information about the countries in the Middle East and North Africa. EUROPA Publication Ltd. London.
—Farjoun, Emmanuel. 1980. 'Palestinian workers in Israel, a reserve army of labour', *Khamsin* no 7. Ithaca Press, London.
—Fisher, G. 1919. *Ottoman Laws*, Humphrey Milford, Oxford University Press, London.
—Foster, Carter A. 1978. 'The modes of production controversy', *NLR* no 107. (Quoted from Immanuel Wallerstein's *The Modern World System*, New York. 1974, also numerous recent articles.)
—Galtung, J. 1971. 'A structural theory of imperialism', *Journal of Peace Research*. no 8.
—Ghandor, S. 1983. in *Samed Al-Iktisadi*. no 44. Amman and Beirut.

—Givati, Chaim. 1984. *A Hundred Years of Settlement*. Jerusalem.
—Goldfield, Steve. 1985. *Garrison State, Israeli Role in US Global Strategy*. Palestine Focus Publications. San Francisco, EAFORD. London and New York.
—Goodman, D, & Redcliff. 1981. *From Peasant to Proletarian Capitalist Development and Agrarian Transitions*. Camelot Press, Southampton. Great Britain.
—Grannot, A. 1952. *The Land System in Palestine. History and Structure*. Eyre and Spottiswoode. London.
—Harari, H. 1976. *Israeli Arabs in Figures*. Givaat Havivah. Tel Aviv.
—Harris, John. 1984. (ed.) *Rural Development*. Hutchinson University Library. London.
—Harris, W. William. 1980. *Taking Roots*. New York Research Studies Press. John Wiley.
—Herzl, Theodor. *The Jewish State*. Quoted in Maxime Rodinson, 1973, *Israel a Colonial Settler State*. pp. 9-14. New York Pathfinder Press.
—Himadeh, Said. 1938. *Economic Organization of Palestine*. Beirut.
—Hodgkin, Thomas. 1986. (ed. E.C. Hodgkin). *Letters from Palestine*. London and New York.
—Horowitz, David. 1972. *The Enigma of Economic Growth—A Case Study of Israel*. New York, Praeger.
—Istanbuli, D. 1981. *AlInsan Alzira'ai (The Agricultural Man)*, Arab Thought Forum Publications. Jerusalem.
—Istanbuli, D, Abu-Arafa, A and Azzah, Y. 1981. *Alwaqi Alzira'ai fi Almanatiq Almuhtalah (The reality on Agriculture in the Occupied Territories)* Arab Thought Forum. Jerusalem.
—Jarar, G. 1986. *Samed Al-Iktisadi*, no 61. Amman and Beirut.
—Kayyali, A.W. 1978. *Palestine A Modern History*. Croom Helm Ltd.
—Kazi, Omar. 1984. *The Impact of the Israeli Technology on West Bank Agriculture*. Memoi.
—Keyder, Caglar. 1981. *The Definition of Peripheral Economy. Turkey 1923-1929*. Cambridge.
—Keyder, Caglar & Huri Islamoglu. (ed.) 1981. *The Ottoman Social Formation*, in Anne M. Bailey and Josep R. Llobera's *The Asiatic Mode Of Production*. Routledge & Kegan Paul. London.
—Kahan, David. 1983. Agriculture and water in the West Bank and Gaza. *West Bank Data Project*, Jerusalem.
—Khouri, Fred J. 1976. *The Arab-Israeli Dilemma*, Second Edition, Syracuse University Press.
—Lenin, V.I. 1972. *The Development of Capitalism in Russia*. Collected Works. V 3. Progress Publishers, Moscow.
—Leon, A. (1970). *The Jewish Question: a Marxist Interpretation*, Pathfinder Press, New York.
—Lipshitz, I. 1970. *Economic Development in the Administered Areas. 1967-1969*. Jerusalem.
—Loutsky. 1980. *Tarikh Alaktar Al-Arabiah Alhadith (Modern History of Arab Country)*. Al-Farabi Publications. Beirut. (Arabic).
—Mansour, Antoine. 1983. *La Cisjordanie—Une Economie de Resistance*. Paris. Quoted in PLO London Office, Department of Information, *The Economic Destruction of the Occupied Territories*. 1986. p 4.
—Migdal, Joel. 1980. *Palestinian Society and Politics*, Princeton University Press, N.J
—Moa'z, M: 1968. *Ottoman Reform in Syria and Palestine. 1840-1861. The Impact*

of Tanzimat on Politics and Society. Oxford, Clarendon Press.

—Marx, K. 1876. *A Preface to the Critique of the Introduction of the Political Economy*. The Publishing House of Foreign Languages. Peking.

—Mommsen, Wolfgang. 1981. *Theories of Imperialism* (English edition). Redwood Burn Publication.

—Mursi, F. 1983. *AlIktisad AlSiasi LeIsrael* (*The Political Economy of Israel*). Dar Al-Mustaqbal Al-Arabi. Cairo.

—Mutawi, S. 1987. *Jordan in the 1967 War*. Cambridge University Press. Cambridge, London, New York, New Rochelle, Melbourne and Sydney.

—Nathan, R, Gass, O, & Creamer, D. 1946. *Palestine—Problem and Promise, An Economic Study*. Public Affairs Press, Washington.

—Nikitina, G. 1973. *The State of Israel; A Historical, Economic and Political Study*. Moscow. Progress Press Publications.

—Owen, Roger. 1982. ed. *Studies in Economic and Social History in Palestine in the Nineteenth and Twentieth Centuries*. Macmillan Press Ltd. London.

—Petras, James. 1980. 'The US and the Middle East: recolonization or decolonization', in *Arab Studies Quarterly*, vol 2, no 2. Spring 1980. AAUG. Inc.

—Polk, Stamler and Asfour. 1957. *Back Drop to Tragedy*. Beacon Press.

—Porath, Y. 1974. *The Emergence of Palestinian Arab National Movement*. Vol. 1, 1918-1929. London. Frank Cass.

—Riyad, M. Al-Baheth Al-Arabi (in Arabic). *Arab Researcher*. no 6 January 1986.

—Roi, Yaacov. 1986. 'The Zionist attitudes to the Arabs' in *Middle Eastern Studies*, vol 2, April 1986.

—Saad, Ahmad. 1984. *Harb lubnan. Azmit alIktisad alIsraeli* (*Lebanon War, The Crisis of the Israeli Economy*). Al-Aswar publications, Acre. Israel.

—Saad, Ahmad. 1984. *Samed Al-Iktisadi* nos 50/51. Amman and Beirut.

—Sayigh, Rosemary. 1979. *Palestinians From Peasants to Revolutionaries*. Zed Press, London.

—Samara, A. 1977. *Iktisad Almanatiq Almuhtalah. Altakhaluf Uaamiq Alilhaq* (*The Economy of the Occupied Territories. Underdevelopment Deepening Integration*). Salah Al-Din Publications. Jerusalem.

—Samara, A. 1979. *Iktisadiat AlGou fi AlDiffah Walqtaa* (*The Economics of Hunger in the West Bank and Gaza Strip*). Dar Al-Amel Publications. Ramallah, West Bank.

—*Samara, A. 1983. Hiwarat wawathaiq fi almanatiq almuhtallah* (*Dialogue and Documents in the Occupied Territories*) in *Al-Shira* Bi-Weekly, no. 50. Jerusalem.

—Samara, A. 1986. 'Arab nationality, Palestinian question and an economic scenario for Arab unity' in *Khamsin*, no 12, London.

—Samuel Viscount Herbert. 1945. *Memories*, London.

—Sawalha, F. 1984. *Intaj AlKhodrawat fi AlDiffa AlGharbiah* (*Vegetable Production in the West Bank*). By the Rural Research Center, Al-Najah University, Nablus, West Bank.

—Sawalha, F. 1984. *Ziraait wIntaj alKhodrawat fi alDiffah alGharbiah* (*Vegetable Planting and Production in the West Bank*). March 1984. Al-Najah University, Nablus, West Bank.

—Scholch, A. 1982. (ed Roger Owen). *Studies in the Economic and Social History of Palestine in the Nineteenth and Twentieth Centuries*. Macmillan Press Ltd London.

—Senghass, D. 1973. (ed.) quoted in Wolfgang Mommsen, 1981, *Theories of Imperialism*. Weidenfeld and Nicolson, London.

—Shiblak, Abbas. 1986. *The Lure of Zion*. Al-Saqi Books, London.

—Shehadah, R, and Kuttab, J. 1980. *The West Bank and the Rule of Law*. Interna-

tional Commission of Jurists and Law in the Service of Man, NY.
—Shuqair, A. 1983. *Samed al-Iktisadi* no 46. Amman and Beirut.
—Simpson, John Hope. 1930. *Report on Immigration, Land Settlement and Development.* London.
—Stein, Kenneth. W. April 1985. *The Land Question in Palestine. 1917-1939.* University of North Carolina Press. Chapel Hill, London. First printed 1984.
—Stein, L. 1961. *The Balfour Declaration.* Simon and Schuster, New York.
—Sussman, Z. 1986. *Israel's Economy: Performance Problems and Policies,* Institute of Jewish Affairs, London, and the Jacob Levinson Centre of the Israeli-Diaspora Institute, Tel Aviv.
—Szereszewski, Robert. 1968. *Essays on the Structure of the Jewish Economy in Palestine and Israel.* Jerusalem.
—Taggart, Simon. 1985. *Workers in Struggle—Palestinian Trade Unions in the Occupied West Bank.* Editpride, London.
—Taylor, John. 1983. *From Modernization to Modes Of Production.* Macmillan Press Ltd., London.
—Tamari, S. 1983. *The Dislocation and Reconstitutionof a Peasantry: The Social Economy of Agrarian Palestine in the Central Highlands and the Jordan Valley.* 1960-1980. Unpublished PhD Thesis. University of Manchester.
—Tuma, Elias & Drubkin, Haim. 1978. *The Economic Case of Palestine.* Croom Helm Ltd, London.
—Turkkaya, Ataov. 1982 (ed. Ibrahim Abu-Lughud). *Palestinian Rights. Affirmation and Denial.* Medina Press.
—Van Arkadie, B. *Benefits and Burdens: A Report on the West Bank and Gaza Strip Economies since 1967.* New York/Washington: Carnegie Endowment for International Peace, 1977.
—Wallerstein, Immanuel. 1974. *The Modern World System.* New York. (See also numerous articles.)
—Weinstock, Nathan. 'The impact of Zionist colonialism on Palestine Arab society before 1948', Journal of Palestine Studies, Vol 2, no 2.
—Warriner, Doreen. 1948. *Land and Poverty in the Middle East.* London.
—Wolpe, H. 1980. (Wolpe ed.) *The Articulation of Modes of Production.* University of Sussex.
—Wolpe, H. 1980. Capitalism and cheap labour power in South Africa–from segregation to Apartheid in Wolpe (ed), *The Articulation of Modes of Production.*
—Yasin, A. & Saad, A.S. 1974. *alHarakah alwataniah alFilistiniah (The Palestinian National Movement).* Beirut.
—Ziff, William B. 1948. *The Rape of Palestine.* Botolphs Press. London.
—Zvi, Sobel. 1985. 'A lecture in Birkbeck College', University of London.
—Zuraik, Elia. 1979. *Palestinians in Israel: A Study in Internal Colonialism.* Routledge and Kegan Paul, London.

Reports

—*Agricultural Branch in Judea and Samaria.* Central Bureau of Statistics, 1969. Jerusalem. (English).
—Benvenisti M., *The West Bank Data Project.* Jerusalem. 1984.
—Benvenisti, *The West Bank Data Project,* Jerusalem 1986.

—*Civil Administration Annual Report for Judea and Samaria*. 1984. Jerusalem.
—*A Fourteen Year Survey 1967–1981*. 1982. p. 3. (English). Israel's Defence Ministry Publications. Coordinator of Government Operations in Judea, Samaria, Gaza District and Sinai, 1982.
—*Jordanian Development Plan*. Reuters News Agency. 4.8.1986.
—International Labour Conference. 1986 Report of the Director General, appendix III, *A Report on the Situation of Workers of the Occupied Arab Territories*. (English).
—Israeli Pocket Library, *Immigration and Settlement*. Keter Books. Jerusalem. 1973. p 106. (English).
—West Bank Data Project. 1984. *Israeli Population in the West Bank*.
—I.N.S. Momento Economique, La Palestina. Paris 1948. p 8. (English).
—Military Order Series. Published by the Israeli Military Governorate in the West Bank. (Arabic edition).
—*Middle East Report*, vol 3, 1968, Jerusalem: Israel Universities Press, 1971.
—*News From Within*, a weekly independent report published in Jerusalem. (English).
—*Occupied Territories Statistical Quarterly*. Vol. x. no 3. 1982. p 2.
—*Ottoman Land Code*; Ongley, F (translator) William Clowes & Sons ltd. London 1892.
—OXFAM. 1985 *Annual Report for West Bank, Gaza, Israel, and Jordan* (Confidential).
—Oxford Symposium. *Economic Development Under Prolonged Occupation. The West Bank and Gaza*. St Catherine's College, Oxford, 3-5 January, 1986.
—Palestine Government. *A Survey of Palestine, 1945-1949*.
—Palestinian Liberation Organisation. 1985. *Industrial Statistical Bulletin*, no 3, and no 5. Damascus. (English).
—*Palestine Royal Commission Report*. (Peel Report). London 1937, reprinted 1946.
—*Palestine Refugees Today*, U.N.R.W.A. newsletter. (English).
—*Royal Commission Report*. The Secretary of State for Colonies. London 1937.
—*Statistical Abstract of Israel*. Central Bureau of Statistics, 1982, 1985. Jerusalem.
—Shadid, M. *Israeli Policy Towards Economic Development Projects in the West Bank and Gaza Strip*. background paper. no 5, 9 Sep 1985. Delivered to Second International NGOs Meeting on the Question of Palestine.
—United Nations Conference on Trade and Development. 1986. *Recent Economic Development in the Occupied Palestinian Territories*.
—United Nation Document A570, *Terms of League of Nations Mandate for Palestine*.
—*World Development Report*. 1982. New York: Oxford University Press. Table 3.

Newspapers

—*Al-Arab*. Arabic Daily. London.
—*Al-Awdah*. Weekly in English. Jerusalem.
—*Al-Awdah*. Arabic Bi-Weekly. Jerusalem.
—*Al-Bayader*. Arabic Weekly. Jerusalem.
—*Al-Fajr*. English Weekly. Jerusalem.

—*Al-Itihad*. Arabic Daily. Haifa.
—*Al-Jaridah Al-Rasmiyah. 1955-1967*. Jordan. (several issues).
—*Al-Hamishmar*.Hebrew daily, Tel-Aviv.
—*Al-Taliah* .Arabic daily. Jerusalem.
—*Al-Qabas* International Edition. Arabic daily. London.
—*The Economist*. London.
—*Christian Science Monitor*.
—*Eight Days*. (8-Days). London.
—*Haaretz*. Hebrew daily.
—*Financial Times*. London
—*Jerusalem Post*. English. Jerusalem.
—*Jerusalem Post* – International Edition. English.
—*Koteret Rashit*. Weekly. Hebrew. Jerusalem.
—*New York Times*.
—*Tariq Al-Intisar*. Arabic Monthly, Cyprus.
—*Washington Post*.
—*Yediot Acharonot*. Hebrew Daily. Tel Aviv.

Interviews

—Adnan. *Al-Awdah*. Ramallah. 10.5.1980.
—Faisal Hindi. Tulkarem. 9.9.1984. (A trade unionist from Tulkarm town in the West Bank.)
—Tayseer Samara. Ramallah. 10.6.1984. (A truck driver.)

Abbreviations

—ASQ Arab Studies Quarterly
—CAABU Council for the Advancement of Arab and British Understanding.
—CBS Central Bureau of Statistics.
—CGO Coordinator of Government Operations (in the Occupied Territories.)
—CSM Christian Science Monitor
—IAR Israeli Annual Report.
—ICAAR Israeli Civil Administration Annual Report.
—ILO International Labour Organization.
—ISA Israeli Statistical Abstract.
—JPIE Jerusalem Post International Edition.
—JP Jerusalem Post.
—JPS Journal of Palestine Studies.
—J. of PS Journal of Peasant Studies.
—MSEI Map of Settlement in Eretz Israel.
—MER Middle East Report.
—NFW News from Within.
—PLO Palestine Liberation Organization.
—UNCTAD United Nations Conference for Trade and Development.
—WBDP West Bank Data Project.

Toby Shelley

PALESTINIAN MIGRANT WORKERS IN ISRAEL FROM REPRESSION TO REBELLION

FOR OVER A DECADE, West Bank and Gazan labourers in Israel were all but ignored. For sections of the Palestinian nationalist movement, they were an embarassing symbol of the failure of the policy of *sumud* (steadfastness) to prevent the occupation from effecting deep structural changes in the society and economy of the occupied territories. For the international media, migrant labour was undramatic when compared to more newsworthy guerrilla operations or demonstrations. Israeli society, albeit with exceptions, preferred not to notice its Arab labour and, when the 'Jewish' state's embarassing dependence on non-Jewish labour was noticed, particularly on Muslim feastdays, the conviction that the Arabs were more dependent on Israel than vice versa was a comforting reaffirmation of ethnic superiority. The 1980s have seen the development of interest in the migrant workers. The nationalist movement has embarked on attempts to recruit them into unions; the international media has found numerous opportunities to draw comparison with South African migrant labour, together with a plethora of 'human interest' stories; Israeli sociologists have discovered a topic worthy of newspaper articles and treatises; and the Histadrut has been under increasing international pressure to justify its attitude towards Palestinian workers. The Palestinian *intifada* (uprising) which began on 9 December 1987 brought stayaways by migrant workers and, sure enough, sectors of the Israeli economy ground to a halt.

These events have a great significance which the Palestinian nationalist movement and Israeli employers and state will seek to evaluate. The Palestinians have learnt to use a new weapon and Zionism has discovered a weakness forged by its own hand. With this in mind, it is important to understand the conditions under which migrant labourers work because it is only by appreciating the extent of their exploitation that their weaknesses and their strength can be assessed. This article attempts to provide the material for such an understanding.

It should be said that the overwhelming majority of 'noncitizen Arab workers' in the Israeli economy are migrant workers, and it is they who are dealt with here. However, thousands of (mostly women) workers in the West Bank and Gaza Strip work for Israeli employers through the medium of local sub-contractors. They too have played a part in inflicting damage on the occupying state in recent months and this should be examined at another time.

As a final introductory note, readers' attention should be drawn to the excellent article by Emanuel Farjoun in *Khamsin 7 (Palestinian Workers in Israel – a reserve army of labour)*. The following article is more specific in that it deals only with the phenomenon of migrant labour. Nevertheless, it can, in part, be viewed as an update on Farjoun's piece which should be read by anyone with an interest in the Arab workforce in the Israeli economy.

Who are the hewers of wood?

ESTIMATES OF THE SCALE of labour migration from the West Bank and Gaza into Israel vary greatly. Israeli statistics record 20.6 thousand in 1970 (the first year of legal labour migration), rising to 68.7 thousand in 1974 and 90.3 thousand in 1984.[1] As a proportion of the West Bank and Gaza labour force, Israeli statistics show migrant workers as constituting 30% since 1973, rising to over 39% in peak quarters of 1983 and 1984.[2] In 1983, 43% of the Gazan workforce was engaged in migrant work.[3] Yet it is no secret that government figures are incomplete. Unregistered, illegal migrant work began shortly after the consolidation of the occupation and its control and taxation was a factor in the decision to open labour offices in the occupied territories.[4] However, unregistered work continues. Israeli sociologists and Palestinian trade unionists estimate that at least one third of migrant workers are unregistered. This would bring the numbers in the mid-1980s up into the 115-120,000 range. The

ILO has noted estimates of 130,000 and at harvest time,[5] numbers as great as 250,000 (larger than the total labour force in 1984 by Israel's figures) have been mentioned.[6] Some of the disparity here can be explained by the fact that the labour force figures do not include under-age workers, many women workers, and students working in their free time. As far back as 1975, *Davar* reported that 120,000-140,000 migrant workers were active in the Israeli economy.[7]

Even on the basis of the numbers given for registered migrant labourers, the scale of the employment of West Bankers and Gazans is evident. In 1984, 93.7 thousand residents of the occupied territories (excluding East Jerusalem) were employed in these areas as agricultural workers or as skilled, semi-skilled or unskilled workers in industry, mining, building, transport etc., as against 76.7 thousand employed in such work in Israel.[8] If agriculture, which accounts for 37 thousand of those employed in the occupied territories, is removed, it is clear that more workers resident in the occupied territories work for Israeli industry, mining, building, transport etc. firms than work for such Palestinian concerns (63.3 thousand as compared to 56.7 thousand).

According to Mansour, some 70% of migrant workers originate from rural areas.[9] A conference in Paris in November 1984 heard that 46.2% of registered migrant workers come from villages, 29% from refugee camps and 24% from towns.[10] A survey of Palestinians resident in Israel found that in 1974, 91.7% of skilled Arab industrial workers had fathers who were not wage labourers,[11] a clear indication that land expropriation, restrictions on Palestinian farming and enforced competition with subsidised Israeli producers have transformed Palestinian employment patterns. The number of farmers in Gaza fell from 16,700 in 1970 to 7,400 in 1986 while the number of migrant workers rose from 2,400 to 10,500 in the same period.[12] Israeli statistics for 1984 show that 19.5 thousand out of 90.3 thousand migrant workers were also engaged in cultivating farms.[13] Semyonov and Lewin-Epstein note that in 1969 more than 50% of the adult residents of the West Bank and Gaza Strip had no schooling and only 17% had more than nine years of education, that in 1975 half of the 'non-resident Arabs' employed in Israel had six years of schooling or less.[14] But it would be erroneous to depict the migrant worker as an uneducated peasant turned proletarian without making some substantial qualifications. By 1984, only 15% of registered migrant workers had received no schooling and 30% had completed nine or more years.[15] Thus, while 50% of children drop out of school before completing nine years of education[16] (2,000 dropped out of UNRWA schools in Gaza in 1987[17]), unemployment among graduates has thrust many well educated young people into the Israeli labour market. A seminar in Jerusalem in 1986 established that 8,000 graduates from the West Bank and Gaza Strip were unable to find work in their specialist fields. [18] An UNRWA report in 1987 cited evidence that 5,400 West Bank and 2,700 Gazan graduates were unemployed in 1985 [19]. These actual or potential migrant workers (or emigrants) are not trained in 'unproductive' disciplines. The Engineers Association in the West Bank stated that 200 of its 600 members were unemployed in 1985. [20] A report in *al-Fajr* in 1986 notes a chemistry graduate working as a house decorator in Tel Aviv. [21] In 1987, *al-Bayader al-Siyassi* interviewed a Gazan lawyer working in an Israeli factory. [22] Large numbers of teachers work in the seasonal labour market in Israel during holidays. [23]

Getting work

AVAILABILITY FOR MIGRANT WORK is not simply a matter of being unemployed or of dropping out of school. Physically reaching the labour market frequently requires a major investment of time and limited financial resources. Israeli governmental submissions to the ILO claim that:

'The great majority of [migrant] workers live at a reasonable commuting distance from their place of work, and travelling to and from work, often together with people from the same village who work at the same place, can help to reinforce village identity.' [24]

The submissions go on to assert that some 20% of registered migrant workers are given permission to stay overnight in Israel. Such claims have been accepted by some observers (Semyonov and Lewin-Epstein, for example). However, a typical week's return travel from Gaza to Tel Aviv to seek work costs the equivalent of one day's wages and may take four hours per day. [25] Matters are not necessarily better when employers provide transport. In 1985, labourers from Bethlehem working in a bakery in Jerusalem, 20 minutes' drive away, complained they had to leave home at 1am to start their shift at 3am. One of them said:

'We arrive at the bakery before the doors are open and so we are forced to stand in the street without any protection from the cold.' [26]

The cost in time and money forces many workers to stay overnight illegally inside the Green Line. Some do this with the collusion of employers and some even take on nightguard jobs to supplement their daytime earnings. In 1985, the Knesset Interior Committee was told that 50,000 West Bankers and Gazans slept overnight in Tel Aviv alone. [27] The conditions under which such workers live will be dealt with later. In Qalqilia in the north of the West Bank, Gazan workers live in hostels or in the grounds of the mosque in order to be able to reach their places of work. These workers return home between once a week to once a month. Some as young as fourteen years of age have to share sleeping space with people they do not know. [28] But it is not only those who have relatively large distances to travel who live away from home. The majority of Arab workers in Petah Tikva come from the villages of Salfit, Firkha, Qablan and Tel near Nablus and Tulkarm, yet a number of them share rented rooms in order to be able to get to work. In 1985, a room of three by four metres, shared by five to eight men cost $80-120. [29]

The mechanisms through which migrant labour is recruited are worth outlining, not least because they are major factors in maintaining the extent of exploitation faced by Palestinian workers. In theory, all would-be migrant labourers must register at an Israeli labour office in the occupied territories and from there be allotted a job. A payment office is responsible for the worker being renumerated. Seven offices were established in the West Bank in 1968 and a further 30 were set up later. Semyonov and Lewin-Epstein note that procedures have not been adhered to and that, in practice, during the boom of the late 1960s and early 1970s, many workers would find employment (presumably illegally) and then have it regularised *post eventu*. [30] On other occasions, Israeli labour exchange officials actually go into the West Bank and Gaza Strip to seek out workers:

'. . . the Hadera-Samaria labour exchange cannot find enough applicants to fill employers' requests, the State Employment Service said yesterday. It said the director of the exchange, Avraham Bechar, has had to make special recruitment trips to Samaria and local Arab villages to find the 5,000 hands urgently needed by metalworking, food, wood products, and produce-processing and packing plants applying to his office for workers.' [31]

The offices were established in the occupied territories as a means of regulating the flow of Palestinian workers, a flow which had already begun spontaneously. Such regulation was based around three considerations: control over the number of migrant workers; control over their movement inside the Green Line; and control over their wages.

Initially, a quota system was enforced but it was soon relaxed as implied above. This is not to say that any worker who applies for a work permit receives one. Many are ruled out on 'security' grounds and some offices have a reputation for refusing permits to younger workers. Interviews in *al-Tali'a* with workers seeking employment in the Petah Tikva area reveal that the offices actually force workers into the unregistered sector. The interviews indicated two ways in which this happens. Firstly workers claimed that:

'Jewish employers refuse to employ anyone if he is registered with the *lishka* [work office] and so they do not have to observe any of our union or legal rights. And when employers learn that one of the workers wants to be registered, they refuse and say to him, "There is no place for you here. Leave the firm."'

Secondly, they said that:

'... in Petah Tikva the work offices refuse to issue permits to Arab workers ... The Israeli work offices demand [that employers] hire Jewish workers and threaten employers with fines if they take on unregistered Arab workers. However, the employers prefer Arab workers who they take on for donkey work and at half the wages of Jewish workers.'[32]

Permits (of six months maximum) specify the place of work; overnight stays in Israel are generally forbidden. This is clearly a policy related to concerns over security but also affords a means of preventing workers' self-organisation. Even in enterprises employing large numbers of migrant workers, it is rare to find more than a handful from the same village, camp, or part of a town. In other words, there is little chance of workers being able to organise collectively after the day's work and travel is over. Control over remuneration is couched in terms suggesting a concern to ensure that wages should 'be equal to those of Israeli workers with comparable jobs and skills'.[33] The experience of Palestinian workers, however, suggests that the policy is rather more concerned with ensuring that tax deductions of 30-40% of gross pay are made. Thus *al-Tali'a* in 1985, reported the sacking of 33 workers from a Jerusalem bakery.[34] The workers had been on strike, demanding wage parity with Jewish colleagues. When they approached the Bethlehem work office through which they had been hired, they were told by the manager that the matter was one for the Histadrut. Interviewing a leading West Bank union organiser, Taggart quotes cases of registered workers being paid well below the official minimum wage. He also tells of the experience of Musa from Serat who:

'When he asked for his wages he was told to go back in a fortnight. This he did and was told nothing was owed to him. He went to al-Madjdil work office where he was referred to the Gaza office which, in turn, referred him back to al-Madjdil where he was told that there was no proof that he was owed money. He returned to the employer who told him he would be shot if he complained further.'[35]

Israeli sociologist Michael Shalev, accusing the work offices of complicity in the under-paying of Arab workers, has stated that, except for construction workers, the offices simply do not check employers' calculations.[36] Even when formal requirements are observed, Semyonov and Lewin-Epstein note that:

'Monitoring by the payment center, which emphasizes compliance with the law, [thus] legitimizes wage gaps between resident and non-resident employees.'[37]

Parallel to the official mediation of the work office between employer and worker, is mediation by the *simsar* or middleman. Just as the opportunity of making a profit from land sales to settlers has brought unsavoury Arab and Jewish entrepreneurs into alliance, so has the opportunity to profit from the demand for and availability of labour. *Al-Tali'a* interviewed a number of workers employed in Rishon Letzion:

'All the Arab workers of Rishon Letzion work through middle-men who set the pay rates and distribute wages to 'their' workers on the various sites. As they are responsible to the municipality for the work of the labourers, no one really knows exactly how many Arab workers there are. The workers who were interviewed put the number at around 150 with three middlemen.

There is no job security and wages are determined when a man is hired. The pay level varies from middleman to middleman and on the ability of the workers to levy the occasional rise. Workers 'Issa Jibran, Yasser Souayfa, and Khalid Tamizi stated that the average wage varies between 16 and 20 shekels per day but that it depends where the workers come from. Those from Ramallah get 16 shekels, those from Gaza 20 shekels, and those from Hebron 18 shekels. This discrepancy is due to the plurity of middlemen . . .

. . . More than twenty of the Gazan workers have not been paid for a month and a half. The reason? Well, the excuse given by the middleman is that his boss has not yet finished his [annual] military service. The workers never cease to worry about this . . .

The majority of workers who answered questions noted that the middlemen break the workers into work gangs, each dealt with individually by threats, promises and deception. All these show the proficiency of the middlemen in dealing with the workers. Protests about money and hours of work and supervision bring small gain which is lost before long.'[38]

The slave markets' along and inside the Green Line have been well documented in recent years as both the Israeli and the European press have begun to take notice of the migrant worker phenomenon. Unlike the 'mops' or 'hirings' which existed in England well into the 20th century, the slave markets take place every day, in Jerusalem, at the entrance to Gaza, and in West Bank towns like Qalqilia. Beginning at dawn, they are sites where middlemen or direct employers find unregistered labourers. Worker is pitted against worker in the rush for approaching cars and vans. The employer picks the tool deemed best for the job – a healthy looking young worker, a reliable looking older man, someone with a skill. Negotiations are minimal – a wage is offered and if one worker does not accept it, one who has not worked for a while will. The majority of jobs available through the slave market are short term and last a few days at best, so the worker must return to the market frequently. To get three days work in a week is to do quite well. Only a fraction of those who offer themselves for work each day find it. One article, written in 1987, talks of 20 out of 150 workers at one of the Tel Aviv markets finding work on a given day.[39]

The transactions of the markets are, of course, technically illegal: the workers do not have permits and the employers are evading tax. Road blocks and the occasional police raid sometimes force markets to shift to another spot. The Israeli government has stated that in 1984, 6,000 unregistered workers were turned back at road blocks.[40] Shalev believes that the failure of work offices to monitor the wages of registered workers may be a deliberate ploy to persuade employers to comply with registration procedures. He cites the instance of one worker who, had he been paid according to regulations, would have received three times his actual pay and would thus have been a less attractive employee. The complacency of the Israeli authorities is evident, even in the diplomatic language of the 1986 and 1987 ILO annual reports. The 1986 report notes (my emphases throughout):

'No major changes in the level of irregular employment of workers from the occupied territories in Israel were noted in 1985. The Israeli authorities consider this stability – a view shared by the Histadrut – to be proof that the difficult economic situation in Israel has not, as might have been feared, forced employers to turn away from official recruitment channels . . .

The Israeli authorities stressed that they have continued to apply the *usual measures* aimed at reducing irregular employment: *as often noted in the past*, these consist of information campaigns, checks on roads into Israel and penalties imposed especially on employers. They also pointed to the pursuit of the policy of regularisation, intended to assist workers discovered in irregular employment: however, *no figures were provided* enabling an assessment to be made of the number of workers whose situation has been regularised . . . '[41]

The 1987 report observes 'no major changes in the level of irregular employment in Israel of workers from the occupied territories', notes that penalties have been increased and, commenting on Israeli measures, again says, 'However, there is little chance of measuring the impact of such activities since no figures are available.'[42] Arab trade unionists not only deny the existence of Israeli information campaigns but point to the fact that Faisal Hindi, a trade unionist in Qalqilia, was summonsed in 1987 for producing a pamphlet explaining the legal situation of migrant workers.[43]

Work

A BREAKDOWN OF REGISTERED migrant workers in 1982 shows that 37.6% were engaged in unskilled work, 38.2% in semi-skilled work, 23.1% in skilled/craft work, 0.3% in clerical and sales work and 0.8% in professional and managerial work.[44] Semyonov and Lewin-Epstein demonstrate that in order to rectify the imbalance in occupation status between 'non-citizen Arabs' and other ethnic groups in the Israeli labour market, 74% of European-American Jews, 63.0% of Asian-African Jews and (interestingly) 51.9% of Israeli Arabs would have had to change their jobs in 1982.[45] They further show the increasing channelling of migrant workers into certain occupational categories. The concept of 'Arab work' is becoming more a reality as time passes. Thus, 'the lower the status of an occupation, the larger the proportion of non-citizen Arabs who entered it by 1982.'[46] Were migrant workers evenly distributed throughout the Israeli economy, in 1982 they should have constituted around 8.5% of the participants in a given occupational category. In fact, they constituted 60% of agricultural labourers, 23.2% of dyers, and 25.7% of construction workers. [47] It is generally estimated that over half of all migrant workers (registered and unregistered) are engaged in construction work. Israeli figures for registered workers put 48.2% in construction, 17.4% in industry, 16.3% in agriculture and 8.8% in the hotel, catering and commercial sector. [49]

Before further discussing the predominant forms of employment of Palestinian migrants in the Israeli economy, one subsidiary form is worth mentioning. It has already been noted that the slave market phenomenon is technically illegal and that it invites the most gross and unprotected exploitation of labour. The opportunities that the mechanism offers to employers is taken to its logical extreme by Israeli criminals who hire (unwitting) Arabs to carry out the riskier parts of their trade. Five out of the 50 workers interviewed in Qalqilia in 1984 stated that they have been so duped and had ended up being arrested and beaten. One told of how he was hired as a fruit picker, provided with baskets and a ladder and shown where to work. As the end of the day approached, he was assaulted by an Israeli farmer with a rifle who handed him over to the police. His employers had disappeared and he had no way of proving that he was anything but a thief. [49]

Migrant workers are employed in enterprises that range in size from one person outfits to large *kibbutzim* and *moshavim*, Histadrut-owned factories and municipalities (a handful of migrants work for Palestinian municipalities inside the Green Line and some of them have complained of discrimination). Larger, non-agricultural enterprises are more likely to use registered workers since they have more complex accounting systems and are less subject to seasonal fluctuations in labour demand, but they are clearly no less exploitative of their workers. This is apparent from an analysis of some of the techniques of super-exploitation by employer and state alike.

Wages

HAVING NO LEGAL RIGHT to be inside the Green Line, unregistered workers clearly have no real rights at all. However, the statutory safeguard of the legal minimum wage (40% of the average wage in early 1987[50]) and 'accordance with the rates laid down by the collective agreements with the relevant [Israeli] trade unions and employers' organisations',[51] are said by Israel to apply to workers with permits. One case uncovered by Shalev has been cited above but, as he notes, such cases are far from exceptional. Palestinian sources maintain that they are the rule. Taggart cites two cases taken up by the Qalqilia Institute Workers Union where official wage slips revealed that the workers were being paid below the legal minimum wage.[52] Arab submissions to the ILO in 1986 and 1987 claimed that migrant workers are paid 50% less than an Israeli worker doing the same job.[53] This complaint about discrimination within the same job is a common one that recurs in virtually every interview with Palestinians who work alongside Jews. *Al-Bayader al-Siyassi* cites one worker who is paid $15 per day while a Jewish worker doing the same job is paid $23 per day.[54] The baker workers who waited in the cold for their shift to start said that: 'the average monthly wage for the Arab workers is 200,000 shekels whilst the salary of the Jewish worker is between 500,000 and 800,000 shekels.'[55]

In 1986, Arab workers at another workplace (owned by the Dolphin company) said that they were being paid 30 New Shekels per day, half that of Jewish colleagues, but were working much longer hours.[56] The point of long work hours is important, since the deprivation of (and discrimination in) overtime pay and increments is a common method of exploitation over and above that deemed respectable in law. Faisal Hindi stated that:

'West Bank workers are maintained as daily [ie casual] workers even when they have worked somewhere for ten years. This means sacking is easy and family and seniority increments are not paid.
. . . Migrant workers only receive the flat rate for overtime while Israeli workers get time and a half or double time. Israeli workers work five hours on a Friday, Palestinians work eight.'[57]

Semyonov and Lewin-Epstein support such Palestinian claims (even without apparently conducting interviews with them). They note a 1986 survey which showed that even in those firms which agreed to be examined:

'A comparison of gross and net wages . . . revealed that in some cases the wages of Israeli workers were 30 per cent higher than the wages of non-citizen Arabs in the same jobs. In the companies surveyed, the gross earnings of Israeli workers were 17 per cent higher on the average, and, because higher taxes are levied on non-citizen Arabs, the net earnings were 25 per cent higher.'[58]

This being the case for registered workers, Taggart's findings in late 1984 are hardly surprising: unregistered women fruit pickers were earning the equivalent of £1.50 per day, child workers earned £3.50 per day, and adult male labourers got £3.75 per day.[59] A 1987 newspaper report noted that workers aged between nine and fourteen years from the village of Husan, employed at Mafubitar settlement, were being paid five New Shekels for an eleven hour day.[60] Palestinian trade unionists say that it is by no means uncommon for an employer to simply refuse to pay a worker picked up from one of the slave markets, knowing he can do nothing about it.

Taxation and other deductions from the wages of workers in possession of permits constitutes a major source of revenue for the Israeli government (and for the Histadrut). Such deductions, which include levies for the Israeli invasion of Lebanon and for 'security' expenditure in the occupied territories, generally amount to 30-40% of gross wages,[61] but there are cases of net income only reaching 50% of gross earnings.[62] As noted above, many migrant workers are kept on as casual labourers, irrespective of their length of service, and thus lose entitlement to benefits such as holiday pay, sick pay, and redundancy money. The way other benefits are lost is described in the 1987 ILO report as:

'. . . the joint application of the principle of equality of labour costs and the residence qualification required by Israeli law for payment of old-age, survivors', invalidity and unemployment benefit and for child allowance . . .'[63]

In other words, migrant workers pay contributions for these benefits because they work in Israel but are themselves denied the benefits because they do not live inside the Green Line and could not do so even if they wished.

Health, safety, and working conditions

ACCIDENTS AT WORK are a fact of life for migrant workers who do the dirtiest and least desirable jobs. This situation is exacerbated by common lack of provision of protective clothing, inadequate rest facilities and medical treatment:

'At work, we have many accidents – burns, broken bones. If a Palestinian is injured they give him half of what they should . . . Also our medical care isn't good. If we get injured, we are treated at West Bank government hospitals, not by Kupat Holim [Israeli national sick fund]. They give us first aid and then transfer us . . . You can't say that Alia Government Hospital [in Hebron] is like Hadassah [hospital in Jerusalem]. We don't even have a qualified doctor.' [64]

Again, the situation of unregistered workers is even worse, as hospitals require information which regulation-dodging employers are loathe to provide. Arab trade unionists see a conspiracy between state, employers and the Israeli legal profession in the refusals to register accidents with the work offices and in the low levels and long delays in the payment of compensation for serious injuries. A few examples suffice to demonstrate employers' attitudes towards Palestinian employees:

—In 1986, Mohammed Hamidan of Ein Beit refugee camp and Sa'ad Sinouber of Yatmah, near Nablus, were working at the Roukah Man biscuit factory, both paying into the social fund and health fund. Yet, when they were injured there, the supervisor refused to either provide them with treatment or take them to hospital. They finally got themselves to the Radidia Hospital in Nablus but the company administration refused to pay for either treatment or recuperation. [65]

—Isa'ad Ali Jalaita, a young worker from Jericho, had his thumb severed whilst working in the Israeli-owned Mafroumal aluminium factory near Deir Yassin. That was in July 1986. By August 1987, neither management nor the work office nor the Israeli national insurance office had done anything to help him, despite the seriousness of his incapacity. Indeed, the supervisor had initially refused to take him to hospital, only providing him with first aid. He was shipped from hospital to hospital, eventually being detained in one for five days. [66]

—Writing in the *Morning Star*, Taggart cites the cases of one worker who lost a finger on a circular saw and received no compensation, a second who lost a leg which became gangrenous after he was told to patch it up himself, and a third who lost an eye but whose employer still refused to register the accident. [67]

The dangers of injury during working hours are compounded by the frequent attacks on Palestinian workers by their Jewish counterparts and the 'security' forces. Attacks are so commonplace that they barely warrant a a mention in either the Hebrew or the Arabic press. At the lower end of the scale is simple harassment but injuries are often serious and deaths are not unknown.

'. . . Once or twice a week, they are stopped by the police, or the civil guard, in the middle of the street. Some are even held for 48 hours for not having a permit. But usually they are searched, rudely interrogated and then set free. At least once or twice a day they have to endure insults from Israelis. They all speak of getting hostile looks at least once every hour.' [68]

'A 39 year old resident from Jabalya Refugee Camp in the Gaza Strip was hospitalised at Tel Hashomer Hospital after receiving medium injuries. Two Jewish youths attacked the labourer, Mahmoud Jaber Shahin, and stabbed him in his left shoulder. The incident took place in Petah Tikva, north of Tel Aviv, where Shahin works.' [69]

'Three Palestinian labourers were severely beaten recently by three Jewish men who pretended to be Israeli police. The Palestinians were stripped naked and left in an area just outside of Eilat. The Israeli police later arrested the three Jewish men.' [70]

'Three men of the Israeli police from Kfar Saba assaulted two Arab workers from the Tulkaram area as they went about their work on a building site in the Israeli municipality of Ra'anana, inside the Green Line. Worker Tayseer Abd al-Majid Mura'aba (28 years old), from the village of Ras Tira, was seriously wounded in the head when he was beaten with a pistol by one of the policemen . . . The workers also mentioned that the police [later at a police station] would not take their complaints seriously but ignored the two.' [71]

'An Arab worker was stabbed in the back with a butcher's knife while working in the Israeli coastal town of Ashdod, October 19. Two other Gaza residents were also attacked by three Israelis posing as policemen while working in Bat Yam on October 20. Many Arab workers are refraining from going to work in Israel for fear of more attacks against them.' [72]

'The body of 21 year old Abdul Fattah Shuqir, who was reported missing two weeks ago, was found July 1. Shuqir, a resident of Zawyeh village near Tulkarm, worked in an Israeli restaurant in Tel Aviv.' [73]

It has already been noted that (according to the Israeli government) only 20% of registered workers are permitted to stay overnight in Israel but that many thousands more do so. Conditions are hardly ideal for those with permits. Thus, Rosenbluth states:

'By law, Palestinians must be in their assigned lodgings at night and are not allowed to walk freely in Jewish areas. Even with a sleeping permit, a worker from the West Bank or Gaza caught in a Jewish area after midnight can be arrested or imprisoned.'[74]

The testimony of labourers, registered or unregistered, demonstrates that sleeping accommodation provided by Histadrut companies such as Solel Boneh, moshavim and kibbutzim, are as bad as any 'cowboy' employers. The two examples below demonstrate this:

'The [Solel Boneh] company hostel was more like a jail. At night they would lock us in. The rooms we slept in were four metres square and we had six workers sleeping in them. There weren't enough beds for everyone so four would sleep in the beds and two would sleep on the floor, and we would take turns. The blankets were dirty and had holes in them. Sometimes we had mice bigger than cats running around us . . . Only a few days a week would we have hot water. The food was no good, but they took 10% of our wages just for the food.'[75]

'Some of the workers on the moshav sleep in chicken houses, some of us just in the open air. None of the chicken houses have electricity. We cook on fires outside . . . Some of the houses for the animals have heat and electricity because the animals cost money. We used to say we lived like chickens, but the chickens live better . . . The labour office don't see and they don't come to see. Sometimes, though, the border police come around to see if any workers are sleeping illegally. The moshav [residents] hide us or we run into the fields. Sometimes we get caught and they beat us or take us to jail. If we get taken to jail, the moshav won't have anyone to pick their crops. That's the only reason they hide us. One evening when we were talking and joking together, the manager came and said we shouldn't speak to each other because the noise would attract the army. He brought two people from the moshav to watch us . . . We get our washing and drinking water from the irrigation pipes. It really is a prison: we can't leave and our families can't visit us and we are guarded with guns . . .'[76]

Because Palestinian migrant workers tend to be treated as casual workers, it is easy for employers to make them redundant. The turnover of workers is high even on the basis of figures used by Israeli apologists which (necessarily) exclude unregistered workers. Statistics quoted in late 1984 maintained that 46% have worked in one place for between one day and one year, 18% have been in one workplace *or trade* from one to two years, 16% for two to four years, and 20% for four years or more. [77] Migrant workers are often sacked just before they would qualify for severance pay. A worker quoted in *al-Fajr* in 1986 said:

'. . . If the employer is good, when he fires you he'll give you a piece of paper saying you are released so you can go to the labour office and get compensation. But most of the time you don't get anything . . . ' [78]

Migrant workers have been summarily dismissed even after periods of 13 years at a workplace. [79] The ILO report for 1987 cites a case in which the management of a cardboard box factory in Lod had decided that large scale redundancies were to be made. Half the workforce was Arab and half Jewish. The Jewish workers demanded that the Arabs be fired on the grounds that 'they were generally considered to be "temporary"'. Eventually, the Histadrut sided with the management and agreed that there should be equality of treatment according to length of service. However, as the ILO observers noted:

'The favourable and equitable outcome of this affair was acknowledged to have been closely linked to the personality and convictions of the employer, thus graphically illustrating how haphazard equality of treatment and the protection of Arab workers from the occupied territories could be in practice.' [80]

The Histadrut

AS WE HAVE SEEN above, the Histadrut [the Zionist Labour Federation] which owns 25% of Israeli industry and which employs and exploits migrant labour like any other Israeli firm, is also willing to subject Palestinian workers to inhumane living conditions. Its support for police action against unregistered workers has also been mentioned. The Histadrut has a direct financial interest in ensuring that as many migrant workers as possible are unregistered; this and the contempt in which it is held by Palestinians of the West Bank and Gaza must be noted. (The discrimination of the Histadrut against Palestinians living inside the Green Line will not be dealt with here)

Whilst membership of the Histadrut is a voluntary commitment which very few migrant workers wish to accept and which costs approximately 3.5% of gross wages, all workers pay a compulsory levy of 1% of gross wages. [81] This is refered to as the 'organisation contribution' and is paid directly to the Histadrut, bringing in millions of dollars per year. In return for these deductions, Histadrut is supposed to defend migrant workers. Yet, as Michael Shalev points out:

'On the ground, though, local Histadrut officials and workers' committees at best demonstrate a lack of enthusiasm for the task, and a tendency to deny or to shrug off their responsibilities.

Nevertheless, the problem in the labour movement begins at the top. The leadership has cynically tied the Histadrut's willingness to take its responsibilities seriously to the government's readiness to offer it a more generous cut from the pay pockets of workers employed through the Employment Service. Insofar as Histadrut leaders raise the issue of labour from the territories in public, it is not to indict the splitting of jobs and workers along nationality lines, but rather to rage against the evils of "unorganised labour".' [82]

The 'more generous cut' which Shalev mentions refers to attempts to persuade the Israeli government to approve a trial year in which the Histadrut would collect wage deductions nominally earmarked for pensions, national insurance and other benefits. These sums currently go into the coffers of the Israeli Labour Ministry. [83]

An example of the Histadrut finally agreeing that Arab workers should be treated on the same basis as Jewish workers has been cited. However, this contrasts with the day-to-day experience of migrant workers which reflects the discriminatory nature of the Zionist Labour Federation. Back in 1983, Mordechai Amster, then secretary of the Building Workers Union, made his notorious statement (repeated, in essence, on subsequent occasions) that:

'The building workers from the territories will be the first to be fired if the forecasts regarding the dismissal of thousands of building workers become true; they are not inhabitants of Israel and in every country with unemployment the foreign workers are the first to be dismissed.' [84]

Attempts by Palestinian migrant labourers to organise against their employers are frustrated by the Histadrut. Semyonov and Lewin-Epstein are correct when they say that migrant workers are not represented on most Histadrut workers' committees. However, they are wrong to claim that Arab workers are permitted to organise themselves. [85] Only 40 of their 160 unions are legal [86] and none are recognised as legal entities inside the Green Line and so cannot even be party to court cases on behalf of migrant workers. The Histadrut has joined Israeli state attempts to blacken the name of Palestinian unions which have been described as 'bases for hostile terrorist actions'. Union leaders such as Ali Abu Hilal have been depicted as 'one of the main leaders of the Democratic Front for the Liberation of Palestine . . . in the West Bank . . . ' and excuses made for his deportation. [88] Attempts to set up workplace committees for migrant workers have found a similar response:

'Before I worked in construction, I worked at a factory in Beer Sheba. We had 80 Palestinians and 60 Jewish workers. It was a textile factory. We tried to form a committee for the Palestinian workers. The Histadrut had a representative in the factory but he didn't do anything for us. So we made this informal committee. The employer fired the head of our committee and told us, 'if anyone wants to follow him, he can.' The work office took his work ID so he couldn't work. The rest of us were scared because we had to work. So we lost our committee.' [89]

Unions, resistance and uprising

MIGRANT LABOURERS face gross economic exploitation maintained by structural discrimination and violence, and by enforced separation from home and family. This exploitation is underpinned by their oppression as part of the Palestinian nation. Any expression of Palestinian identity is deemed as troublemaking and is repudiated as unwarranted. Their identity as Palestinian Arabs, according to the ideology of Zionism, enables the treatment they receive; any organisation along such lines is strictly prohibited, for it threatens not only the super profits of their employers but also the fiction around which the Zionist entity is built. Capital seeks to exploit the proletariat as a class whilst publicly denying the existence of class relations and propounding concepts of individualism and social mobility. Post-1967 Zionism, the Jewish labour movement being largely co-opted and capitalist relations of production thus ensured, has also sought to establish a form of super exploitation by recruiting a Palestinian migrant labour force which it has tried to atomise by repressing all forms of self-expression and denying all national rights. However, double exploitation brings with it double jeopardy, for the migrant worker has national grievances as well as class grievances. An important manifestation of the uprising which exploded in December 1987 has been the militancy of the migrant workers of the West Bank and Gaza Strip.

The Progressive Workers Bloc, the Palestine Communist Party wing of the trade union movement and, until the last few years, indisputably the leading faction, has long recognised the need to work with migrant labourers. In the early days, there were those who said workers who crossed the Green Line for jobs were collaborators but the Communist Party had a more sophisticated analysis:

'From the first day of the occupation, we have defended these workers because we have understood that they need to eat . . . Israel thought that migration would help annexation by acclimatising and influencing the workers. This has not happened. These workers have retained their Arabism and it is strengthened by the discrimination that they face.'[90]

In 1984, the Progressive Workers Bloc claimed 25 committees in workplaces inside the Green Line and was attempting to set up committees of migrant workers in villages and refugee camps. Since 1979, the Workers Unity Bloc (sympathetic to the DFLP) has also been involved in such organisation. Union membership offers migrant workers access to information, such as the pamphlet explaining the wage, safety and benefit rights, published by a union in Qalqilia in 1987.[91] The union also offers legal advice, access to a union clinic and limited financial support in times of hardship. Fundamentally, unionisation has often been a way of surviving the rigours of migrant work, more like a Friendly Society than a powerful industrial weapon. This said, despite the recent entry of most migrant workers into wage labour, contemporary Palestinian trade unionism has deep and militant roots. These come not only from the communist tradition but also from the foundation of the movement in the 1920s and from the six month General Strike of the 1936-39 uprising. Despite immense problems, migrant workers have taken industrial action over workplace grievances on a number of occasions. Such action has ranged from small-scale sabotage and job-hopping to strike action.

Al-Tali'a, 26 June 1986, reported that workers in a factory at Tel Bayout, near Jerusalem, organised a committee and went on strike to fight for higher wages and to oppose the exploitative practices of the employer and the middlemen. The same article reported that workers at the Matsadeh Restaurant in Arad had formed a committee to oppose the sacking of one of their number whose offence was to be ill for one day. Similar action was being taken by workers at the Silharime Restaurant over the suspension of four colleagues. One week earlier, the paper noted that the management of the 'Aouf Yerushalayim abbatoir in Bein Shemesh was threatening to call the border guards and to sack a hundred workers who were demanding a reduction in their ten hour working day. [92] In 1985, 35 workers at the Berman Bakery in Jerusalem walked out. [93] Taggart cites a case of 25 sacked sewing workers being re-employed when they threatened to occupy a workshop. [94]

Although tens of thousands of families in the West Bank and Gaza Strip may depend on money coming in as wages from Israeli employers, the employers are also dependent on the workers. Israel's dependence has increased as Israeli Jews grow less accustomed to doing 'Arab work'. This has been noticed over a number of years. A piece in *Ha'aretz* in 1981 made the point:

'Who would have dreamt in those far-away days before 1967, that the Jewish state founded to provide employment for Jewish labour would be almost paralysed on Muslim holiday? We are at the height of the 'Feast of the Sacrifice' at the moment, when the one month fast of Ramadan comes to an end . . . During the thirty days of the Ramadan fast, the output of Muslim workers falls to zero by midday, and every Jewish manager and foreman in every building site, factory and shop knows this. The Jewish employers have learned from years of experience and now take their holidays during Ramadan . . . Even the garbage collection becomes a problem, and special payments have to be made to workers, since the Jerusalem municipality knows that most of its employees in the sanitation department, apart from the drivers and managers, are Arabs.'[95]

In the same month, *Ma'ariv* mentioned some extreme cases:

'The man in the petrol station was behaving very oddly. He was pointing the petrol pipe at my car window, and started to clean it with a strong stream of gasoline. He looked embarrassed. "Ahmed did not turn up today. It's his feast day", he told me with a trembling voice. "I am the owner of the petrol station. This is the first time I have to do this."'

' . . . A company director was arrested after stabbing his wife with a kitchen knife. "The house was filthy and we had been living on bread and water for three days", he explained. A shocked neighbour told reporters: "They used to be so happy. It's just that Fatima did not turn up for a few days. It was her feast day.'"[96]

In 1982, Israeli tanks rolled into Lebanon and migrant workers continued to roll into work. Although they knew that in many cases they were standing in for Israeli reservists, there was neither the organisation nor the confidence to stage mass stay-aways. But both organisation and confidence were present in December 1987 when the killing of five migrant workers by an Israeli hit-and-run driver sparked the uprising. Alongside the mass demonstrations, the stone-throwing, the burning barricades [and the sudden recognition by British politicians that there is a Palestinian people], came the quiet but effective strike of migrant workers. It was weeks before the international press caught on to the significance and impact of the stay-away but the Israeli press was quicker off the mark. On 18 December 1987, *Ha'aretz* interviewed the Israeli owner of orange groves in Kfar Hess:

'The harvest is not yet at its height, which will be at the end of January. Still, there can be no doubt that the absence of the Arab workers messes up the job in hand. Today I heard that Tnuva Export in southern Israel did not pack anything at all, as the workers had not picked any fruit.
... No Jew has been picking fruit since 1967. In our moshav, you are not going to find a single person who would harvest his own crop. There is no such thing. The rest of the agricultural jobs too are all done by Arabs.'[97]

One month later, panic was setting in. *Hadashot* reported that permits had been issued for 550 harvest workers to be brought in from southern Lebanon. Citrus farmers were reported to be 40% behind schedule and fruit was rotting on the trees. *Yediot Ahronot* noted that heaps of rubbish were filling the streets of Tel Aviv. Why? Because less than 30% of West Bank workers and none from Gaza had turned up for work. Responding to blasé talk about finding workers from elsewhere to do Israel's dirty work, the same paper poured on the scorn:

'In construction, 40 per cent of all workers come from the territories. If they stop coming, construction, especially in the private housing sector, will come to a stand-still. Anyone believing that we can import 50,000 foreign building workers within a reasonably short time is deluding himself ... Where else could we find 17,000 share croppers today? The Jewish sector flees from agricultural work ...'

In industry the large firms say they would be unaffected but the smaller ones are worried. The owner of a textile firm tells me: 'A quarter of my workers come from refugee camps near Nablus. There is no substitute for them in Israel, not among Jews or Arabs . . . '

Services are a sensitive matter. 20,000 workers from the territories serve the Israelis ' . . . Somebody proposed to import workers from Portugal. For what jobs? At what price? Are they going to work for 12 or at most 15 dollars a day in a small restaurant kitchen? Workers are not going to come here from any European country. Perhaps from Thailand, but that is far away.'[98]

And how much does the absence of migrant workers actually cost the Israeli economy? In January 1988, the marketing manager of the agricultural marketing board, AGREXCO, stated that $500,000 had been lost in three weeks and that customers such as Marks and Spencer, Sainsbury, and Safeway were 'very upset'.[99] A few days later, *The Independent* quoted an Israeli army report as estimating the cost of work stoppages since the beginning of the uprising at $50 million in lost sales and production. Over 500 permits had been issued to workers from southern Europe to compensate for the absence of Arab labour. Jerusalem building site managers were failing to attract workers, despite doubling wage levels.[100] The impact on tourism will not be known for months.

Conclusion

THERE IS LITTLE POINT in pretending that the Palestinian working class has suddenly arisen from its slumber or that the events of late 1987 have suddenly transformed it from a class in itself into a class for itself. Since 1967, Palestinian migrant workers have understood their double exploitation, resenting it and wanting to be in a position to fight it. The uprising has allowed them to do so because it has offered them something which they have never had before, strategic depth. The uprising has embraced the entire community of the occupied territories (and Palestinians inside the Green Line). Its fury and its all-embracing nature have left little opportunity for wavering. With schoolchildren seizing the streets and old people demonstrating outside mosques, it has been socially impossible for workers to cross the Green Line, whatever the imperatives of feeding their families. The imposition of curfews by the Israeli army and the burning of buses by the *shebab* has reinforced this impossibility and that is precisely what has been needed for the last two decades. Working in enemy territory, migrants are terribly exposed to the wrath of employers and to the fear of losing work and not being able to provide for the family. No amount of distaste at working for the Zionist economy and no amount of private or rhetorical anger at Zionist barbarity in Lebanon has been powerful enough to persuade tens of thousands of workers to put the precarious health of their families on the line. The uprising, however, has provided a guarantee that there is a fate worse than unemployment – isolation from a community paying for its discontent with blood. Strike action is often not only determined at the national level but workers spontaneously refuse to accept jobs left vacant by compatriots from villages on which travel bans have been imposed. [101] This is not to downgrade the day-to-day fortitude of the migrant workers or to dispute their affiliation to the aspirations of the Palestinian people as a whole; rather it is to face up to the reality that neither patriotic words nor bombs on buses can achieve what the unanimous support of a self-organised community can. As to the future, both the Zionist establishment and the Palestinian working class will learn from the uprising, but one side of weakness it had not appreciated and the other side of strength it had never before trusted.

Notes

1 UNCTAD, *Selected Statistical Tables on the Economy of the Occupied Palestinian Territories (West Bank and Gaza Strip)*, Geneva, July 1986, p16.
2 Ibid p15
3 *Al-Bayader al-Siyassi* (English language supplement) 20/11/87.
4 Moshe Semyonov and Noah Lewin-Epstein, *Hewers of Wood and Drawers of Water: Noncitizen Arabs in the Israeli Labor Market*, ILR Press, Cornell University, USA, 1987, pp11-13.
5 *Report to the Director: Appendix III, Report on the Situation of Workers of the Occupied Arab Territories*, International Labour Organisation (ILO), 1987, para. 23
6 Paul Harper, *Labouring Under Oppression: Poles and Palestinians*, CAABU, London, p4.
7 Ibid p3.
8 Semyonov and Lewin-Epstein op cit. p10.
9 Antoine Mansour, *Palestine: une économie de résistance en Cisjordanie et à Gaza*, Paris, 1983, quoted in *The Economic Destruction of the Occupied Territories*, PLO, London, 1986.
10 *Al-Fajr* (English), 22/2/85, Jerusalem.
11 Najouah Makhoul, 'Modifications dans la structure de l'emploi des arabes en Israël,' Perspectives Judéo-Arabes, October-December 1985, Paris.
12 *Al-Bayader al-Siyassi*, op cit.

13 UNCTAD, op cit. p19.
14 Semyonov and Lewin-Epstein, op cit, pp.9-11.
15 *Al-Fajr* (English), 22/2/85, op cit.
16 Sarah Graham-Brown, *Education, Repression, Liberation: Palestinians*, WUS (UK), London, 1984, p68.
17 UNRWA, 'Economic squeeze hits refugees in West Bank, Gaza', *Palestine Refugees Today*, no. 116, 1987.
18 *Al-Fajr* (English), 2/5/86.
19 UNRWA, op cit.
20 *Tanmiya*, August 1986, Welfare Association, Geneva.
21 *Al-Fajr* (English) 13/6/86.
22 *Al-Bayader al-Siyassi*, op cit.
23 *al-Awdah Weekly*, Where to go this summer, 16/6/85, Jerusalem.
24 ILO 1987 op cit. Annex 3, p60.
25 *Middle East International*, 'Letter from Gaza', 27/6/87, London.
26 *Al-Tali'a*, Jerusalem, 21/11/85
27 *Jewish Chronicle*, 12/7/85, London.
28 Simon Taggart, *Workers in Struggle: Palestinian trade unions in the occupied West Bank*, Editpride, 1985, p57.
29 *Al-Tali'a*, 14/11/85.
30 Semyonov and Lewin-Epstein, op cit, p13.
31 *Jerusalem Post*, 3/10/84, Jerusalem.
32 *Al-Tali'a* 14/11/85
33 Semyonov and Lewin-Epstein, op cit, p12.
34 *Al-Tali'a*, 21/11/85.
35 Taggart, op cit., p65.
36 Michael Shalev, 'Winking an Eye at Cheap Arab Labour', *Jerusalem Post International Edition*, week ending 18/1/86.
37 Semyonov and Lewin-Epstein, op cit., p12.
38 *Al-Tali'a*, 15/10/87.
39 *Middle East International*, op cit.
40 International Labour Organisation (ILO), *Report to the Director: Appendix III, Report on the Situation of Workers of the Occupied Arab Territories*, 1986, Annex 3, p65.
41 Ibid, para. 18.
42 ILO 1987, op cit., para 24.
43 Personal communication, 1987.
44 Semyonov and Lewin-Epstein, op cit., pp22-23 (table).
45 Ibid
46 Ibid, p41.
47 Ibid, p29 (table).
48 *Al-Fajr* (English), 22/2/85, See also ILO 1987, op cit., para. 21.
49 Taggart, op cit., p66.
50 ILO 1987, op cit., para. 37.
51 Ibid, Annex 3, p59.
52 Taggart, op cit., p60.
53 ILO 1987, op cit., Annex 2, p43.
54 *Al-Bayader al-Siyassi*, op cit.
55 *Al-Tali'a*, 21/11/85.
56 *Al-Tali'a*, 19/6/86.

57 Taggart, op cit., p60.
58 Semyonov and Lewin-Epstein, op cit., p88.
59 Taggart, op cit., p15.
60 *Al-Tali'a*, 1/10/87.
61 Taggart, op cit., p60.
62 *Al-Tali'a*, 14/11/85.
63 ILO 1987, op cit., para. 38.
64 *Al-Fajr* (English), 2/5/86.
65 *Al-Tali'a*, 19/6/86.
66 *Al-Tali'a*, 13/8/87.
67 *Morning Star*, London, 7/11/84.
68 *Al-Fajr* (English), 5/10/84.
69 *Al-Fajr* (English), 9/5/86.
70 *Al-Fajr* (English), 10/10/86.
71 *Al-Tali'a*, 20/8/87.
72 *Al-Fajr* (English), 24/10/86.
73 *Al-Fajr* (English), 11/7/86.
74 International Labour Reports, no. 24, Barnsley (Britain), November-December 1987.
75 Ibid.
76 *Al-Fajr* (English), 2/5/86.
77 *Al-Fajr* (English), 22/2/85. See also ILO 1987, op cit., para. 21.
78 *Al-Fajr* (English), 2/5/86.
79 *Al-Fajr* (English), 26/4/85.
80 ILO 1987, op cit., para. 36.
81 Ibid, para. 44.
82 Shalev, op cit.
83 International Labour Reports, op cit.
84 *Ha'aretz*, 18/11/83.
85 Semyonov and Lewin-Epstein, op cit., p104.
86 ILO 1987, op cit., para. 49.
87 International Labour Reports, op cit.
88 Histadrut Executive Committee reply to letter from British trade unions.
89 *Al-Fajr* (English), 2/5/86.
90 Taggart, op cit, p58.
91 One-off publication of Qalqilia Union of Municipal and Public Institute workers on subject of migrant workers' rights, 1987.
92 *Al-Tali'a*, 19/6/86.
93 *Al-Tali'a*, 21/11/85 and *Kol Ha'ir*, 8/11/85 (translated in *Israeli Mirror*, London).
94 Taggart, op cit., p39.
95 *Ha'aretz*, 2/8/81, quoted in Harper, op cit., pp4-5.
96 *Ma'ariv*, 4/8/81, quoted in Harper, op cit., pp5-6.
97 *Ha'aretz*, 18/12/87, translated in *Israeli Mirror*, op cit., 24/12/87.
98 *Yediot Ahronot*, 15/1/88, translated in *Israeli Mirror*, op cit., 16/1/88.
99 *Financial Times*, London, 28/1/88.
100 *The Independent*, London, 30/1/88.
101 *Intifadah wa al-Ard*, one-off publication of Dar al-Sharara, West Jerusalem, March 1988.

Ben Cashdan

COLONIAL LAW AND IDEOLOGY – ISRAEL AND THE OCCUPIED TERRITORIES

Introduction

SINCE THE BEGINNING of its occupation of the West Bank and Gaza Strip, Israel has pursued an uninterrupted policy of Jewish settlement in those territories. Early calls for an exchange of land for peace quickly faded to the background, and successive Israeli governments have differed only in their strategies where settlement is concerned. Thus, in the first twenty years of occupation, over 125 Jewish settlements have been established by both Labour and Likud, home to over 50,000 Jewish settlers. [1] The establishment of settlements in territories inhabited by over a million native Palestinians has required widespread land expropriation and the suppression of Palestinian social and economic development, accompanied by repression of Palestinian resistance to Jewish settlement.

For a minority of Israeli Jews, Jewish settlement in the West Bank and Gaza Strip (like that which took place in Israel's 1948 borders) is regarded as a religious imperative – the fulfilment of a biblical promise – and thus the indigenous Palestinian inhabitants are merely temporary custodians with no enduring rights to property or life there. For this radical minority, land expropriation is simply the return of the territory to its rightful owner, and suppression and repression are the necessary means to purge the land of gentiles (or to rebuild the upright and proud Jewish soul).

But how are Israeli policies explained and justified by the majority of religious and secular Jews who have little truck with such outspoken Jewish religious fundamentalism? Why are the vast majority of Israeli Jews prepared to serve in the army of occupation and actively concerned to defend Israeli policies in the face of widespread international condemnation? Naturally there are dissenters: conscientious objectors, peace protestors and so on; but still the fact remains that Israeli settlement and repression continues with the support and consent, albeit contradictory and ambivalent, of the majority of the Israeli Jewish population. As the Palestinian uprising prepares to celebrate its first anniversary, and international calls for a peace settlement are more numerous than ever, the Israeli bulldozers roll on: demolishing Palestinian homes and building new villas for Jewish immigrants.

At the economic level there is a simple answer to this question. The occupation generates a large workforce of cheap Palestinian labour and constitutes a private and highly lucrative market for Israeli consumer goods. Racism is always founded on economic exploitation, and this relationship is especially marked in a settler-colonial context. With the huge US subsidy to pay for the machinery of repression in the territories, Israeli Jews benefit economically from the exploitation of Palestinian labour and the Palestinian market. Colonialism distorts the basic capitalist class contradictions in favour of national oppression and brings the economic interests of the colonial working class more into line with its own bourgeoisie: thus Israeli Jews actually have a material interest in continuing the process of settlement.

In this paper I will examine some of the legal and ideological mechanisms which are active in distorting the class contradictions in Palestine and which continue to win the support of the majority of Israeli Jews for Israeli colonialism. I will look at the legal and judicial apparatus which facilitates and legitimises land expropriation, Jewish settlement, suppression of the Palestinian economy, and repression of Palestinian resistance, and I will attempt to fill in the ideological framework within which Israeli writers, politicians, legislators, judges and soldiers operate when explaining and justifying their actions.

Although my study is intentionally restricted to Israel and the occupied territories (and in particular the West Bank), many of the issues covered sound a distinct echo in the political culture of Western countries. The ideological mechanisms which are active in winning support amongst Israeli Jews for Zionist expansionism are reflected in those which operate in Britain and elsewhere in gaining the support of Jews and non-Jews for Israel. It is with this in mind that I hope that this paper will contribute something to the project of demystifying Zionism in the West and winning support for the Palestinian national liberation struggle.

Settling in

THERE IS NO SINGLE authoritative document which outlines the policies and objectives of Israeli settlement in the West Bank, although several plans have been proposed and are no doubt used as guides by the state.[2] Common to all of them are the following basic themes:

1. The permanent transfer of population (identified as 'Jewish') to the West Bank, whether present Israeli citizens or new immigrants.
2. The establishment of a supporting infrastructure able to sustain the settler communities (roads, basic services, communications, etc.).

Since the settler infrastructure is to be incorporated into that of the Israeli state proper, and the settlers are to be regarded as citizens of the State of Israel, all the plans imply the permanent annexation of all or part of the West Bank. Clearly the Palestinians living in the areas to be annexed cannot be franchised within the Israeli political system as this would preclude full Israeli control over settlement plans (and would in the long term threaten the Zionist character of the state). Thus the following problems have also had to be confronted:

1. The extension of Israeli citizenship to and the political enfranchisement of the settlers, but not the indigenous population.
2. The administration of the settler communities separately from the indigenous population.
3. The support and development of the settler economy.

Of course the Palestinians cannot simply be ignored. Putting the policies outlined above into practice has necessitated:

1. The active accommodation of the Palestinian infrastructure, administration and economy to their Israeli settler counterparts.
2. The accommodation of the Palestinian population to Israeli settlement, including the suppression of resistance.

The use of the law in securing these objectives has both a coercive and a consensual aspect. In fact the two are mutually dependent, since repression achieved through legal and judicial practices relies on the representation and objectification of these practices for its legitimation. Thus, at the same time as the legislatory and juridical apparatus is used to put settler-colonial objectives into practice, it also plays a central role in justifying the objectives themselves. These legal justifications, when superimposed upon and inserted within discourses around the interests of various collectivities ('the public', 'the Jews', etc.), provide Israelis (and to a much lesser extent Palestinians) with a means of 'making sense' of Israeli settlement in the West Bank.

I will now look at two strategic and ideologically significant legal practices in some detail, namely the acquisition of land and the extension of Israeli law to settlers.

At the outset, it was essential to seize control of government and law. Thus, in the proclamation on law and administration (No.2) of 7 June 1967, the commander of the Israel Defence Forces (IDF) on the West Bank assumed 'any power of government, legislation, appointive, or administrative'. In addition the following principle was agreed by the Israeli government on 11 October 1968: 'The Area Commander is the exclusive formal authority within the area. He [sic] is the legislator, he is the head of the executive and he appoints local officials and local judges'.[3]

With total control concentrated in the hands of one individual, the ground was cleared for putting the settlement objectives into practice.

Creating facts on the ground[4]

ONE OF THE FIRST PROBLEMS to be confronted was that of acquiring land on which to build the settlements. Three bodies of secular law have been drawn upon in a highly eclectic manner by the Israeli authorities in order to acquire land in the West Bank.[5] The oldest of these dates back to Ottoman times. Where no appropriate legislation could be found, the Area Commander has simply used his [sic] own authority to issue a military order. All the methods employed have tended either to *define* the land in question as *the property of* the state or to render Palestinian claims to the land *illicit* or *inapplicable*.[6]

Expropriation of ownership: By virtue of the above proclamation on government of the territories, all land which was previously registered in the name of the Jordanian government immediately became the property of the Israeli state. In addition, through a combination of two Israeli laws passed in 1950,[7] plus a military order specially designed for the purpose,[8] all property owned by persons who left the area in, or before, 1967[9] was considered 'abandoned', and was transferred to the Israeli

'Custodian of Abandoned Property'. The burden of proof of ownership of 'abandoned' land rests with the individual claiming rights. The most successful method of land expropriation was adopted in 1980, whereby all uncultivated, unregistered land is considered *liable for* declaration as state land by virtue of an Israeli interpretation of the Ottoman Land Code (1855). Declarations of state land are not made through judicial process of land registration, but rather preempt it. The only judicial redress open to inhabitants is appeal to a review committee, composed of military government officials. The final method of expropriation of ownership is based on a Jordanian law,[10] which allows for 'Land Expropriation for Public Use', as long as this is in the 'public interest'. This method is thus used to acquire land for arterial and access roads which bypass Arab towns and villages, as well as public buildings in the Israeli settlements. These acquisitions are justified as being in the interest of a rapidly expanding Jewish public.

Seizure of possession: This is effected in individual cases by military order. The Area Commander is free to declare an area of land 'closed' for reasons of 'military security' or to seize possession of land for 'military purposes'.

Restrictions on use: These are also contained in military orders. Restrictions range from prohibitions on building and construction to restrictions on cultivation without express permission. In addition, certain areas of land have been declared 'nature reserves' or 'combat zones', in the latter case the authorities disclaiming any responsibility for damage incurred by military action.

Often a number of these methods will be tried in turn, beginning with offers to buy land. If the owner will not sell, then the area in question may simply be declared state land, or requisitioned for military purposes.[11] In the first case, the burden of proof of ownership rests with the present occupier, whose Ottoman deeds will normally be declared invalid.[12] In the latter, there is no appeal.

Making sense of the law

ALL THESE METHODS of land expropriation are themselves legitimised by being *within the law*.[13] This legitimation relies on a representation of the law as the protector of the interests of the collectivity against the individual who seeks private gain, and thus as the protector of the rights of the 'law-abiding individual'. [14] In addition it relies on traditional perceptions of the law as the force of rationality, somehow 'objective' [15] or 'scientific'. Thus the law operates as a powerful force in the ideological field, defining what is in the *public interest* and what is in the interest of *national security*, and therefore who is outside the national collectivity and the national interest. And indeed, *national security* and the *public interest* are often mobilised to justify the laws which define them. For instance, it is often said that West Bank settlements are important in maintaining the security of the Israeli state. [16] This assertion has the powerful ability to conjure up images of 'war', 'invasion' and 'terrorism' in the minds of the receptive Israeli audience, appealing to the very real fear of many Israelis of the 'Arab Threat'. [17] Whether or not the settlements are *actually* likely to reduce the risk of such occurrences is not important in this context. What counts is the connection which has been made and its strong potential to mobilise support for continued settlement, by drawing upon the everyday image-stock and experience of its audience.

The same goes for the notion of serving the 'public interest', which appeals to a deeply experienced sense of the importance of *justice within the law*. After all, fair's fair; the Palestinians may sometimes get a bad deal, but the law is only doing its best to cater for the needs of everyone in the territories. Individuals always have to make concessions to the public interest, as defined by the law, otherwise society would cease to function. [18] Of course, what is missing in this line of reasoning is the potential of the law to define the 'public interest' in such a way that it actively excludes the interests of the majority of the population. But this contradicts directly the prevailing representation of the law as the protector of the interests of *all* its subjects, except those whose deviant actions conflict with the 'collective interest'.

Whose land is it anyway?

THE NOTIONS OF 'national security' and the 'public interest' have an important role to play in mobilising support for the law in all modern nation states. In Israel, however, the law is further supported by a set of ideas which draw on images particular to the experiences and continually represented history and traditions of 'the Jews'. These centre on the idea that the 'Land of Israel' either *belongs* or is of *peculiar importance* to 'The

Jewish People'. This idea is expressed in a myriad of contradictory forms, both religious and secular, fundamental and utilitarian, as the subject of history, and as its object. The central images which lie beneath these various expressions are those of 'Jewish Tradition', 'Jewish Religion' and 'Jewish Culture' on the one hand, and 'Anti-Semitism' (connected in Israel to the 'Arab Threat') and the danger of 'Assimilation' on the other. The roots and mutual interplay of such ideas in the history of Israeli political culture are extremely complex and I do not intend to unpack them in any detail. [19] What is important here are the perceptions of Israel associated with these ideas and images: Israel solves problems, satisfies aspirations or fulfils requirements of 'The Jewish People'. Thus Israel is a haven from anti-Semitism, a place where 'Jewish Culture' may be preserved and developed freely, a locus of biblical destiny and spiritual redemption, a fulfilment of ancestral tradition or simply a state machine which defends the present Jewish population from the 'Arab Threat'. In all these cases a clear idea emerges: Israel in some sense either belongs or is of peculiar importance to 'The Jewish People'. This I will call the 'special relationship' (SR) notion.

The ideas which form the basis of the SR notion are constantly reproduced and represented in schooling and in the media, rooted in and appealing to the very real experiences of their audience. Thus the notion allows people in Israel to give meaning to their own actions. In whatever complex and contradictory way the notion is understood, it will serve as a filter, a conceptual apparatus, through which to 'make sense' of the individual's actions and experiences. [20] Thus the soldier who is called upon to evict a Palestinian forcibly from a piece of land will have the conceptual apparatus at his or her fingertips to explain his or her actions. The judge whose job it is to evaluate a convincing Palestinian land claim which conflicts with a planned Israeli settlement will be able to make some sense of his or her ruling that the land deeds are invalid by virtue of the SR notion. And the 'innocent' Israeli citizen, who reads in the paper that his/her government has just sanctioned another settlement in an area of dense Arab population will be able to find ways to explain it in terms which make sense to him or her. Thus the appeal to the idea that there exists a 'special relationship' will often provide the only way of making sense of the world.

And the SR notion is often appealed to directly in dealing with specific land claims. When the 'extremist' settlers 'took the law into their own hands' and established a settlement in the heart of Arab Hebron, there was initially no way to legitimise the action by existing legislation or a new military order. Thus, the settlers made use of several forms of the SR notion. For example, they claimed that 'there have always been Jews in Hebron', and that the present inhabitants were no more than custodians of 'Jewish property'. They also referred to the religious significance of the city to the 'Jewish People'.[21] Thus these different formulations appealed to differing systems of justification embedded in the SR notion. It is precisely the diverse and ambiguous nature of the images underlying the notion which make it a powerful ideological force as a mobiliser of different constituencies of support. And the appeals in this case were successful in averting a legal crisis until the authorities could find a way to justify the settlement by legal means.

The 'special relationship' is much more than a last resort in times of crisis. It inhabits the realm of 'common sense', of 'how things are'. It simply makes no sense to suggest that land and property in East Jerusalem were taken from Palestinian Arabs illegally immediately after the occupation began. Jerusalem – East or West – is a part of Israel; that's just the way it is. There is simply no other way of thinking about it, so strong are the images mobilised around the SR notion in this context.

A final example of the significance of the 'special relationship' in acquiring land in the West Bank is offered by those groups who believe that all of *Eretz Israel*,[22] including the whole of the West Bank, belongs to 'The Jewish People' by virtue of its centrality in 'Jewish Tradition', and that the Palestinians have no rights of ownership whatsoever. *Amana*, the settlement division of Gush Emunim,[23] subscribes to this belief, asserting that 'the only justification for Jews to be living in this Palestinian area is because it was the land that was maintained as a part of our tradition for all these years'. And further, 'you cannot apply practical political rules to the way the Jewish state operates'. 'If your philosophy is placed on a sideline and practicality takes its place exclusively, then you may end up with something that's very practical but you'll lose the game.'[24] Thus 'practical political rules' (that is 'regular' state law), although used extensively as a way of securing ownership of land in the West Bank, are not the real justification. This lies elsewhere, in the realm of absolute rights of possession based on 'national tradition'. *Amana* is now an official settlement organisation of the Israeli state and consequently receives extensive funding from the Israeli authorities. Thus *Amana*, although represented as a bit 'extreme', is used by the state to put an extra-legal version of SR into practice.

In summary; Israeli expropriation of land in the West Bank is achieved by ingenious manipulation of the law, so that land acquisition can be described as falling entirely 'within the law'. This legitimation process relies on the traditional notion that the law is the impartial defender of the collective interest, and of the rights of the individual. In addition, the whole process takes place within a particular ideological climate, in which the idea that there exists a 'Jewish People' with a special or peculiar relationship with 'The Land of Israel', is extremely pervasive. This idea takes on many contradictory forms, which only serve to broaden its appeal, and thus to increase its importance in adding extra legitimation to Israeli settlement. It achieves this by helping to 'make sense' of the experiences and actions of individuals in relation to the acquisition of land for settlement, or through 'fundamentalist' adherents it provides a direct route for extra-judicial settlement. Thus the two important themes here are *traditional*: one centres around traditional notions of the nature of the law, the other around that of the 'Jewish People'.

Thus, Yitzhak Shamir, Prime Minister of Israel, was able to say in a 1984 interview with *Time* magazine, 'We are not taking land from anybody. Nothing.'[25]

Within and without the law

IT IS CLEAR from the settlement objectives outlined above that a strict legal distinction had to be made between the Israeli settlers in the West Bank and the indigenous population. How else could the two populations be administered separately, and political enfranchisement within the Israeli system be denied exclusively to the latter? Similarly, the idea of planning in the 'public interest' in the context of Israeli settlement relies on a definition (within the law) of 'the public', which explicitly or by ommission excludes Palestinians.

By 1984, this problem had been all but solved. A way had been found to extend full Israeli citizenship to all West Bank settlers, and to bring them under the jurisdiction of Israeli law and Israeli courts, without extending the same privileges to the Palestinians. The method used was to define the jurisdiction of Israeli law and Israeli courts in tems of *who* it covers, not its territorial extent. As in the case of land acquisition, this solution makes use of a definition of the community or collectivity of souls referred to as 'The Jews'.

The solution was put into practice by making a succession of amendments to a set of Emergency Regulations which were introduced at the start of the occupation.[26] Initially these regulations had served to extend the jurisdiction of the Israeli courts to Israeli nationals who committed an offence whilst travelling in the occupied territories. This was necessitated by the relative ease of travel which was now possible across the Green Line.[27] Explicitly excluded from the jurisdiction of the courts were 'residents' of the 'regions', i.e. the occupied territories. This meant that Israeli settlers were excluded along with the Palestinians. Thus, in their initial form, these regulations simply served to extend the territorial extent of Israeli jurisdiction, without incorporating those persons resident in the appended territory.

However, in July 1975, an amendment to the Emergency Regulations was introduced[28] which qualified the definition of the group excluded from Israeli jurisdiction. It now read, 'any person who at the time of the act or the omission was a resident of one of the regions *and was not registered in the Population Register*' (my emphasis). Naturally, Palestinians living in the occupied territories do not qualify for an entry in the Israeli Population Register. Apart from present Israeli nationals or permanent residents of Israel,[29] the only persons who are eligible for registration are 'Jews', and their families, as defined in the Israeli *Law of Return*.[30] This extension of legal jurisdiction to 'Jews' was consolidated in a final amendment to the regulations in January 1984.[31] This set out a list of Israeli laws which were henceforth to apply to 'any person whose place of residence is in the region [the occupied territories] and who is an Israeli citizen or entitled to acquire Israeli citizenship pursuant to the *Law of Return*'. This list is extendable by the Israeli Minister of Justice.

Thus, strictly speaking, a legal distinction had been made between those permanent residents of the occupied territories who are defined as 'Jewish',[32] and those who are not. The former are now Israeli citizens who fall under the jurisdiction of Israeli law and Israeli courts; the latter are merely 'residents' of the 'areas'.[33]

The importance of establishing this distinction cannot be over-emphasized. It means that as far as regular Israeli law[34] is concerned, Palestinians in the occupied territories simply do not exist–they are *outside the law*. Furthermore, they have been *defined out* of the national community (identified in the Law of Return), which Israeli law claims to serve, since they are 'non-Jews'. They have no claims to Israeli state land, and their interests do not have to be taken into consideration when planning in the 'public interest'. Thus, in the words of Meron Benvenisti, 'All communal lands are the patrimony of the Jewish community, being the only legitimate collective'.[35] 'Closed areas are closed for Palestinians only, and open for Israelis.'[36]

Israeli settlements in the West Bank are now served by their own local and regional councils, which have been incorporated into the government administration in Israel proper. Funds for settlement are allocated by the Ministry of Housing and Construction, the budgets being fully integrated with those for construction inside Israel. Local councils are also regularly allocated funds by the Ministry of the Interior and Religious Affairs. Land planning is carried out by the responsible bodies in Israel, in conjunction with the 'High Planning Committee' in the West Bank, which superseded the Palestinian/Jordanian planning authority. The latter had provided for the full participation of members of the local community in land planning. The new 'High Planning Committee' is made up entirely of Israeli government representatives, with negligible local participation. So far its plans seem to be oriented towards developing an infrastructure for the Israeli settlements entirely separately from that which serves the Palestinians, the latter being neglected in the main. Official blueprints refer to the following objectives: 'interconnection between existing Jewish areas in order to create continuity in Jewish settlement patterns; fragmentation of Arab settlement blocs; and encouragement of new Jewish settlement blocs'.[37]

Thus, having lifted the Israeli settlers up into the cradle of the law and the nation, whilst leaving the indigenous population down on the ground below, legislative and administrative power could quite 'legitimately' [sic] be used to actively promote the interests of Israeli settlement and to accommodate the 'natives' as required. This accommodation was achieved by military rule.

Law, crime and the Palestinians

ON ASSUMING GOVERNMENTAL and judicial authority over the West Bank, the Area Commander (AC) proceeded to set up a Military Government (MG), staffed by Israeli army personnel. These Military Government officials were appointed by the Area Commander who delegated to them a wide range of administrative and legal functions. Where existing Jordanian/Palestinian administrative and judicial bodies were not dismantled, they became ultimately accountable to the Area Commander.[38]

Thus the Military Government was able to exercise a great deal of control over almost every conceivable aspect of the lives of Palestinian inhabitants of the occupied territories, from land-use, distribution of water, and construction of buildings; through investment and employment; to freedom of movement, organisation, expression, and assembly.

Since the very existence of an indigenous population presents an obstacle to increased Israeli settlement, extensive use has been made of these powers to control and restrict the normal functioning and development of Palestinian society and economy.[39]

Like the state bodies directly responsible for Israeli settlement planning, the Military Government has considerable leeway to define what is, and what is not, 'in the public interest'. Thus it is not in the 'public interest', as defined by the MG, to permit the expansion of Palestinian towns and villages into areas which may be designated for future Israeli settlement – building permission is frequently denied.[40] Nor is it in the 'public interest' to allow Palestinians to make extensive use of water, if this is needed by the settlements – permission to sink wells is often refused.[41] And the 'public' is best served by introducing special financial incentives for Israeli businesses moving to the West Bank, whilst imposing strict trade restrictions on Palestinian produce.[42]

Palestinians who have grievances against decisions made by the MG can take them to the Military Objections Committee,[43] which itself consists of MG officials. In the last instance, the Israeli High Court of Justice will take petitions and hear appeals on behalf of West Bank Palestinians, as long as they are represented by Israeli lawyers. However, it is not clear whether the High Court actually has the authority to overturn MG rulings, particular if they are presented as masters of 'security'. In explaining his refusal to scrutinize one such appeal, High Court Judge Justice Vitkon declared, 'security matters, like matters of foreign policy, are not justiciable'.[44]

Reference to 'security' is the most commonly-used explanation of laws and rulings by the MG which are likely to be contested. The 'security' justification is used in the overwhelming majority of cases where the freedom of Palestinians is restricted by military order or by reference to the Emergency Regulations (1945) enacted by the British Mandate Government; e.g. prohibitions on membership in Palestinian political parties; censorship, including prohibitions on publishing or displaying anything with 'a political significance', such as the Palestinian flag; restrictions on travel into Israel;[45] the requirement that all Palestinians carry an identity card at all times; the temporary closure of universities[46] and trade union offices[47]; the banning of trade union meetings[48]; and cultural events[49]; as well as curfews on whole towns or camps.[50] Specific restrictions are also placed on individuals, for example, 'Town Arrest,' or 'House Arrest,' which confine the individual to her or his place of residence (town or dwelling) for the specified period (normally six months), thus precluding the possibility of continuing employment.[51] Persons under 'Town Arrest' are normally required to report to the nearest military headquarters each day, at their own expense.

Palestinians charged under military law are tried in military courts operated by the MG. However, since 'security' offenders are often not given a trial, or even told the reasons for the restrictions imposed upon them, it is not easy to make a clear distinction between punitive and preventative measures. All that is required is that the Area Commander (AC) judge the restriction necessary in the interests of 'security'. The AC may imprison any Palestinian without trial for a period of up to six months, the term of imprisonment being indefinitely renewable. This is known as 'Administrative Detention'. [52] Other sanctions which are frequently used against 'security' suspects are the demolition or 'sealing' of the house of the suspect and his or her family, [53] or deportation. [54]

Individual and collective freedoms are also restricted by means of policing practices. The West Bank is policed by a civilian force under the aegis of the MG, backed up by IDF soldiers. It is the latter who deal almost exclusively with matters relating to military orders or restrictions. In addition, IDF soldiers regularly set up road blocks in carefully selected locations, such as on the approach road to a university. Passage may be refused, again usually on the grounds of 'security'. [55] Frequent raids on university campuses and dormitories, as well as private residences, have been reported. And there have been numerous reports of various forms of harassment, intimidation, and torture of Palestinians by the IDF, both on the streets and in custody. [56]

In 1981, the Israeli authorities established a Civilian Administration in the West Bank, with certain secondary legislative and administrative responsibilities. However all primary legislative power remained with the Area Commander of the IDF, who was responsible for appointing the head of the Civilian Administration. Thus, although this move served a cosmetic function by appearing to follow the spirit of the Camp David accords, [57] it did not significantly alter the distribution of power. [58]

Thus the Israeli state, through the IDF, assumed responsibility for all the administrative and legal affairs of the West Bank Palestinians. By virtue of this highly-centralized concentration of power, it has had considerable space within which to define what consitutes a crime and what does not. These definitions of criminality are, in the main, reliant on the terms 'public interest', and in particular 'security'.

Since the normal functioning and development of Palestinian society is an obstacle to Israeli settlement plans, it is also contrary to the 'public interest' as defined by the Israeli authorities. As a result a very great range of Palestinian activities, from building houses to writing newspaper articles and poetry, is *criminalised*; it constitutes a resistance which must be confronted and removed by the Military Government.

For the vast majority of the Israeli population, the criminalisation of Palestinian resistance is not a conspiracy. On the contrary, these criminal definitions are simply the only way of making sense of what is happening. For the IDF soldier on duty in the West Bank, they are the only way of understanding his or her own actions.[59] On the other hand, these definitions are not simply fed to the masses. Rather, individual Israeli citizens are active in bringing them into existence, developing them, articulating their own experiences through them, and swapping them with each other. The discourses around the 'crime problem',[60] or around 'Palestinian disruption of Israeli settlement',[61] or around 'attacks by the Arabs on those "extremist" settlers in the territories',[62] are not open discussions in which full representation is given to conflicting interpretations. The discourse takes place within the framework of existing ideological systems and is highly structured, largely by the media, and through the media by the state. The result is that the representations of Palestinian criminality emerge as common sense explanations of the personal experiences of people living in Israel.

An extremely important set of such experiences are those associated with armed or military Palestinian resistance. Experiences of bombings or knifings, and in particular the way they are presented in the media, form powerful images, which, when conjured up at other moments, serve to strengthen and consolidate the criminalisation of many different forms of Palestinian resistance.

The discourses which form the basis of the criminalisation process further draw on numerous ideological fragments which have been left behind by more developed ideologies. I will now look at two such ideologies which are important in understanding the criminalisation of Palestinians in the West Bank. One is associated with the colonised 'native', the other with the 'Goy' (i.e. the non-Jew).

The 'Native', the 'Goy', and the 'Arab'

IN THE COLONIAL and post-colonial world there is a stock of images which has become embedded in our common sense thinking about law and, in particular, crime. These comprise representations of the 'native'. In a highly evocative passage, Hall describes the representation of the 'native' in the British media:

'The good side of this figure is portrayed in a certain primitive nobility and simple dignity. The bad side is portrayed in terms of cheating and cunning, and, further out, savagery and barbarism. Popular culture is still full today of countless savage and restless "natives", and sound-tracks constantly repeat the threatening sound of drumming in the night, the hint of primitive rites and cults. Cannibals, whirling dirvishes, Indian tribesmen, garishly got up, are constantly threatening to overrun the screen. They are likely to appear at any moment out of the darkness to decapitate the beautiful heroine, kidnap the children, burn the encampment or threatening to boil, cook and eat the innocent explorer or colonial administrator and his lady wife. These "natives" always move as an anonymous collective mass – in tribes or hordes.'[63]

There is a great deal of overlap between the picture painted here and the dominant representations of the 'Arab' which El Asmar identified in a recent study of children's literature in Israel.[64] According to this study, the 'Arabs', like the 'natives', are anonymous, moving in gangs and mobs. The 'Arabs' are dirty, they carry contagious diseases. They are thieves and untrustworthy. They are fighters, infiltrators, saboteurs.

But contemporary Israeli representations of the 'Arab' do not only draw on classical colonial mythology. They are also bound up with certain selected representations of the 'other' of 'Jewish Tradition'. Like the 'special relationship' notion (see above), the way in which the 'Goyim' are different from the 'Jews' has been expressed in a wide range of conflicting forms, spiritual, genetic, cultural and so on. For example, some claim that 'the Jews' are different from 'the Goyim' by virtue of divine selection or genetic code, others that they have something to protect from them, such as 'Jewish Culture', or 'Jewish Tradition'. The latter corresponds to the threat of 'Assimilation'. Another threat which has been of central importance to the 'Jew'/'Goy' distinction, and the representation of the Goyim, is anti-Semitism. This is either an intrinsic characteristic of the Goy, or it arises out of the incompatibility of Goy and Jewish culture, or it is a result of the active stigmatisation of things Jewish by certain Goyim, in pursuit of their interests.[65]

The 'Arabs' are perceived as 'Goyim', and they are 'natives'. Thus they threaten the integrity, the purity, the sanctity and the order of the Jewish space. Filled with a hatred of Jews and things Jewish, they mean to invade, to penetrate, to kill, and to steal the land. At the same time, they are noble primitives and unfortunate victims of Fate or Chance.[66] It is within this fragmented and contradictory field of images that discourses around Palestinian crime take place.

Making sense of Palestinian crime: A study of the criminalising discourse

ON 4 DECEMBER 1986, two young Palestinian students were shot dead by Israeli soldiers after a sit-down protest at a roadblock set up near Birzeit University in the West Bank. In the week that followed, several more violent confrontations took place between the military and Palestinian inhabitants, in the course of which two more Palestinians were killed and several wounded. During December, a large number of articles appeared in the Israeli press, reporting or reflecting on what had taken place.

In those articles appearing in the Jerusalem Post,[67] the following expressions were used to refer to the response of Palestinians all over the occupied territories to the first two shootings: 'wave of disturbances', 'unrest', 'wave of demonstrations', 'eruption', 'outbreaks', 'turmoil', 'disorder', 'riots', 'disturbances swept the West Bank', 'widespread disturbances continued to rock the Gaza Strip'.

The actions of the IDF officers, however, were represented by the following expressions: 'self defence', 'preventing further violence', 'breaking up a demonstration', 'quelling the disturbances', 'maintaining law and order', 'troops used "maximal restraint" '. In addition, their actions were defended, or described as too lenient: 'the IDF has acted correctly in the circumstances, acted as it must act', 'the security forces had acted according to regulations', 'the security forces should show less "restraint" and . . . greater punishment of law-breakers should be imposed if order is to be maintained'. Explanations were offered or implied as follows: 'It's actually like a tetanus shot we have to administer every three months in order to keep things in check'; 'Israel's policy is to maintain law and order and peace for all the territories' inhabitants'; 'force will get the Arabs nowhere and will solve nothing'; 'life in the West Bank is returning to a semblance of normalcy'.

Statements also pointed to the 'unusual' or 'exceptional' nature of the 'disturbances'. Thus: 'The wave of incidents is unusual but it is not a major outburst'; 'Israeli officials have characterised the worst unrest in the territories for years as an "unusual" development'; 'momentary ephemeral occurrences'.

Israeli settlement was referred to both as the solution to, and the justification for, the confrontations: 'The disturbances should prompt the government to set up more settlements in the territories. Settlements are an assurance of security'. An IDF soldier who admitted to shooting one of the two Birzeit students argued, 'We were caught in an impossible situation. Had we retreated, no Israeli from the nearby settlements would be able to travel on the main road leading west'.

Another common assertion in the articles surveyed explicitly or implicitly blamed the PLO for the occurences: 'The disturbances at Birzeit University . . . are part of an attempt of the PLO to murder prospects for peace by inciting to riot'; 'there may be some guiding hand behind the eruption of simultaneous demonstrations throughout the West Bank and Gaza'; 'It's only a few PLO activists who incite the others. Most people who live in the territories want peace and quiet'. However, in this context the PLO is not a political organization with a set of intelligible, if unacceptable aims, rather it is the ultimate symbol of criminality, a 'murderer of peace'. (Membership of the PLO or any communication with its members by Israeli citizens is a criminal offence under Israeli law.)

It is easy to see how these expressions and assertions draw upon and reproduce the discourses on 'The Law' and 'Crime' which I identified above. They mobilise images of the 'restless native', the 'diseased Arab', the 'Order' of 'The Law'. The problem was basically one of an eruption of 'unrest' (by far and away the most common descriptive term used), a spurious outbreak of disorder. The solution is to 'quell' this outburst, to restore normality and order, to administer the medicine, and thus to put the troublemakers back to rest. Clearly settlement must go ahead – and so the criminals had to be dealt with. In fact, increased settlement would help prevent the same thing happening again.

One slightly more critical position was also represented, which suggested that the IDF soldiers had acted a little harshly, and a less violent way must be found to solve the problem. ('Israel . . . must . . . reduce tensions in the sphere of settlement'.) But still the basic problem was the same. And on this occasion, disturbances had unfortunately broken out and had to be dealt with, a little less harshly if possible. Thus, even in this more critical formulation the basic issues were the same.

Amongst all the articles, just one line of argument was offered which broke away from the dominant framework. This asserted that 'the disturbances are not marginal. They are politically very serious, grave and worrisome. Israel must not relate to them only militarily or in terms of maintaining law and order'. This certainly constitutes a move onto new ground. However the argument was preceded by the following: 'The disturbances were an attempt to block the political process leading towards peace.' Thus the politically serious nature of the disturbances, which were not simply breaches of the law by criminals, were aimed at blocking 'the political process leading towards peace'. Thus the 'politics' associated with the 'disturbances' is the 'worrisome' politics of 'saboteurs'. In such a context, this is hardly a very radical departure from the dominant defining frame.

Here lies the importance of the media in enabling the state to *define the situation*; to set out the basic issues to be evaluated. The articles I surveyed contained a preponderance of direct quotes from Israeli government and army officials, regularly contacted by the press as spokespersons and experts. Thus it is through the institutional relationship between the state and the media that representatives of the state become what Stuart Hall calls 'primary definers'[68] of the situation at hand.

In the context of Palestinian crime, one extremely important defining representation is that of 'terrorism'. 'Terrorism' is the purest expression of Palestinian criminality, drawing on images of irrationality, of savagery and barbarism, anti-Semitism and Evil. In Israel, 'terrorism' is almost exclusively what Gilroy calls a 'racially distinct crime'.[69] Israeli Police Minister Haim Bar-Lev refers to the need to deal with both 'Arab terrorism' and 'extremist reaction from Jews', since 'there is the same law for every resident in the country'.[70] Thus, in the words of Noam Chomsky, 'Palestinians carry out terrorism, Israelis then retaliate, perhaps too harshly'.[71]

There have been numerous recorded incidents of Israeli settler attacks on Palestinian persons and property in the West Bank, often including the use of arms.[72] According to an Israeli government report, whose publication was suppressed for two years, the perpetrators of these attacks 'are not perceived by the police as offenders in the usual sense';[73] their actions are 'not the usual criminal delinquency', since they are seen as 'springing from the desire to demonstrate 'rights' on the ground'.[74] Thus 'Jews' who attack 'Arabs' are not criminals at all – they have simply 'taken the law into their own hands'.[75] Palestinians, on the other hand, who are active in student or trade unions, or who write about 'Palestine' and the 'self-determination of the Palestinian people' are not simply law-breakers, they are 'terrorists' too. What's more, 'terrorism' is a fact, a reality that cannot be explained; it is irrational, outside 'Jewish' understanding. Hence, 'Terror is a situation I have been living with since I arrived in this country.' And, 'There is no single way to end terror once and for all'.[76] Similarly, 'Our policy was to fight terror with every legal means available'.[77]

Thus, through the media, the Israeli state is able to mobilise extremely powerful images, rooted in the dominant representations of the real experiences of (some) Israeli citizens, and articulated through the fragmentary traces of more developed 'traditional' ideologies of prior epochs, against those actions which conflict with its interests. What is important about these ways of understanding the world is not their *direct correspondence* to a 'reality' outside themselves, nor their logical consistency – indeed, they contain many inherent contradictions – but the connections that are made within them and their success as ways of 'making sense' of the problematic and contradictory nature of human experience. If they appeal, if they 'hail' the majority of the population into the community of group identity and group interest which they claim to represent, then they will often become the only available means of thinking about the problems which are posed.

The collectivity or community is itself constructed and defined by the problems it is said to face, and by the 'other' which is the source of its problems. Thus it is the traditional discourses of 'Jewishness' and the 'native', re-expressed in terms of law and crime, national security and the public interest, which define the notion of 'Arab terrorism' for the community of 'civilised', 'law-abiding' Jewish citizens of Israel.

Notes

1   Benvenisti (1986b), p47 puts the figure for 1985 at 104.
2   Examples are the *Allon Plan* (1967, 1968, 1969, 1970), based on the idea of 'secure borders' along with limited territorial concessions to a 'Jordanian-Palestinian' state, the *Drobless Plan* (1978, 1980, 1981), which proposed total annexation of the occupied territories and intensive settlement in and around areas of dense Arab population, the *Sharon Plan* (1980), close to the maximalist approach, although excluding a couple of individually-selected areas of dense Arab population, and the *Development Plan, Judea-Samaria (1983-1986)* (1983), concentrating on the surburban areas around Jerusalem and Tel Aviv. For brief outlines of all these proposals, see the appropriate entries in Bevenisti (1986a).
3   Source: Al-Haq
4   An expression used by advocates of annexation to describe their strategy, namely, the preemption of politically-motivated territorial concessions by the state, through the establishment right now of 'facts on the ground', i.e. settlements.
5   *The Ottoman Land Code (1855)*, Jordanian land law, and legislation passed by the Israeli Knesset.
6   See Shehadeh, pp 15-58 and Benvenisti (1986b), pp25-36.
7   *Absentee Property Law No. 28 (1950)* and *Development Authority (Transfer of Property) Law No. 62 (1950)*, cited in Shehadeh, p34.
8   *Military order 58, (July 1967)* in Ibid., p35.
9   Including those who fled through fear, intending to return.
10   *Law of Land Expropriation for Public Purposes, No. 2 (Jordan 1953)*, in Ibid., p37.

11   Declaration of state land has now almost completely replaced *Requisition for Military Purposes*.
12   See, for example, the case of *Sabri Ghuraib*. He refused to sell a piece of land adjacent to an expanding Israeli settlement. Soon afterwards he found a portion of his land fenced off, and his house was left on a little island in the middle! Sabri is unusual in that he has copies of deeds to his land, issued by the Turkish and Jordanian authorities. These have been rejected as proof of ownership by the Israeli authorities.
13   Apart from exceptional cases, they are within the local and national law, as interpreted by the Israeli state. Often, inconsistencies and inadequacies are found, and an attempt is usually made to patch them up. Israeli settlement is, however, in direct contravention of international law.
14   The 'individual in the eyes of the law' is a legal construction of bourgeois law used to define the rights and responsibilities of the individual within capitalist social relations.
15   'The Israeli court system is certainly well known as an objective court system', Chaim Mekovsky of Gush Emunim, interviewed by author.
16   See, for example, *Jerusalem Post* 8.12.86.
17   The fear is experienced, whether or not it is justified.
18   This line of argument was offered by Chaim Mekovsky of Gush Emunim in an interview with the author.
19   For obvious reasons this is highly contested terrain. There are a multitude of studies of Jewish political culture, in particular Zionism. One good survey of the themes I have touched on in the context of the Israeli state and its interests is contained in Seliktar.
20   See, for example, Hall (1981), p31.
21   From interview with Mekovsky.
22   *The Land of Israel*. Normally denotes the maximalist view, which extends in theory from the Nile to the Euphrates and right across the Jordan into the eastern desert.
23   Literally '*The Bloc of the Faithful*'. A political pressure group with a strong religious underpinning which advocates increased settlement in the whole of the West Bank.
24   Chaim Mekovsky, in an interview with the author, January 1987.
25   *Time*, 9 April 1984. Cited in Shehadeh, p17.
26   *Emergency Regulations (Areas Held by the Defence Army of Israel–Criminal Jurisdiction and Legal Assistance)*, 5727-1967, cited in Hillier, p1.
27   The line separating Israel in pre-67 borders from the occupied territories.
28   *Emergency Regulations (Areas Held by the Defence Army of Israel–Criminal Jurisdiction and Legal Assistance) (Amendment) Law*, 5735-1975, in Ibid., p3.
29   Not including the occupied territories.
30   'For the purposes of this Law, "Jew" means a person who was born of a Jewish mother or who has become converted to Judaism and who is not a member of another religion.' Citizenship rights are also extended to 'a child and grandchild of a Jew, the spouse of a Jew, the spouse of a child of a Jew and the spouse of a grandchild of a Jew except for a person who has been a Jew and has voluntarily changed his religion'. Cited in Davis (1987), p32.
31   Cited in Hillier, p6.
32   Or who are registered as Israeli nationals. In any case, all those people defined by the *Law of Return* as 'Jews' are eligible for Israeli citizenship.

33   Thus, since I satisfy the definition given in note (30) above, if I were to visit the occupied territories, presumably I would immediately come under the jurisdiction of Israeli law, although a 'non-Jewish' companion of mine would not!

34   As opposed to Military Orders specifically aimed at the Palestinian population.

35   Benvenisti (1986b), p26.

36   Ibid., p30.

37   Ibid., p30.

38   Or their powers were drastically reduced, rendering them no more than cosmetic remnants. Or both. For example, the Jordanian courts still operate, but they are now under the charge of the MG officer responsible for the judiciary. In addition, the court facilities and supplies (e.g. stationery) have been allowed to run down, and they are offered very little assistance in terms of policing from the IDF. Increasingly, civil cases are being heard in the military courts. See Shehadeh, pp 76-81. Information also supplied to the author by Andre Rosenthal, an Israeli advocate practicing in Israel and the occupied territories.

39   Examples are restrictions on import of capital, capital transfer, banking, trade, purchase of plant, construction, trade union organisation, publication and distribution of press, educational provision and academic freedom, legal practicing. See Shehadeh, Benvenisti (1986b), and special reports of Al-Haq and Birzeit University Public Relations Department for detailed studies of the nature, extent and effect of the many different forms this control has taken.

40   Both Birzeit University and the Islamic University in Gaza have been refused permission to continue construction of new buildings for long periods. In the latter case, permission to build on an existing site has been denied.

41   'In 1990, 60 million cubic meters will be available to some 30 Israeli agricultural settlements, only one third less than the amount available for 400 Palestinian villages.' Benvenisti (1986b), p21.

42   In addition, West Bank farmers have repeatedly been prevented from travelling to East Jerusalem to sell agricultural produce.

43   See Shehadeh, pp 87-91

44   Cited in Shehadeh, p97.

45   It is a criminal offence for a Palestinian Arab of the West Bank or Gaza Strip to remain in Israel after 12 midnight.

46   In the period 1979-86, Birzeit University was closed by Military Order nine times, for a total of over 15 months (from BZU Special Report on Academic Freedom).

47   The office of the General Federation of Trade Unions in Nablus was ordered closed by Military Order for a period of one month from 24 August 1986 for 'security' reasons. The office of the Services and Free Professions Union in Nablus was ordered closed for one year from 19 September 1986. The office of the Institutions and Skilled Professions Union in Nablus was ordered closed for six months from 23 September 1986.

48   The Annual General Meeting of Palestinian teachers was prevented from taking place on 12.12.86. The venue, the Al-Hakawati Theatre in East Jerusalem, was simply ordered closed for a period of 24 hours.

49   The Al-Hakawati Theatre has been closed by order, and theatrical performances have had to be cancelled.

50   Examples are Ramallah 7.12.86, Balata camp 8.12.86, Ramallah 9.12.86.

51   In 1986, 62 persons were placed under Town Arrest in the West Bank. (source: Al-Haq).

52   Imprisonment without trial: 1985: 131 1986: 37 (source: Al-Haq). 'Administrative Detention is justified only to avert a danger to state security or public security', Itzhak Zamir, Israeli Attorney General, 1982. See Playfair (Al-Haq).

53   House Demolitions/Sealings (West Bank) 1985: 55 1986: 47 (source Al-Haq).

54   Deportation Orders (West Bank and Gaza) 1985: 31 1986:5.

55   Birzeit University was 'seized' by means of military checkpoints on 36 separate occasions in the academic year 1985-6. This method seems to be used to hinder specific events, such as visits by Israeli academics, or work camps. (source: BZU Report).

56   See Reports by Al-Haq and by the World Council of Churches.

57   Signed by Israel in 1978, the accords called ambiguously for the 'withdrawal' but not necessarily the 'abolition' of the Military Government.

58   In any case, the Civilian Administration is now run by Israelis, including military personnel.

59   And this is an important case, since those actions are part of institutional practices which have the criminal definitions 'built in'. 'Terrorism' is a 'problem' the IDF has to 'deal with'. It would be extremely difficult for a soldier on duty, following orders etc., to bring in alternative definitions of the situation.

60   See *Jerusalem Post* 19.12.86, 'What the Police learnt from the unrest', 'Israel is in a better situation than most western countries when it comes to the level of crime and murder with which it is expected to deal'

61   See *Jerusalem Post* 12.12.86, 'Arab villages engage in pre-emptive activity: Building site selected to block Jewish settlement'

62   The slightly more critical position, i.e. the settlers are 'extremists', but the Palestinians are still the 'criminals' for attacking them.

63   Hall (1981), p40.

64   El Asmar, esp. pp73-103.

65   It is certainly not the case that these ideas are confined to Israelis or to 'Jews'. The idea of an essential difference between 'Jews' and others (culture seen as essential here too) has gained considerable purchase in the consciousnesses of many of those people who constitute the 'Goyim'. The images which were mobilised around the perceived 'Goy'/'Jew' divide (which were very similar to some of those images of the Arab identified above) clearly had an important part to play in the rise of European fascism, which led to the murder of millions of people identified as 'Jewish'. When pogroms were instigated against 'the Jews', the idea of a 'Jew'/'Goy' difference was irresistible. What is important in the present context is the role of these ideas in constructing representations of the 'Arabs' in Israel today, and in particular criminal representations of West Bank Palestinians.

66   I am dealing with a dominant and yet contradictory field of images; I do not mean to suggest that all 'Arabs' are stereotyped by all 'Jews' in all these ways.

67   I have collected every article reporting on the West Bank between 5.12.86 and 2.1.87. In the analysis that follows, I have endeavoured to include all the modes of description and representation offered (except straightforward factual statements like 'two Palestinians were shot at close range') and all the lines of argument and explanation. Quotes are all taken directly from the articles, and are

chosen as representative or typical examples. Descriptions and explanations included as specifically 'Palestinian viewpoints', as opposed to official statements or authoritative descriptions, have been excluded from this study. Specifically excluded are two reflective articles written by Palestinians from Birzeit. Naturally they did not take on board the dominant frame, but nor could they ignore it. One of them was a direct attempt to expose the dominant representations of Palestinian criminality; it was entitled 'Because we are Human Beings' (JP 24.12.86).

68 Hall (1978), p57 ff.

69 'Jewish Terrorists' have been identified in the press, but they are highly exceptional.

70 JP 19.12.86.

71 Chomsky, p9.

72 See Karp Report, and Abu-Shakrah.

73 Karp Report, p42.

74 Ibid., p35.

75 An instance is also cited in the Karp Report (p30) of a case against settlers accused of stabbing a Palestinian being closed since 'all are reconciled to the incident because of the particular background'. This background was that the Palestinian had been having 'relations' (!) with a 'Jewess'. So it seems that all are reconciled to the extra-judicial punishment of a Palestinian who has sex with a Jew. (cf. threat of assimilation).

76 Police Minister Bar-Lev, JP 19.12.86.

77 Yitzhak Shamir, commenting on Israeli policies in the occupied territories during 1986.

Select Bibliography

Books; Articles in Books and Journals

—El-Asmar, F, (1986), *Through the Hebrew Looking Glass: Arab Stereotypes in Children's Literature*, (Zed)

—Benvenisti, M, (1986a), *The West Bank Handbook: A Political Lexicon, [The West Bank Data Base Project]* (The Jerusalem Post)

—Chomsky, *'Middle East Terrorism and the American Ideological System'*, in *Race and Class*, Vol 28, No 1, Summer 1986

—Davis, U, (1987), *Israel: An Apartheid State*, (Zed)

—Fanon, F, (1967), *The Wretched of the Earth*, (Penguin)

—Gilroy, P, (1987), *There Ain't No Black in the Union Jack*, (Hutchinson)

—Hall, S, et. al., (1978), *Policing the Crisis*, (Macmillan)

—Hall, S, (1981), 'The Whites of their Eyes: Racist Ideologies and the Media', in Bridges, R, & Brunt, R, (eds.), *Silver Linings*, (Lawrence & Wishart)

—Orr, A, (1983), *The unJewish State: The Politics of Jewish Identity in Israel*, (Ithaca)

—Seliktar, O, (1986), The unJewish State: The Politics of Jewish Identity in Israel, (Croom Helm)

—Shehadeh, R, (1985), *Occupier's Law: Israel and the West Bank*, (Institute for Palestine Studies, Washington DC)

—Sivanandan, A, (1983), *A Different Hunter: Writings on Black Resistance*, (Pluto Press

—Weisburd, D, & Vinitzky, V, (1984), *Vigilantism as Rational Social Control: The Case of the Gush Emunim Settlers*, in Aronoff, M.J, (ed.), *Political Anthropology Vol 4: Cross Currents in Israeli Culture and Politics*, (Transaction Books, New Jersey)
—Sumner, C, (1982) '*Crime, Justice and Underdevelopment: Beyond Modernisation Theory*', in Sumner, C, (ed.), *Crime, Justice and Underdevelopment*, (Gower)
—Sumner, C, (1979), *Reading Ideologies: An Investigation into the Marxist Theory of Ideology and Law*, (Academic Press)

Special Reports

1 The West Bank Data Base Project:
Benevenisti, M, (1986b), *The West Bank Data Base Project 1986 Report: Demographic, economic, legal, social and political developments in the West Bank*
2 Al-Haq/Law in The Service of Man: West Bank affiliate of the International Commission of Jurists
Faloon, V, (1986), *Excessive Secrecy, Lack of Guidlines: A Report on Military Censorship in the West Bank*
Hillier, T, (1984), *The Israeli Knesset and the Annexation of the Occupied Territories*
Hilterman, J R, (1986), *Israel's Deportation Policy in the Occupied West Bank and Gaza*
Kuttab, J, & Shehadeh, R, (1982), *Civilian Administration in the Occupied West Bank*
Playfair, E, (1986), *Administrative Detention in the Occupied West Bank*
Rishmawi, M, (1986), *Planning in Whose Interest? Land Use Planning as a Strategy for Judaization*
Shehadeh, A, Shehadeh, F, and Shehadeh, R, *Israeli Proposed Road Plan for the West Bank: A Question for the International Court of Justice*
Al-Haq/LSM Staff, *Torture and Intimidation in the West Bank*
Programme Report (1986) Newsletters Nos. 9-14
3 Palestine Human Rights Campaign
Abu-Shakrah, J D, (1985), *Israeli Settler Violence in the Occupied Territories: 1980-1984*
4 Birzeit University Public Relations Department
Academic Freedom at Birzeit University 1985-6
Reports of harassments of students
5 Israeli Government
Karp, Y, (1984) *The Karp Report* (An Israeli government investigation of the enforcement of law in the Occupied Territories) (Published by the Institute for Palestine Studies)
6 *World Zionist Organisation*
WZO (1984) *New Dimensions: Aliyah to Judea, Samaria and Gaza* (Immigration and Absorbtion Division, World Zionist Organisation)
7 World Council of Churches
Commission of the Churches on International Affairs, (1983), *Human Rights Violations in the West Bank: In Their Own Words*

Newspaper Articles

Jerusalem Post: Monitored by the author between 1.12.86 and 3.2.87.

Interviews

Mekovsky, C, spokesperson for Gush Emunim, interviewed by author, January 1987.
Rosenthal, A, Israeli advocate, interviewed by author, January 1987.

Richard Thomas

DEMOGRAPHY AND SETTLER POLITICS IN THE OLD CITY OF JERUSALEM, 1980-88

ISRAELI GOVERNMENT CONTROL and sovereignty over East Jerusalem and the Old City has been characterised by a single and over-riding concern: how to guarantee and consolidate Jerusalem as the 'undivided' and 'eternal' capital of the state of Israel.[1] The chief method which successive Israeli governments have used to pursue this objective has been to establish an Israeli Jewish demographic majority over Palestinians within the boundaries of the Municipality of Jerusalem. This article will argue, in the first place, that despite being successful in this objective in statistical terms, the full picture seriously challenges Israeli Jewish numerical dominance in the long-term. Second, it will examine how an awareness of this development among Israeli government officials and planners has led to overt and covert government encouragement of the settlement activities of Israeli Jewish religious groups in the Muslim Quarter of the Old City. Finally the article will assess possible developments relating to demography and settlement in the Old City. Two areas are beyond the scope of this article: the role of the Jordanian *Awqaf* (Endowments) Administration in the politics of the Old City and, by its very currency, the full implications of the Palestinian uprising on the Old City.

The Jerusalem municipal area.

THE ISRAELI ANNEXATION of Jerusalem and the enlargement of the Jerusalem municipal boundaries to include parts of the West Bank in 1967, led to the incorporation of 70,000 Palestinians into the new capital of Israel. Government policy since then has dictated that the demographic dominance of Israeli Jews over Palestinians should be maintained at a ratio of approximately 7:3 at least, and that future planning should be determined by this objective.[2] Table 1 shows that, by and large, this objective has been achieved:

TABLE 1: Population growth in Jerusalem of non-Jews (Palestinian) and Jews (Israeli) 1967-1984[3]

	Total	Palestinian %	Israeli %
1967	267,800	26.7	73.3
1972	313,800	26.7	73.3
1980	407,100	28.2	71.8
1984	446,500	28.4	71.6

The fact that, in the face of a high natural increase in the Palestinian population and significant Palestinian immigration into the Jerusalem municipal area, this objective has been attained can be explained by two interlinked government policies. First, the Israeli government expropriated Palestinian land in and around the Jerusalem area and placed restrictions on the usage of the remaining Palestinian land. This effectively halted the expansion of Palestinian suburbs and villages within the Jerusalem municipal boundaries.[4] Second, new Israeli immigrants were encouraged to settle in the new housing estates or 'settlements' built upon these expropriated lands. Indeed, in 1970s it was proposed that 80% of all new immigrants to Israel should be channelled to Jerusalem for the very purpose of asserting Israeli Jewish demographic dominance in the city.[5] While this proposal was never implemented in full, the inducements for the new immigrants were sufficient to result in Jerusalem comprising in 1984 10.6% of the total population of Israel as opposed to 9.9% in 1972.[6]

These statistics, however, do not reveal the complete picture or the dilemmas that the Israeli government has had to confront. In the first place, the municipal boundaries of Jerusalem were drawn up in such a way as to exclude large concentrations of the Palestinian population. For example, although the road leading northwards out of Jerusalem to Ramallah is inside the municipal boundaries, the suburban Palestinian villages of Al-Ram and Bir Nabala on either side of the road have been excluded. In the second place, government restrictions on land use and housing inside municipal boundaries led to the emigration of Palestinians to areas just outside the municipal boundaries. Both these groups of Palestinians use and work in Jerusalem and thus make up the daily reality on its streets and buses, and in its shops, offices and factories but cannot live within the formal juridical boundaries of the Municipality. In these two ways the statistics exclude a large number of Palestinians who would still regard themselves as Jerusalemite. Demographically, then, Jerusalem is the centre of a much wider metropolitan area than its municipal boundaries suggest.

This fact is ultimately recognised by planners in the Jerusalem Municipality who plan according to a 'functional' city and insist on participation in the planning of areas outside the formal jurisdiction of the Municipality. The 'functional' area is consequently defined as including the Palestinian-dominated sub-districts of Ramallah and Bethlehem. In 1984, only 52% of this wider metropolitan area was estimated to be populated by Israeli Jews and most of these were found to be in West Jerusalem.[7] Viewed from this perspective, the Palestinian challenge to Israeli Jewish demographic dominance is a serious and growing one for the Israeli government. It is further underlined by two dilemmas confronting Israeli planners.

First, the land available for the construction of Israeli Jewish housing estates within the municipal boundaries is rapidly being depleted. To simply extend the municipal boundaries again would not necessarily solve the problem. As we have seen, this would unavoidably result in the inclusion of the newly-established areas of Palestinian settlement on the municipal borders of Jerusalem into the municipal area, thus cancelling out the demographic gains such an extension intended. Second, the construction of new Israeli Jewish housing estates would repeat the already established pattern by which employment is provided for thousands of Palestinian labourers from the West Bank who are then tempted to seek accommodation in the Jerusalem area. This would also off-set the demographic gains for the Israeli government that the housing construction was supposed to provide.[8]

In the mid-eighties it became apparent to Israeli planners that they could not outstrip the growth of the Palestinian population. Running to stand still, the Israeli government needed to increase the Israeli Jewish population in Jerusalem through immigration in order to match the Palestinian natural increase. Its options, however, are increasingly limited and its only alternative is to adopt a policy of reducing the Palestinian population in the Jerusalem area with greater severity. In the Old City of Jerusalem we can see how the demographic pressures building up in the municipal area will lead to the reduction of the Palestinian population. This article will focus on the Muslim Quarter.

The Old City

THE DEMOGRAPHIC FACTS in the Old City present a disturbing picture for the Israeli government. In 1972, 98% of the Old City population was Palestinian. Following the reconstruction of the Jewish Quarter and its settlement with exclusively Israeli Jewish families and *yeshiva* students, this figure changed to 93% in 1981. Table 2 gives the population figures of the Old City by traditional quarters:

TABLE 2. Population of the Old City by Quarters – non-Jews (Palestinians) and Israeli Jews [9]

	Christian	Armenian	Jewish	Muslim	Total
1972	4,195	2,079	1,647	15,506	23,427
1981	5,056	2,093	1,823	20,125	28,097
1983	4,322	2,008	2,042	17,106	25,478

It should be noted that after a high point in 1981, the population of the Muslim Quarter dropped by nearly 16% in 1983. However, the accuracy of these statistics must be qualified since some of the Old City residents who have moved out of the Old City keep a nominal presence in their former dwelling, staying one night a week for example, in order to maintain their claims for Israeli National Insurance benefits to which a Jerusalem residency entitles them. One can nevertheless still conclude that the Palestinian proportion of the population is likely to continue to diminish and it is merely the speed of this reduction which remains to be seen.

Israeli municipal planners work on the assumption that the desired maximum for the Old City population should be no more than 20,000 people. [10] They also aim to increase the Jewish population of the Old City to 5,000, following the completion of the reconstruction of the Jewish Quarter. This has extremely important ramifications for the Palestinian population in the other quarters of the Old City, particularly the Muslim Quarter. If this projected figure of 5,000 for the Jewish Quarter is added to the population of the Christian and Armenian Quarters for 1983 (Table 2), one arrives at the figure of approximately 9,500. Thus in order to meet the projected target of 20,000 for the whole of the Old City, the Palestinian population in the Muslim Quarter would have to drop to 10,500 – a reduction of over 40% of the 1983 figure of 17,500. The severity of this reduction in the Muslim Quarter may be mitigated by reductions in the Armenian and Christian Quarters. (There are some indications that the church hierarchies are encouraging their congregations to emigrate outside the Old City by providing subsidized housing). However, it is quite clear, as will be seen, that the main focus of the government's plans will continue to be the Muslim Quarter. If the Jerusalem Municipality and the Israeli government are to be successful in reaching their target of 20,000 in the Old City, then possibly up to 7,000 Palestinians will have to leave the Muslim Quarter. At this point we can begin to see the connections between the long term development plans of the Municipality for the Muslim Quarter and the unofficial support for the Israeli settler groups active in the same area.

Since the mid-seventies, the Jerusalem Muncipality has been trying to introduce a programme of 'slum clearance' in the Old City in order to reduce the density of housing and thus the Palestinian population. In addition, it wishes to create 'open spaces' to allow more room for leisure and recreational activities within the walls of the Old City. [11] Not wishing to antagonise the Jordanian-controlled *Awqaf* which manages the greater part of the housing and commercial properties in the Muslim Quarter, the Jerusalem Municipality has so far only proceeded with piece-meal projects. But with the demographic situation in the Jerusalem area becoming more serious from an Israeli perspective, it is increasingly likely that the Israeli government will be prompted to overrule the Municipality's sensibilities in this respect, and pursue a more aggressive policy of Palestinian 'resettlement'.

Confirmation of this development is found in a further point. The Municipality is unable to secure firm government backing for its opposition to the activities of the Israeli settler groups now operating in the Muslim Quarter. While individual officials and councillors in the

Municipality may not necessarily object to the political aspirations of the settler groups its official policy, backed by Mayor Teddy Kollek, is to oppose the autonomous and uncoordinated activities of these groups.[12] From the Municipality's point of view, the communal tensions these settlers engender in the Old City hamper its works in other fields and, more importantly, may affect its revenues if tourists are deterred by the violence their settlement provokes. Thus an examination of the settler groups in the Old City will illustrate both the demographic gains to be had by their encouragement and the political forces lined up against a continued Palestinian presence in the Old City.

Settler groups

A BRIEF HISTORICAL introduction is required. Prior to 1900, Jewish settlement in the Old City was concentrated in the Jewish Quarter in a position similar to the area currently known officially as the Jewish Quarter but much smaller. Severe overcrowding led to small Jewish groups moving to the Muslim Quarter, mostly in the *Aqabat Khalidi* area but also some along *Tariq al-Wad* and in the *Bab al-Huta* area near *Bab al-Zahra* (Herod's Gate).[13] Due to increasing Arab-Jewish tensions in the 1930s, these Jewish communities migrated to the New City districts that sprung up in West Jerusalem outside the city walls. Their properties in the Muslim Quarter were either sold or leased to Palestinians or left empty and subsequently occupied by Palestinian squatters. Following the 1948 war and the annexation of East Jerusalem by the Hashemite Kingdom of Jordan, the leased, occupied or abandoned properties were placed under the jurisdiction of the Jordanian 'Guardian of Enemy Property'.

In many cases the Jordanian 'Guardian' leased out these properties to Palestinians so that in 1967, when Israel occupied the Old City and the 'Guardian's' responsibilities were transferred to the Israeli 'Custodian of Absentee Property' or to the Israel Lands Administration, the Palestinian tenants continued to pay rent to one of these Israeli institutions. At this point it should be noted that one of the key planks of the Municipality's platform has been the espousal of a 'mosaic' policy in which a territorial homogeneity (or residential segregation) of the Palestinian and Israeli Jewish communities is encouraged as a means of reducing inter-communal tension. In this context, there seemed little prospect that the leases signed by Palestinians with the different Israeli state institutions would be affected and, in this way, that there would be little change in the demographic composition Palestinian–dominated Muslim Quarter.

The victory of the 'Greater Israel' parties (Likud, Tehiya and the National Religious Party) in the 1977 Israeli elections changed this situation. A number of settler groups were formed which challenged the Muncipality's position. While intending to pursue their long term objective of building a Jewish temple in the *Haram al-Sharif* area, they also decided to establish a Jewish presence in the Muslim Quarter by taking over the former Jewish properties already mentioned. In this latter aim they received assistance from individuals within key Israeli ministries and departments controlled by the 'Greater Israel' parties such as the Ministry of Religious Affairs, the Ministry of Housing, the Custodian's Office in the Ministry of Justice and the Israel Lands Administration. [14]

There are four main settler groups. Two, *Ateret Cohanim* and *Torat Cohanim*, are an offshoot of *Gush Emunim*, the main national settler organisation active in the West Bank and Gaza Strip. Another smaller group, the Young Israel Movement, was founded by Meir Kahane's brother and has close links with the Kach party. The last group, *yeshiva Shuvu Banim*, has attracted much media publicity due to its confrontational tactics. While all the groups have separate membership and engage in independent fund-raising activities, the first three groups share a common strategy in seeking to establish a vibrant Israeli Jewish presence in the Muslim Quarter through the establishment of seminaries and residence.

Three aspects of these groups' activities are relevant to this article. First, the activities of the settler groups correspond to the long-term plans of the Israeli government and, indeed, in this respect, of the Jerusalem Municipality itself, which, as has been argued, is to maintain the demographic upperhand in the Old City by reducing the Palestinian population. In occupying and renovating former Jewish properties in the Muslim Quarter, in buying other Palestinian-owned properties, in evicting tenants and precipitating the departure of their Palestinian neighbours through harassment and intimidation, the settler groups are contributing to the execution of these long-term plans. The Municipality's objections are not so much to do with the end result, as to the uncontrolled and often violent methods employed.

Second, the overt and covert support the settler groups receive from the government allow them to bypass any Municipality objections. This has put the Municipality in a weak position *vis-à-vis* the settler groups and it is no longer able to maintain its 'mosaic' policy in the Old City. For example, although it was able to enforce building regulations regarding the illegal construction of a floor by the *Shuvu Banim* settler group, it was not able, as it wanted, to evict the group itself.[15]

In addition the groups were able to approach the government directly and receive grants for renovation and settlement activities. The extent and strength of their support is impressive. Both Zevulun Hammer of the National Religious Party and a former Minister of Religious Affairs and David Levy, Deputy Leader of the Likud Party and Minister of Housing, have indicated their support vocally and through their respective ministries. The Ministry of Religious Affairs, for example, granted *Atara Leyoshna*, the real estate body set up by three of the settler groups, the sum of $250,000 in 1984.[16] It also set up a commission to investigate the possibility of restoring a number of small synagogues in the Muslim Quarter.[17] In 1986 the Ministry of Housing granted $40,000 to *Ateret Cohanim*, the largest of the groups, for reconstruction work in the Muslim Quarter despite the fact that this sum was not allocated in the annual budget.[18] In May 1987, Ariel Sharon, the Minister for Trade and Industry, called on the government to increase the resources available for settlement in the Old City and directly challenged the Municipality by moving in to a former Jewish property belonging to *Ateret Cohanim* on *Tariq al-Wad*. Sharon has also been linked with another settler group running the *Shuvu Banim yeshiva* through his friend Avaraham Dweik, a New York financier, who funded the *yeshiva*'s legal defence against the Municipality in the dispute mentioned above.[19] Professor Yuval Ne'eman, leader of the Tehiya Party, has expressed his support for the settlers and called for a renewal of the charter for the Company for the Reconstruction and Development of the Jewish Quarter and for its work to be extended into the Muslim Quarter.[20] In sum, the settler groups have collected a formidable array of political support that wields powerful governmental influence.

The third and final point to note is that the settlers appear to have a clear strategic plan in choosing properties for occupation and renovation. Former Jewish properties under the jurisdiction of the Custodian of Absentee Property along *Aqabat Khalidi* have been given priority (See Map 2). From this initial base, properties adjacent or close to them are then selected and the existing Palestinian tenants are encouraged to vacate through a mixture of violent harassment and financial inducements.[21] In this way, a chain of settler-occupied properties is being created in the heart of the Muslim Quarter from the top of *Aqabat Khalidi*, which can be reached from the Jewish Quarter across the roofs of the covered markets, down to the old Hungarian synagogues on *Tariq al-Wad*, beside which an army post guards the underground passage-way to the Western (Wailing) Wall plaza. Similar 'chains' have been created in the northern section of *Tariq al-Wad* and in the *Bab al-Huta* area near *Bab al-Zahra* (Herod's Gate). It is interesting to observe that the establishment of such territorial linkages is consistent with traditional forms of Zionist colonisation and settlement.

The future for the Palestinians in the Old City

THE OPEN REVOLT of the Palestinians against the Israeli occupation of the Old City in the first half of 1988, sparked off in part by the activities of the settlers and Sharon's provocative move into the Muslim Quarter, has made conjecture as to future developments extremely difficult. While the Palestinian uprising has had an immediate affect in freezing the situation in the Old City, it is not likely to alter the situation in the medium and long-terms unless, of course, there is a political settlement between the PLO and the Israeli government.

In the medium-term, given the weakness of the Municipality in the face of the settler groups' operations and government support for them, and given the strength of their financial base and legal position, it would seem that the existing properties held by the settlers will continue to remain in their possession. This means that the 'chains' of settler-occupied property have already become the *status quo*. Without stiff Palestinian resistance, the next few years will see the gradual depopulation of the *Aqabat Khalidi* area of Palestinian residents. One can project that within five years the Jewish Quarter will be enlarged to absorb this part of the Muslim Quarter. Growth of Israeli Jewish settlement in the northern *Tariq al-Wad* section and the *Bab al-Huta* area is likely to be more gradual and more dependent on governmental intervention but will be along similar lines.

The longer term is quite likely to see the clearance of areas of Palestinian residence, leaving only the major historical sites, museums and schools. The commercial areas of the bazaars and *suqs* will be left for touristic reasons while Christian premises along the Via Dolorosa will be retained so as not to alarm the Western church hierarchies. Israeli Jewish settlement will increase in the Muslim Quarter but will be restricted to *yeshiva* students, the main emphasis being the restoration of synagogues and Jewish sites of historical interest. In conclusion, if the Israeli occupation of the Old City continues without major changes, by the end of the century we are likely to see an Old City 'Disneyworld' featuring variously-clad religious personnel with Palestinian shopkeepers providing an exotic biblical backdrop for tourist excursions.

Notes

1 This status was conferred on Jerusalem after the passing of the Basic Law 1980. From a juridical point of view, it merely reaffirmed what had been established in previous laws incorporating East Jerusalem into Israel, notably the Law and Administrative Ordinance (Amendment) Law and the Municipal Corporations Ordinance (Amendment) Law both passed in 1967.
2 See Benvenisti, M., *Jerusalem: The Torn City*. (Minneapolis: Israelitypeset Ltd. and the University of Minneapolis, 1976) p.250.
3 *Statistical Yearbook of Jerusalem, No.3 – 1984* (Jerusalem: Jerusalem Institute for Israel Studies, 1985) p.89.
4 This is a well-documented area of study but for Jerusalem, see Mattar, I., in N. Arur: *Occupation: Israel over Palestine*, (London: Zed Books Ltd. 1984) p.138.
5 Benvenisti, *op. cit.* p.252.
6 Statistical Yearbook, *op. cit.* p.31
7 Hyman, B., Kimhi, I., Savitzky, *Jerusalem in Transition: Urban Growth and Change, 1970s-1980s* (Jerusalem: Jerusalem Institute for Israel Studies, 1985) p.37.
8 Benvenisti, *op. cit.* pp. 253-4.
9 Statistical Yearbook, *op. cit.* p.107.
10 Sharon, A. *Planning Jerusalem – The Old City and its Environs* (Jerusalem: Weidenfield and Nicholson, 1973) p.82.
11 See Kroyanker, D. *Jerusalem Planning and Development 1982-1985: New Trends* (Jerusalem, The Jerusalem Foundation, 1985) pp. 23-5.
12 The Municipality's position has been expressed clearly in *Out of Jerusalem*, Winter, 1983, Vol. 4, No.1, pp. 5-7. *Out of Jerusalem* is published by the pro-Kollek Jerusalem Committee.
13 Ben Arieh, Y. *Jerusalem in the Nineteenth Century: The Old City* (Jerusalem: Yad Izhak Ben Zvi Institute, 1984) pp. 377-386.
14 See articles by Nadav Shragai in *Ha'aretz*, 23.4.86 and 25.4.86.
15 See *Jerusalem Post* article entitled 'Yeshiva in Moslem Quarter Likely to Retain its Lease', 24.1.84 and articles from 13.12.83 and 14.12.83.
16 Nadav Shragai, *op. cit.*
17 See article by Nadav Shragai in *Ha'aretz*, 11.5.87 and by Hadar Horesh in *Kol Ha'ir*, 1.3.85 and 6.12.85.
18 Report by Avi Temkin in *Jerusalem Post*, 27.3.86 entitled 'Yeshiva gets $40,000 to buy Moslem flats'.
19 See *Jerusalem Post* articles "Old City Yeshiva", 19.12.83., 23.12.83.
20 See interview with Professor Ne'eman in *Kol Ha'ir*, May 1987.

21   See Abu Shakr, J. *Israeli Settler Violence in the Occupied Territories, 1980-84*, (Chicago: Palestine Human Rights Campaign, 1985) pp. 23-4.

Ehud 'Ein-Gil

THE TWENTY-FIRST YEAR: NEW IDEAS

The writer, a militant of the Socialist Organization in Israel (Matzpen), was active in the various solidarity committees mentioned in this article, in the section entitled The Years of Deadlock.

BOTH MAJOR ZIONIST POLITICAL BLOCS–Labour as well as the Likud–are entrenched behind an ideological parapet: the denial of the rights and even the very existence of the Palestinian people. However, a few cracks appeared in this parapet even before the outbreak of the Palestinian uprising in the occupied territories. Paradoxically, the largest shift occurred within the ranks of the Herut Movement, the most ideologically committed component of the Likud. Moshe 'Amirav, member of Herut's Central Committee and the movement's candidate for the headship of the government's Press Office, had drawn up his own peace plan, which he proceeded to discuss over a period of several months in secret talks with West Bank Palestinian figures known to be PLO supporters. According to 'Amirav, some of these meetings were also attended by other representatives of his party, including Knesset members. He continues to claim that senior leaders, including Prime Minister Yitzhak Shamir, were briefed about what was said in these meetings.

'Amirav met the head of the Centre for Arab Studies in East Jerusalem,

Faisal al-Husseini, and Dr Sari Nusseibeh, a lecturer at Birzeit University. He showed them his proposals and asked for their comments. Indirectly, he enquired what position the PLO would take regarding his peace plan. Eventually he received a reply: his proposals could serve as a basis for Israeli-Palestinian negotiations. In order to advance the launching of such negotiations, 'Amirav agreed to go to Geneva to meet the PLO leader, Yasser 'Arafat; but the planned meeting never took place.

The person who torpedoed this project was probably the Minister of Defence, Labour's Yitzhak Rabin. After Menahem Begin succeeded where Labour had failed for years and signed a peace treaty with Egypt, Rabin was afraid of a possible success by the Likud in advancing an Israeli-Palestinian settlement. The Labour Party, rigidly adhering to its ridiculous Jordanian Option even after it has become clear that nothing is less realistic, had to prevent the Likud scoring a success where Labour was unwilling to try. Faisal al-Husseini was put under administrative detention, following which 'Amirav's proposed journey to Geneva was cancelled. The existence of the secret talks was then revealed by other participants, who wished to convince public opinion that al-Husseini had been detained for holding talks with Israelis rather than for taking part in organizing demonstrations and disruptions of order, as claimed by the Security Services.

When the affair blew up, 'Amirav became a target of attacks by his comrades and rivals in Herut. Those who had known about the talks were less courageous than him and disclaimed any part in the affair. He was supported by only four or five second-rank Herut functionaries, including Shim'on Dar'i, head of Herut's youth movement, *Beitar*. 'Amirav was brought before a Herut disciplinary tribunal, but refused to recant. Quite a few Herut people who did not support him were nevertheless opposed to expelling him from the movement, even after he dared stage a one-man demonstration against Ariel Sharon's move into a house he had acquired in the Muslim quarter of the Old City of Jerusalem. Eventually 'Amirav was forced to resign all his official positions in Herut and was banned from speaking publicly as member of any of the movement's bodies. Thereupon he tore up his membership card and shortly afterwards joined the small Centre Party, in which he is still noted for being relatively dovish. Shim'on Dar'i was forced to resign his position in the Herut youth movement but has not recanted.

Most interesting was the fate of another Herut functionary, who was interviewed by an East Jerusalem newspaper and expressed a position similar to 'Amirav's. Colonel (res.) Shmu'el Pressburger, one of Ariel

Sharon's supporters in Herut, published an article in the Israeli newspaper *Ma'ariv* (12 November 1987). 'Compared to *Islamic Jihad*' he wrote, 'the PLO is a moderate body, with whom it is almost possible to live; and herein lies a solution that requires unconventional thought and action.' Shortly after the publication of that article, Pressburger was selected by Herut's Jerusalem branch as their official candidate for the mayorship of the city.

The interesting, and original, element in 'Amirav's proposals is his attempt to bypass what can so far be regarded as the most widely accepted political solution: Israeli withdrawal from all the territories occupied by it in 1967, and the creation there of an independent Palestinian state. This solution is at present supported by the vast majority of countries around the world, by the central trend in the PLO and by most of the Israeli left: the Communist Party, the Progressive List and the various groups attached to them. Within the Zionist left as well there are voices supporting such a solution with added provisos like 'demilitarization of the Palestinian state' or 'minor border changes'. 'Amirav, whose search for a compromise solution started off from a position of Zionist maximalism that aspires to preserve a single political entity between the Jordan and the sea and even dreams of including in it the Jordan's East Bank, finally arrived at a sort of federalist idea.

Almost in parallel, a small group calling itself the Confederation Group got organized inside the Labour Party. It is led by Arieh Hess who, just like 'Amirav, lives in Jerusalem. He too tried to meet Faisal al-Husseini and Sari Nusseibeh, and he too declares that he is prepared to meet Yasser 'Arafat; but, as a faithful pupil of the 'left' Zionist school, he stipulates, as a precondition for such a meeting, that 'Arafat declare his support for his (that is Hess's) confederal solution. Paradoxically, although their ideas are essentially similar, the 'right-winger' 'Amirav is much more consistent and courageous than the 'left-winger' Hess.

'Amirav's scheme

APART FROM SMALL CIRCLES of Herut members, few Israelis are familiar with the writings of Valdimir Ze'ev Jabotinsky. The general public knows little about him except that he was the founder of so-called 'revisionist' Zionism and Menahem Begin's mentor. In the Zionist labour movement he is branded as a fascist, although during recent years some labour Zionists have occasionally quoted several of his more liberal sayings in order to embarrass the Likud. The fact is that the same

Jabotinsky who inspired the hawkish policy of the Israeli right wing is also claimed by Moshe 'Amirav as an inspiration for his own ideas. Since 'Amirav is not an isolated individual but expresses a certain trend within Herut, it may be of some interest to have a brief look at Jabotinsky's doctrine as reflected in 'Amirav's eyes today, in the 21st year of the occupation.

On 14 October 1987, when he was still member of Herut's Central Committee, Moshe 'Amirav published in *Ma'ariv* a detailed exposition of his position entitled 'Historical Revisionism as a Possible Basis for a Peace Settlement'. This is what he wrote in that programmatic article:

'Not necessarily in the topical connection of my meetings with pro-PLO Palestinian leaders, I have recently found myself reflecting on the problem of legitimation. "Your meetings help to legitimize the enemy," I have been told. And this subject, in a broader historical context, deserves to be publicly discussed.

'The more I reflect on this subject of de-legitimizing the enemy, I find in it the root of the conflict, the tragic seed of calamity, that prevents us, Jews and Arabs, from relating to each other without stereotypes and prejudices.

'Right from the very beginning of the conflict, the de-legitimation of one's rival is clearly evident not merely as a tactic but as a heavily emotional ideological attitude.

'The Palestinians refused to recognize the Zionist enterprise as an authentic national liberation movement of the Jewish people. At first their attitude to Zionism was one of contempt, giving rise to a belief in the ephemerality of the Zionist enterprise. In the atmosphere of the 1920s, when European colonialism was flourishing, it was convenient for the Palestinians to persuade themselves that this is just another colonial enterprise that the Jews of the European metropolis had chosen as a branch for their own settlement.

'In a later development, the colonial view of Zionism acquired the meaning of [regarding Israel as a latter-day] Crusader State. Both conceptions implant in the mind of whoever believes in them a feeling that the existence [of Zionism and Israel] is historically ephemeral. The Zionists, for their part, out of almost the same kind of obstinacy, also refused at that time to recognize the national existence of this country's Arabs. In the Zionist vocabulary of those days they were referred to as a "population", never as a "people". According to the same vocabularly, the country was described as "empty" or "desolate".

'As opposed to the Revisionists, who were the first to recognize the national existence of the Palestinians, the [Zionist] socialist labour movement suffered from conceptual confusion, from which it has never managed to rid itself. The socialist Zionist leaders regarded the conflict merely in class terms: The Jewish proletariat, which has the well-known socialist right to "develop desolate countries", is struggling against the "Arab effendis"; when the ignorant Arab peasant tenants are freed from the effendis' yoke, they would be glad to co-operate with the Zionists bearing of the banner of fraternity and development.

'Typical of that attitude was Ben-Gurion's claim that "the [Jewish] national home can be developed without depriving a single Arab child". Even when the Arab Rebellion broke out in 1936, the leaders of the *Yishuv* refused to regard it as a national uprising and called it "riots" or "events" – that is, mob actions.

'The mutual de-legitimation policy has in fact persisted to this very day: Israel refuses to recognize the Palestinians as a people and is pleased with UN [Security Council] Resolution 242, which describes them [merely] as refugees. The Palestinians, for their part, refuse to recognize the existence of Israel and are pleased with the UN [General Assembly] resolution that equates Zionism with racism.

'Some of the Zionist conceptions to which we still hold on took shape in those stormy times [of the 1920s]. It was not for nothing that the main dispute raged between the socialist labour movement and the nationalist revisionist movement. The difference between them was not only over the goals and the means of achieving them, but over the very perception of reality. Ze'ev Jabotinsky, unlike the leaders of the labour movement, recognized the Palestinians as "a specific national entity", and even noted that they have a patriotic consciousness.'

'. . . Jabotinsky's perception of the reality of national conflict between two peoples also led him to outline the way to a just solution of the problem. His formula was "One country in which there are two nationalities". Since he was opposed to partitioning the country, he put forward an interesting distinction between national *rule* and national *sovereignty*, a distinction which makes it possible today to propose a federal solution, which I shall describe in detail in the sequel. The rise to power of the Herut movement in 1977, was not only a political victory of Jabotinsky's disciples, but also re-introduced into the public debate about the conflict some of his conceptions and principles.

'Jabotinsky's disciples were not surprised when Menahem Begin was the first Jewish leader to recognize the Palestinians as a nationality and even signed a document recognizing their "legitimate rights". The autonomy proposal that he put forward also comes straight from the political doctrine of Jabotinsky, who already in 1922, in his famous Parity document, noted that he preferred to make a concession in the matter of sovereignty rather than give up part of the territory.

'Starting from the historical positions of the Revisionist movement, it is now possible and necessary to arrive at a principle that will guide us towards finding a solution to the conflict: the principle of partnership over the country, while recognizing the legitimacy of the Palestinian people's demands.'

Of course, 'Amirav is still a faithful Zionist; but his emphases are worth noting. Most important perhaps is his attempt to present the Revisionists as the first Zionist current to recognize that the Palestinians are a nation. Hence his critical appraisal not only of the classical positions of the Zionist labour movement, but also of Resolution 242, on which the Zionist consensus insists as a basis for political negotiations. Note that the official position of both the Likud and Labour is opposed to any talks with the PLO, not only because it is branded as a terrorist organization but also because it refuses to accept Resolution 242.

So, 'Amirav is criticizing several Zionist dogmas: the country was neither empty nor desolate; a Palestinian people did exist and had a patriotic consciousness; the problem to be solved is not merely that of refugees but a national problem; and the national aspirations of the Palestinians must somehow be responded to. Based on his historical analysis, 'Amirav formulates a series of proposals that, taken together, add up to a scheme for resolving the Israeli-Palestinian conflict.

'The historical Greater Land of Israel, which stretches over an area of over 100,000 square kilometres, from the Mediterranean Sea to the desert, is at present inhabited by seven or eight million people, about half of whom are Jews. In the centre of this land there is a relatively small area called Judea and Samaria [i.e., the West Bank – ed]. On the basis of the principle of partnership, it is possible to arrive at a settlement of Minor Partnership over Judea and Samaria, and in parallel with it a Major Partnership over the historical Land of Israel.

'Within the Major Partnership – or, to use international terminology, the Confederation – the two states on either side of the Jordan River will form an association by means of various economic treaties, like the European Economic Community, and will co-operate in developing regions such as the Dead Sea, the Gulf of Eilat, a common port on the Mediterranean, irrigation projects in the Jordan valley, and so on. Co-operation is also possible in other areas, as is now customary between states that have mutual confederal ties. Within the Minor Partnership, an autonomy will be set up in Judea and Samaria, which will enable its Arab inhabitants to exercise a large measure of self-rule. Within this framework, they will be able to have national paraphernalia such as currency, postage stamps, a flag and a national anthem. The administration capital of the autonomy will be in East Jerusalem. Israel will continue to run the spheres of security and foreign relations, as well as to be the source of authority. The settlements will remain where they are and the zone will be open to [free] movement. According to the Jabotinskian model, the Arabs in this zone will exercise ''national rule'', whereas we shall exercise ''sovereign rule''. This is the only possible meaning of ''partnership'' over the country.

'The advantages to Israel of a settlement of partnership over the country are clear: national security without territorial compromise; peace without a demographic problem.

'The advantages to the Palestinians are no less important: the settlement of Minor Partnership will enable them, for the first time in their history, to exercise self-rule. The option of self-determination or a state will always be open to them in Jordan. They can continue to aspire to a state in Judea and Samaria as well, but in a situation of peace this aspiration will be expressed by diplomatic means rather than terrorist actions.

'At this point the reader may well ask whether the Arabs would agree to this scheme. In order to find an answer to this, I went to talk with Palestinian leaders who are PLO supporters, to hear from them whether they would agree to this scheme.

'In our talks my Palestinian interlocutors surprised me almost as much as I surprised them with these ideas of mine.

'They admitted that after the defeat in Lebanon, there are new tendencies for moderation and sobriety within the PLO, and the ideas I raised seemed fairer and more realistic than the prospect of establishing a Palestinian state at present, which they know to be unattainable. They declared unambiguously that the PLO is prepared to recognize Israel – if Israel will recognize the Palestinians as a nationality. And here I should like to end with what I said at the start of my article: I am increasingly convinced that this business of ''de-legitimation'', of each side denying the existence of the other, is the root of the problem. It is our duty to adopt the views of Jabotinsky; to recognize the Palestinians as a nationality, to conduct peace negotiations with them – not with Hussein – and to make them a fair offer, an offer of true partnership over a Greater Land of Israel.

'This is the duty of the Likud, its most important task for the next few years. There are two reasons for this. First, only the Likud can make peace; a settlement proposed by the [Labour] Alignment and opposed by the Likud will not pass, but a settlement proposed by the Likud will be accepted by the Alignment.

'Second, only the Likud, loyal to the historical views of the Revisionist Movement, has a realistic solution that is capable of satisfying the national aspirations of the Palestinians, as well as [Israel's] national security and the integrity of the country. Will the leaders of the Likud rise to do what Ze'ev Jabotinsky would do where he living among us today?'

The drawbacks of 'Amirav's scheme are clear. Palestinian self-determination, he says, can be realized only in Jordan. In this he follows Ariel Sharon, who has repeatedly proposed helping the Palestinians to overthrow King Hussein and set up a Palestinian state in Jordan. More importantly, 'Amirav's scheme does not actually include an end to the Israeli occupation. In essence, he takes the autonomy proposed in the Camp David agreements and extends it, but does not go much further than this.

How then can 'Amirav claim or hint that he received positive responses from the Palestinian side? Can any Palestinian seriously regard 'Amirav's scheme as a fair offer? In order to answer these questions, one needs to read 'Amirav's formulations carefully. Actually, he says, he is only proposing a temporary settlement. As he puts it, the Palestinians 'can continue to aspire to a state in Judea and Samaria as well, but in a situation of peace this aspiration will be expressed by diplomatic means rather than terrorist actions'.

On the other hand, on several important points 'Amirav's proposals depart from the historical Zionist consensus, and for this reason they deserve to be taken seriously. First, 'Amirav lays some of the historical blame for the conflict upon the Zionist movement. Second, he understands why Resolution 242 cannot be acceptable to the Palestinians. (In this connection it is worth mentioning that, until some time after the October War of 1973, even the Israeli Communist Party refused to co-operate with leftist groups that rejected Resolution 242 as the sole basis for a solution.) Third, 'Amirav speaks of the 'principle of partnership over the country, while recognizing the legitimacy of the Palestinian people's demands'. Partnership over the country means partnership over the whole of it. 'Amirav demands for Israelis rights beyond the Green Line (Israel's pre-1967 border), but at the same time he is prepared to accept that the Palestinians have legitimate demands also inside the Green Line.

Fourth – and this is perhaps the most important element in 'Amirav's approach – is his idea of including Jordan in a joint Israeli-Palestinian political framework, thereby extending a little the confined horizon within which the Israeli-Palestinian conflict is viewed by almost everyone. If a solution is to address the problem of all the Palestinians, it cannot ignore that part of the Palestinian people living in Jordan. In the longer term, a tripartite Israeli-Palestinian-Jordanian confederal framework may serve as basis for a larger federal union of the Arab *Mashreq*. This option is certainly never considered by the racist Zionist doves, whose sole wish is to preserve a small Jewish polity with as few Arabs in it as possible. Their faces turned towards western Europe and North America, those Zionist doves are prepared to immure themselves in a small Jewish ghetto, to turn their backs on the surrounding region and live happily ever after as a small western enclave. 'Amirav's scheme, therefore, even if it does not include an independent Palestinian state, may be much more attractive to nationalist Palestinians, who do not wish to see a rigid border between themselves and Israel in its pre-1967 borders.

Hess's Confederation

ALTHOUGH DESERTED by virtually all his friends when it came to the crunch, 'Amirav is nevertheless representative of a group within the Likud who are prepared, under certain conditions, to recognize at least part of the Palestinians' rights.

The Confederation Group in the Labour Party is actually one person's baby. Like 'Amirav, Arieh Hess lives in Jerusalem; and like him he is very energetically active in propagating his ideas, which are, however, less consistent than 'Amirav's. He publishes a newsletter called *On Both Sides of the Jordan* whose motto is 'For the Advancement of Federalism in the Land of Israel'. In the first version of his scheme, Hess speaks of subdividing the land between the Jordan and the sea into Swiss-like cantons, which will have confederal ties with Jordan. He even composed a draft constitution whose main points are the following. The Confederation of the Land of Israel will consist of ten cantons, of which seven will be Israeli (together comprising the present territory of the State of Israel) and three Palestinian, centred around Nablus, Hebron and Gaza. The Confederation's capital will be Jerusalem, which will have a joint umbrella municipal administration as well as two separate administrations for its Israeli and Palestinian parts. Security will be exclusively the responsibility of the Israeli government, which will be elected in the same way as in present-day Israel. The Palestinian cantons will have their own representative in the UN, and will have full authority in the spheres of education, economy, law, police, external relations and rehabilitation of refugees. This Confederation will offer to form wider confederal ties with Jordan, but the Palestinian cantons will also be free to form such ties on their own, without the Israeli cantons.

In a pamphlet (undated) published by the Confederation Group, the ideological implication of their scheme is explained as follows:

'The confederal scheme is a political and ideological compromise in the matter of the West Bank and the Gaza Strip. Confederation does not mean partition of the country; but neither does it mean annexation of the territories of Judea, Samaria and Gaza to Israel, or for that matter to Jordan. This scheme also does not lead to the creation of an independent Palestinian state in the territories, that is, to the formation of a third state between Israel and Jordan. At the same time, the confederal scheme recognizes the right of the Palestinians to develop their own political, cultural and spiritual life. The confederal scheme recognizes the Palestinians as a people, but does not recognize their claim over the country. The confederal scheme recognizes and accepts that in the historical Land of Israel there are now three political protagonists: Israeli, Jordanian and Palestinian; and it accepts all the implications of this. At the same time, this scheme takes into consideration and recognizes the historical and geographical affinity of both Jordan and Israel for the districts of the West Bank.'

The same pamphlet also says:
'The Tripartite Confederation scheme accommodates both the Principle of Return, which is sacred to the Palestinians, and the Israeli Law of Return. Every Palestinian now living outside Jordan, the West Bank and Gaza Strip will have the choice of returning to settle there.'

Like 'Amirav, Hess too is prepared to go towards the Palestinians only so far as this does not threaten the Zionist basis of the Israeli state. Since both, though differing in their ideological origins, had similar pragmatic motives in developing their ideas, their schemes are rather similar and equally vague. This vagueness need not be held against them. 'Amirav and Hess, whose schemes are not completely worked out, have left them rather fluid, and in this respect are perhaps open to further development. To the extent that they are more than isolated curios, but rather reflect an increasingly widespread feeling that something must be done, the appearance of these schemes is encouraging.

The flexibility of Hess's thinking, for example, was demonstrated shortly after the outbreak of the uprising in the Gaza Strip, before it spread over the West Bank. He published then a 'Gaza plan for solving the Palestinian Problem', whose main points are as follows:

'Israel shall propose that the Gaza Strip be recognized as a Palestinian city-state, like Singapore in the Far East; this city-state shall be completely demilitarized, without any military presence or a local army. The Gaza city-state shall become a member of the UN and the Arab League and have diplomatic legations all over the world. The Gaza city-state shall have its own flag, national anthem, currency and all other paraphernalia of a modern sovereign state. The identity cards and passports of its inhabitants shall be Palestinian.'

The plan also had another component, which was in fact an adaptation of Hess's original confederal scheme to the new situation and to the freshly awakened awareness of Gaza's special position:

'Israel shall propose that the West Bank be divided into two Palestinian cantons, working and organized according to the Swiss model. These cantons shall be responsible for releasing land for construction, running various economic and community projects, taxation, economy, education, postal services, telecommunication, and issuing identity cards and passports. The identity cards and passports shall be Palestinian or Jordanian, according to the inhabitants' choice. The Gaza city-state and the Palestinian cantons shall gradually establish a series of central organs of power, such as a legislature, a federal cabinet and other central authorities. Representatives of the Palestinian cantons shall be incorporated into the delegations of the Gaza city-state abroad, in the UN and in the Arab League. Gradually, the Gaza city-state and the Palestinian cantons will grow into a Palestinian political federation.'

On the subject of sovereignty Hess wrote:

'On the West Bank, there shall be [joint] Israeli-Palestinian sovereignty, for a period of 20 years. Sovereignty in Gaza shall be Palestinian. Jewish settlements in the Gaza Strip and the West Bank shall be in all spheres directly under the authority of the State of Israel and the Knesset. Arab villages in Wadi 'Ara and the Triangle [i.e., parts of Israel bordering on the West Bank] shall be able to joint the West Bank cantons, although they shall remain under Israeli sovereignty. Jewish settlements in the West Bank will be allowed to absorb new members, each settlement according to its capacity; no new settlements shall be established. Any Jew wishing to settle in a site where there is no existing Jewish settlement will have to do so of his own accord and using his own resources.'

As for Jerusalem, this new version of Hess's scheme repeats the idea about one umbrella municipal authority and two separate sub-municipalities. But now the Arab inhabitants of East Jerusalem are offered the choice of carrying Palestinian documents and passports and voting in elections to the federal Palestinian parliament.

It is easy to see that the Palestinian uprising prompted Hess to take a big step forward. This second version of his plan implies the creation of a Palestinian state, albeit federally tied to Israel. His doctrinal flexibility allowed him to break yet another Zionist ground rule, which forbids any Israeli concession whatsoever regarding the Green Line. He is prepared to consider a scenario in which Arab villages that are now inside Israel would incorporate themselves in a separate Palestinian structure.

Of course, the schemes of 'Amirav and Hess have many drawbacks. They fall short of regarding Palestinians and Israelis as two groups having equal rights, both of which must be allowed to be implemented in full. Being Zionists, they necessarily load the scales in the Israelis' favour. But – unlike the main dovish current in Israel, including most of those who support the creation of a Palestinian state alongside Israel – 'Amirav and Hess start from the premise that there is nothing wrong in having Arabs and Jews living together. They do not keep looking for ways to separate people according to origin and national affiliation but, on the contrary, keep trying to reduce this separation and temper it with some measure of partnership.

Lately, however, 'Amirav has joined the Council for Peace and Security, a group composed mainly of pro-Labour Party retired army officers. Under the influence of his new milieu, he too has begun to stress the 'demographic danger', the Zionist doves' argument in favour of withdrawal from the occupied territories.

Both 'Amirav and Hess have continued their activities after publishing their respective schemes. 'Amirav has taken part in gatherings, public meetings and conferences against the occupation; and Hess too has sought various ways to push his ideas. In March 1988, for example, he published a proposed form of Palestinian identity card, for distribution in the occupied territories, as an illustration of the situation advocated by him.

Ideas similar to those of 'Amirav and Hess are occasionally voiced by other people as well. Thus, on 8 February, *Ma'ariv* published an article entitled 'A Confederal Settlement as a Realistic Utopia' by Yosef Gorni, a Labour Zionist and lecturer in modern Jewish history at Tel-Aviv University. Gorni's ideas are essentially similar to those of 'Amirav and Hess; but he deserves special mention because his 'realistic utopia' contains an additional element. Gorni does not forget the ties of Egypt with the Gaza Strip and of Israel with the Sinai Peninsula (in both cases, ties that were formed as a result of military occupation), and therefore his confederation scheme includes not only Israel, Jordan and the Palestinians, but Egypt as well. He writes:

'First, I should like to point out that the federal idea has accompanied Zionist political thought from the time of the Second 'Aliyah [1904-14], through the Weizmann-Faisal Agreement following the Balfour Declaration, to David Ben-Gurion's proposals in the 1930s and it is worth emphasizing that Ze'ev Jabotinsky too was not opposed to it.

'On the face of it, there is no substantive connection between these proposals, which cropped up at different times and under different historical circumstances. But on second and deeper thought they can be seen to have common elements. They followed from a recognition of the rights of Jews and Arabs alike to national determination; they combined national autonomy with a political unity of the peoples of the Middle East; they based the political settlement upon large-scale economic co-operation; and they tied the settlement to a democratic superpower that has interests in this region. These principles may also form foundation stones for a present-day regional political settlement. Because all other solutions – whether the one aspiring to absolute Jewish sovereignty over the entire Land of Israel, or the one that speaks of its re-partition into two absolutely independent states, or even that proposing to return most of the territories of Judea and Samaria to Jordan – have apparently gone up in the smoke of the burning tyres and the rubber bullets that fly in the Palestinian camps.'

The details of Gorni's scheme are as follows:
'1. Creation of a federal or confederal political entity, consisting of three sovereign states: Egypt, Jordan and Israel, and an autonomous Palestinian region in Judea, Samaria and the Gaza Strip. The internal and international status of the autonomous region will be similar to that of

the large Soviet republics, the Ukraine and Byelorussia. Territorially, it will have two focuses: Judea and Samaria, and the province of Gaza. To the latter shall be added the western part of Sinai, including the town of al-'Arish, in order to solve the problem of population density in that part of the country.

'2. Israel's security borders shall be drawn according to the Allon Plan, with territorial corrections in Judea and Samaria, and the de-militarization of Sinai.

'3. The walled part of Jerusalem shall have extra-territorial status, like the Vatican in Rome, and shall be run by representatives of the three religions, Judaism, Islam and Christianity.

'4. Jewish settlement in Judea, Samaria and the province of Gaza shall be allowed at an extent equal to the proportion of members of the Arab nationality living in Israel within the Green Line.

'5. The Jewish inhabitants of the autonomous Palestinian territory and the Arab inhabitants of Israel shall be allowed to choose between citizenship according to their national affiliation and citizenship of the state in which they live.'

Gorni's scheme is much worse than those of 'Amirav and Hess. It is much more typical of the hypocritical aspect of 'left-wing' Zionism, which in the guise of moderation tries to get more than even the right dreams of achieving in the foreseeable future. In his compromise scheme he tries not only to extract acceptance of additional Israeli annexations (Point 2), but also to squeeze a few hundred thousand additional Israeli settlers into the occupied territories (Point 4). For some reason he also wants to embarrass the Egyptians, and perhaps also foment a quarrel between them and the Palestinians, by proposing the annexation of parts of Sinai to the province of Gaza. The idea of turning the walled part of Jerusalem into an extra-territorial zone does, it is true, undermine its annexation to Israel; but the conceptual world it belongs to is that of the Middle Ages. While 'Amirav and Hess propose a municipal division of Jerusalem along national lines, Gorni has the city divided according to religion.

Despite the blatant shortcomings of Gorni's scheme, it reflects at least an attempt to react in a new way to a changing situation. Like the Schemes of 'Amirav and Hess, it gives expression to a feeling which is seeping into the Zionist camp, that solutions must be sought in new directions.

The years of deadlock

THE 1980S HAVE BEEN YEARS of political deadlock in the region. Israeli withdrawal from the occupied territories seemed far off, a growing number of Israelis went to live across the Green Line, and some voices began to say that the occupied territories had in fact (if not in name) been irreversibly annexed to Israel. The clearest among them was the dovish voice of Meron Benvenisti, formerly vice-mayor of Jerusalem, who repeatedly claimed that the status of the occupied territories is indeed irreversible; and therefore the Israeli left, as well as the Palestinians, should stop the useless struggle for Israeli withdrawal and struggle instead for equal rights under Israeli rule.

The political deadlock, and probably also the internal situation in the PLO, led some Palestinians in the occupied territories to see a greater need for contacts with sympathetic Israelis. Encounters of this kind were made easier due to a resolution of the Palestinian National Council that approved of contacts with Israeli 'democratic forces'.

Such contacts, which had hitherto been sporadic, became more regularly established. The Committee for Solidarity with Birzeit University, whose activists included members of all Israeli leftwing tendencies, first declared its existence in a demonstration on the campus of Birzeit University, which had been closed by administrative edict.

Shortly after that, on 29 November 1981, about 250 supporters of the committee arrived in the centre of Ramallah to demonstrate against the closure of the university, and in effect against the occupation. The demonstration was dispersed using tear-gas–hitherto unprecedented where Israeli demonstrators are concerned–and dozens were arrested. The brutal suppression of that demonstration broke many mental barriers on the Palestinian side and prepared the ground for real co-operation. In February 1982, the Birzeit Solidarity Committee held another demonstration in Ramallah. On the following day, 21 February, the Israeli daily *Yediot Ahronot* reported:

'A military force called to the site started trying to disperse the demonstrators, who were aided by local youths who threw stones at the security forces. Tear-gas canisters were used, which the demonstrators threw back at the security forces.'

Two years later, conditions had ripened for the creation of a joint organization of Palestinians and Israeli leftists. This was an ad hoc body, a Committee in Defence of the Rights of 'Abd al-'Aziz 'Ali (Abu-'Ali) Shahîn. Not surprisingly, two of the Palestinian founding members of the committee were to be three years later Moshe 'Amirav's interlocutors: Faisal al-Husseini and Sari Nusseibeh.

Shahîn was a Fatah member who had been caught and condemned to 15 years' imprisonment. After his release from Israeli jail, he was exiled from his home in Rafah to Dahaniah, a small Beduin village on the Gaza Strip's border with Egypt, where he was held in isolation. After one year's exile, the Israeli authorities decided to deport him from the country. The committee in his defence, which met in East Jerusalem, held several protest actions, culminating in a demonstration held in the grounds of Kibbutz Keren Shalom overlooking Dahaniah where Shahîn was being held. This demonstration was unprecedented in several respects. For one thing, it was the first one in which Israelis and Palestinians from both sides of the Green Line took part on an equal footing. Also, for the first time Palestinians from the occupied territories agreed to take part in a demonstration inside Israeli territory, and even accepted the hospitality of a *kibbutz* (some of whose members were active in the committee).

In the end, Abu-'Ali Shahîn was deported to Lebanon. But before dissolving itself, the committee held one final symbolic demonstration. Several dozen Israelis and Palestinians gathered on the site of the village of Bashit, Shahîn's birthplace, whose inhabitants were expelled or fled in 1948 and which is now a Jewish settlement. On the hill of Bashit's old graveyard the demonstrators planted several dozen olive trees. They were attacked by the present inhabitants, who after the demonstration was over tore out all the olive saplings.

During the committee's last meeting, all those present expressed a wish to continue working together. Faisal al-Husseini then raised a novel idea, as food for thought: the creation of a joint organization of Israelis and Palestinians, which would work out plans for joint future activity for the day following the creation of a Palestinian state in the West Bank and the Gaza Strip.

The reasoning behind this idea was quite simple. Among Palestinians as well as within the Israeli left, there are differences of opinion as to the genuine solution of the Israeli-Palestinian conflict. Inside Israel, those such as Rakah (the Israeli CP) and parts of the Zionist left, who regard the two state solution as the ultimate one, refused in those days to collaborate with those for whom the creation of a Palestinian mini-state alongside Israel is not the be-all and end-all. Similarly, among the Palestinians there were then deep differences between mainstream Fatah supporters, who really favoured the creation of a Palestinian state in the West Bank and Gaza Strip, and those who were prepared to raise the demand for such a state merely as a tactical step, and yet others who in those days still opposed it altogether. Al-Husseini's suggestion, that one should start planning for the 'day after', was designed not only to encourage some long-term thinking – not a bad thing in itself – but also to enable all concerned to work together within one common body, and thus to facilitate collaboration that is not confined to the struggle for a Palestinian state. As far as the future is concerned, clearly one has to think in terms of a form of coexistence that goes beyond normal relations between two states.

For various reasons, al-Husseini's idea was not taken up. But the experience gained in the Shahîn Defence Committee served as a basis for the creation of another joint Palestinian-Israeli organization, the Committee against the Iron Fist. Its first militants belonged to the nucleus that had been active in the Shahîn Committee, but they were soon joined by others. New forms of protest actions were tried. For the first time, use was made of the fact that East Jerusalem has been officially annexed to Israel, which meant that licence could be obtained for demonstrations there. These demonstrations, although held in occupied territory, were legal and many Palestinians could join them without risking immediate arrest. Later, use was made of the Israeli law that allows holding a picket with less than 50 participants without obtaining prior police permit. Such pickets were repeatedly held near the Damascus Gate in East Jerusalem.

At the same time, meetings were held with Israelis belonging to other groups with the hope of enlarging the Committee against the Iron Fist. As a result, a few militants of the East For Peace movement (a group of dovish Oriental Jews) joined the committee; but on the whole there was no great success on the Israeli side. Nevertheless, it seems that the committee's activities were in tune with the need felt by Palestinians in the occupied territories to develop new forms of action that might help break the deadlock.

New forms of action often go together with new ideas. A new idea had been raised by Sari Nusseibeh in 1985. On 19 October of that year, he published an article against autonomy in the East Jerusalem paper, *al-Mawaqif*. Here are a few excerpts:

'By definition, autonomy does not give full political rights. On the contrary, it gives individual human rights, such as the rights of expression and movement. It would also grant some collective human rights (such as conducting municipal affairs), but it does not allow the individual or the community to implement their sovereign right to conduct their affairs.

'The sovereign capacity for self-determination, which is acquired by means of full participation in the implementation of the political rights enjoyed by the ordinary citizen in his own country, including the right to elect his representatives to the legislature and to be elected to executive authority . . . that capacity does not exist in an autonomy but would exist in a framework of full incorporation in the State of Israel.

'We, inhabitants of the occupied land, should think a little about these possibilities. For it is possible that at some stage it might be better for us to raise the banner of Incorporation and get equal rights. If we find that the present slogan, demanding an independent state as a people with its own identity, is unrealizable and that what we are offered instead of it is autonomy, then it would be better to struggle for this goal [of incorporation in Israel].'

On the face of it, what Nusseibeh is saying goes in a totally opposite direction to 'Amirav's scheme. Whereas the latter proposes an extended form of autonomy, Nusseibeh prefers incorporation into Israel over autonomy. Nevertheless, in an interview with the Israeli weekly *Koteret Roshit* (13 November 1985), Nusseibeh stressed that 'the ultimate aim is to liberate myself from you and set up a state of my own, with my own parliament and government, a state in which I would be able to participate in building my own future and that of my children. But it seems to me that if matters continue to move in their present direction the possibility of realizing this ideal would melt away. One should find something else that would be best for us.'

The Palestinian uprising two years later succeeded in reversing several developments. For one thing, it cut off many of the ties between Israel and the occupied territories and re-asserted the latter's separate identity. But the ideas born during the preceding period of deadlock will not just fade away. The Palestinians wanted to put an end to the occupation, and during the 1980s some have realized that there is more than one way in which the occupation could come to an end. It may end by the withdrawal of Israel's forces from the occupied territories; but it can also end in other ways, such as the one outlined by Sari Nusseibeh. A situation in which all the inhabitants of the occupied territories become Israeli citizens and are able to participate in all aspects of Israeli political life, sharing all the duties as well as all the rights enjoyed by Israeli citizens – this too is a form of abolition of the occupation. In such a situation, Nusseibeh told *Koteret Roshit*, 'I shall continue my struggle as part of an ongoing historical process leading to the secular democratic state, but the struggle will have to employ democratic means. I shall propose to amend the Law of Return so that it will include Palestinians as well as Jews.' He also talks about establishing a party whose programme would include the return of all

Palestinians, and full equality of rights for Arabs and Jews. 'If we have a majority, I would also change the name of the state and its flag.'

A similar voice has also been heard on the other side of the Green Line. Muhammad Kiwan is a well-known militant of the Palestinian nationalist movement inside Israel since the 1950s; he is one of the founders of the *Abna' al-Balad* movement in Umm al-Fahm and practises as a lawyer in the nearby town of Hadera. In an interview with *Koteret Roshit* (20 April 1988) he was asked to describe the ideal state of which he dreams. Since this is the first time that the secular democratic idea of Palestinian nationalism has been given such detailed interpretation by a Palestinian citizen of Israel, it is worth quoting him at some length:

'I dream of a secular democratic state for both peoples together. Such a state can only come into being in the very very long term, after a strenuous and prolonged activity of mutual persuasion. It will mean that instead of today's partial democracy for Jews there will be true democracy, without a ruling people and a subject people. My state will allow the right of return to the exiled Palestinians, and the right of immigration for Jews who would want to live here, but the structure must be secular because through religion it is impossible to set up true democracy.

'As I am aware that the Jewish public in Israel has always been taught to believe that a secular democratic state means the liquidation of the State of Israel – an interpretation quite different from my own ideal – it is clear to me that such a state can only come about after we prepare the ground for it by mutual education, and by giving equal opportunities, and by co-operation between both peoples on a truly equal basis. Only then will it be possible to convince the Jewish public that such a state is really for the benefit of both peoples, not just one.

'... If we make use of this period by educating people for equality, there will not be any ground for suspicion or fear; because the coming generations will not have our complexes, and will live as human beings, not as rulers and subjects. In the Switzerland of today, for example, a citizen's ethnic origin is of no importance; what counts is what an individual can contribute to society and its welfare. The right criterion is: the right person for the right place. That is to say, not as in the bad Lebanese model, whereby the prime minister must belong to one ethno-religious community, the president to another, the chief of staff to yet another; but each [should be chosen] according to suitability.

'The flag will have five colours: black, red, green, blue and white [that is, the colours of both the Palestinian and the Israeli flags].

'The national anthem must be based on love for human beings, on their contribution to society, on full equality.

'The official languages will be Hebrew and Arabic, but not as at present. For example, I have recently lodged a complaint with the Administration of Lawcourts in Israel against the practice that has become prevalent in the Hadera Magistrates' Court whereby an Arab citizen who does not understand Hebrew must, in a civil case, pay for translation [although Arabic is nominally an official language]. Recently I had a client who had to pay 200 New Shekels for the translation of the cross-examination of a single witness.

'The political regime will be based on a free parliament. It is enough to mention that at present one of the conditions for being allowed to run for the Knesset is that the party in question recognize Israel as the state of the Jewish people. It is enough to mention that what exists today in Israel's Knesset is democracy for Jews, not for Arabs. My parliament will not be called Knesset, because this term means Jewish Congregation. I want a parliament that is democratic in the full sense, with a constitution that shall guarantee that if even that parliament deviates from the fundamental principles of human rights, then one would be able to appeal to the Supreme Court, which shall have the right to overrule discriminatory laws. That is, a Supreme Court whose authority is anchored in the constitution, so that the parliament cannot deprive it of the right to overrule discriminatory laws.

'Equal rights for women. This is very important; it also includes the right to have an abortion, because every person is responsible for his or her body and has a sovereign right to decide. There should be legislation to guarantee that homosexuality shall not be illegal, and whoever wishes to have such relations would be free to do so.

'As for the Law of Return, in practice it is a dead letter in the lawbook, because as we know Jewish immigrants are not coming. But in principle it is a law based on racial privilege, on granting priority to anyone who was born Jewish over any other race. . . .

'If such a Utopian state comes into being, it will be open not only to persecuted Jews but also to exiled Palestinians as well as to other ethnic groups, such as the Kurds.

'As for the economy, in the long run it will have to be socialist, especially in Palestine-Israel, in view of all the injustice done to the Palestinian Arab people, particularly in the matter of land ownership, where Israel's Knesset took care to enact draconian laws to rob Arabs of their lands. In order not to inflict an injustice on the other people [i.e. Israeli Jews] the land and means of production must belong to those who work them, and in this way we can solve this knotty problem.'

Thinking about the day after, that is after the creation of a Palestinian state in the West Bank and Gaza Strip, is not merely a theoretical exercise in Utopia-mongering. Contrary to the belief of many who support the creation of such a state, it will not be a solution of the Zionist-Palestinian conflict. It will leave unchanged the Zionist character of the State of Israel and may even put the Palestinian minority living inside it at greater risk. Their remaining lands may be in danger of expropriation, and the plans of 'transfer' – that is, mass deportation – may receive a big impetus. Every complaint of the Palestinian minority will be met with the reply: 'You have your own state just across the border, so you can go there if you don't like it here'. A Palestinian mini-state will also not solve the problem of masses of refugees, who would adhere to their dream of return.

The question is whether socialists can propose a plan of their own, which can serve as a programme for immediate struggle, and which also encapsulates a long-term solution to the national problem of Palestinians and Israelis alike. It seems to me that socialists have so far confined themselves to proposing principles for a long-term solution, whereas it is possible to be a little more specific, without sliding into nationalism.

The autonomy solution

ABOUT SIX YEARS AGO, a debate on the national question was reopened in the Socialist Organization in Israel (Matzpen). Some comrades felt that for the needs of propaganda it was no longer sufficient to insist – as the SOI had traditionally done – on recognition of the rights of both the Palestinian Arab people and the Israeli Jewish people to self-determination; and that something more positive, more concrete, must be proposed. In other words, a particular form of implementing the right to self-determination ought to be recommended. The idea they offered for debate was that the SOI should call for struggle for an Israeli-Palestinian bi-national state. One option was to support the creation of such a state in the whole of the area between the Jordan and the Mediterranean (that is, in what is now Israel plus the occupied territories); while a second option was to call for Israeli withdrawal from the occupied territories, and the transformation of Israel itself (within the Green Line) into a bi-national state.

Those comrades went on to suggest that Matzpen should formulate a draft constitution for the proposed bi-national state. When they tried to formulate their ideas in some detail, it transpired that in order to make the state – that is to say, the state institutions – bi-national, they proposed the creation of two parallel structures of national institutions which would share power between them: Palestinian Arabs and Israeli Jews would each elect their own respective national representatives, and these two bodies together would compose the legislature and the executive power. The practical implication would be that every citizen in the bi-national state would have to be labelled by nationality, and this would apply not only to international socialists who are not in the habit of identifying themselves by nationality, but also to members of national minorities who belong to neither of the large national groups, such as Circassians, Armenians and Black Hebrews (members of a Black sect who immigrated to Israel from the US). When one goes into greater detail, it turns out that the proposed constitution would divide even the members of Matzpen along national lines: members of Arab origin would have to vote together with all other Palestinian Arabs, for Arab candidates only, while those of Jewish origin would vote for other bodies, made up of Jews only.

True, the proposed scheme envisaged absolute equality between both national groups, irrespective of their numerical size, but it nevertheless implied an element of separation between citizens according to national origin; moreover, the separation would have to be institutionalized and anchored in the constitution. Those comrades who proposed this idea claimed that separation also exists at present, except that in the Zionist State of Israel there is separation plus anti-Arab discrimination; so their proposed constitution would be a step forward. The trouble was, however, that this bi-national scheme was supposed to be a solution to the national problem – the Palestinian problem and the Jewish problem in the Middle East. Although it represented an advance compared to the existing situation, it was a large retreat from the socialist solution to the national problem.

Four years ago, the bi-national idea was put into practice in the formation of the Progressive List for Peace, which ran for the 1984 general elections. Ever since its foundation, it is a bloc of two sections, one Jewish and one Arab, and membership in this movement is only possible through one of the two national sections. Members of Matzpen who in 1984 were active in the PLP's election campaign, had to resign from it for this very reason: it was impossible to belong to it without joining one of the national sections; and the demand to allow the formation of a third, mixed, section was rejected. Some members of Matzpen who nevertheless decided to stay in the PLP (in its Jewish section, *Alternative*) thereupon left Matzpen.

There are, nevertheless, certain ways of implementing the right to self-determination that are quite compatible with a socialist structure of society. Of course, there is the classical bourgeois unitary form, whereby all citizens are legally equal; and the state in its laws and institutions does not separate, let alone discriminate, people according to national origin. Within such a political framework, it is possible also to satisfy the linguistic, cultural and educational requirements of groups belonging to different ethnic backgrounds, without however discriminating against any group.

But there is yet another form of political structure, examples of which can likewise be found in existing bourgeois states. Namely, a federal form of state. In this connection, it is worth reminding all those groups and individuals who call themselves Marxist-Leninists, what Lenin's position was: 'As far as autonomy is concerned, Marxists defend, not the "right" to autonomy, but autonomy itself, as a general universal principle of a democratic state with a mixed national composition . . . ' (The Right of Nations to Self-Determination, 1914)

Every state (other than a city-state), no matter how centralistic, devolves and distributes power in some form. Some of its powers are distributed functionally (into various departments) and some are devolved geographically. Even in the centralist Zionist State of Israel there are elements of distribution of power; for example, some aspects of power, albeit rather limited, are devolved to local authorities. This is a limited form of local autonomy. Another example is the administrative division of the country into districts, each with its own district commissioner with rather extensive local powers. Similarly, the police and the courts of law are organized along regional lines.

Regional division of power does therefore exist. But two questions need to be asked in relation to it. First, how democratic is the power exercised by the sub-divisions? Second, what are the criteria for drawing the boundaries of these sub-divisions?

As far as Israel is concerned, it is easy to answer both questions. As to the first quesiton, only the power of municipal authorities is an elected autonomous power, albeit to a rather limited extent. The power of democratically elected local authorities is severely limited by state control. It is also clear that local authorities are treated very unequally, because the subsidies provided by the central government are determined by undemocratic criteria, according to partisan considerations and even more so according to considerations of nationality and ethnicity.

All other sorts of regional administration are not autonomous at all, because they lack the minimal ingredient of autonomy – involvement of the local population in policy decisions. The district commissioners are appointed from above, by the Ministry of the Interior. The 'development of the Galilee', for example, is entrusted to a senior government official, the Co-ordinator of Government Activities in the Galilee. This person does everything possible not for developing the Galilee, but for Judaizing it, against the express wishes of the majority of the Galilee's inhabitants.

As for the second question, it is clear that the boundaries of the various districts are gerrymandered so as to prevent Arabs being in a majority. Wherever the most logical boundary of a district would have included more Arabs than Jews, the authorities manipulated the boundary to include big Jewish towns.

It is clear that in a country where there is more than one national group, one of the most important criteria in drawing the boundaries of administrative sub-divisions is the national composition of each district. Proper democratic administration requires this. If the majority of the Galilee's inhabitants are Arabic-speakers, the interests of proper democratic administration demand that the boundaries of the Galilee should be fixed so as to include as many Arabic-speakers and as few speakers of other languages as possible. In this way, the local inhabitants would have a local administration that speaks their own language. On the contrary, there is no justification (other than a purely formal geographical one) for including the north-eastern 'finger' of the Galilee, almost all of whose inhabitants are Hebrew-speakers, in the main Galilee district.

Sub-division of the country into districts with wide local powers and democratically elected local authorities, and the drawing of boundaries between them with utmost consideration for their national composition – this is a programme that socialists support not only because it advances democracy, but also because it is part of their struggle for transferring all political, social and economic power in society to democratically elected bodies of delegates. It is not merely a blueprint for greater democracy, it is also a foreshadowing of socialism.

This programme has no 'positive' or 'constructive' national ingredients. its logic would have been just as valid if the majority of the Galilee's inhabitants had been Jews, or if the Galilee were to be part of a secular democratic Palestinian state. But it is particularly pertinent in the existing situation, in which, in addition to the particular interests of the inhabitants of the Galilee as a geographic-economic region, and in addition also to the requirements of proper democratic administration, the Galilee has a different national composition the rest of the country. As Lenin said,

' . . . it is beyond doubt that in order to eliminate all national oppression it is very important to create autonomous areas, however small, with entirely homogeneous populations, towards which members of the respective nationalities scattered all over the country, or even all over the world, could gravitate, and with which they could enter into relations and free associations of every kind. All this is indisputable, and can be argued against only from the hidebound bureaucratic point of view.

'The national composition of the population, however, is *one* of the very important economic factors, *but not the sole* and *not* the most important factor. Towns, for example, play an *extremely important* economic role under capitalism . . . ' [and, we may add, under socialism as well.]

'To cut the towns off from the villages and areas that economically gravitate towards them, for the sake of "national" factor, would be absurd and impossible. That is why Marxists must not take their stand entirely and exclusively on the "national-territorial principle.' (Critical Remarks on the National Questions, 1913.)

Territorial autonomy of regions, whose boundaries are determined to a great extent (though not solely) by the 'national factor', is indeed an integral part of democracy.

There are, it is true, national problems to which neither total political separation nor territorial autonomy are applicable. Such is the case where a national minority is dispersed, without constituting a majority in any district. Where separation and territorial autonomy are out of the question, other guarantees must be sought against national oppression. This was, for example, the situation of the Jews in Tsarist Russia, where the Bund tried to deal with the problem by demanding a non-territorial 'cultural-national autonomy'. I shall not enter into a discussion of this demand, because it is irrelevant to our present problem. In this country it is in principle possible for both peoples to separate from each other and form two separate national states; and it is also possible to sub-divide the entire country into autonomous regions.

At this point we should mention a very different concept of autonomy, the one included in the Camp David agreements. The autonomy offered to the Palestinians by the Likud government was emphatically non-territorial; it was 'an autonomy for people, not for a given territory'. This formula shows at once that something is very wrong with the whole concept. When an oppressed national group is denied the right to exercise authority over a territory in which it constitutes a large majority, and is only allowed to run its own cultural and municipal affairs, the purpose of such 'autonomy' can only be to preserve a position of inequality. When it is possible to sub-divide a country into autonomous districts in each of which one national group has a clear majority, this is a preferable democratic solution.

It may be asked what the demographic situation would be if and when the Palestinian refugees are allowed to return. Would it still be possible to sub-divide Israel into geographically and economically reasonable districts with clear national majorities? In my view, a detailed analysis of the data shows such sub-division to be possible. The district boundaries may, it is sure, be as tortuous and 'illogical' as the Green Line or (perhaps more to the point) the borders of the 1947 UN partition resolution. So what? These boundaries will be analogous to municipal boundaries, which have purely administrative significance and do not hamper the citizens' freedom of movement across them. The district boundaries will exist on the map; in reality they will be of interest only for the purpose of elections to the district council, taxation and other matters that will be under the authority of the autonomous district. Crossing them will be as uneventful as crossing from one town to the next.

A favourite trick of those who oppose the democratic solution of the national problem is to point out examples of countries where the national problem has not been solved, as proof that it cannot be solved. Paraphrasing Lenin, we can say that there is only one solution to the national problem, in so far as such a thing is possible in a non-socialist world, namely: consistent democratism. As proof of this we can point out Switzerland, for example.

Those who wish to evade the core of the problem do not like this example. They try to refute or devalue it. Switzerland is an exception, they say. In Switzerland there is a special kind of decentralization, a special history, special geographic conditions, a special distribution of linguistic groups, and so on and so forth. All this is just an attempt to evade the essence of the argument. It is true that Switzerland is exceptional inasmuch as it is not a uniform national state. But it is far from being the only such 'exception'. Spain and Iran are other examples of this kind. It is true that special historical and geographic conditions have enabled Switzerland to develop a more consistent democratism in the national question than Spain or Iran. But this is not a valid argument against our position. Surely, when one is looking for a paradigm, a model to be studied or copied, one should single out the best examples rather than the worst. In the present world, countries in which any kind of institution has been founded on consistent democratic foundations are rare, even exceptional. Does this prevent us from defending consistent democracy in all institutions?

Switzerland, which Lenin often quoted as an example, has one other advantage not pointed out by him. Unlike other federal countries, in which every national or ethnic group is concentrated in a single autonomous region where it constitutes a majority, Switzerland has no such concentrations. Each of its three major national groups has more than one canton. This has great long-term importance. No national group has a single geographical focus for its national aspirations, or a single legislative council around which its political ambitions might rally. Local questions, and even a measure of local-patriotism, tend to weaken national uniformity and allow other kinds of inter-personal and inter-communal ties to develop.

The Swiss example is a good one for another reason. Its way of dealing with the national question is compatible also with a socialist structure of society, and can be applied in widely differing areas. It can be applied within the 1948 borders of Israel (the Green Line), or in the whole area between the Jordan and the Mediterranean, or in a united socialists Arab east. It can also be applied in a united Europe, divided not into large states but into many smaller cantons, which are more suitable for self-management.

And yet another advantage: division into relatively small administrative units, provided they are run democratically, facilitates maximal mass participation in the political process. From here it is not a far cry to a form of social self-rule based on a system of councils.

Haim Bresheeth

SELF AND OTHER IN ZIONISM: PALESTINE AND ISRAEL IN RECENT HEBREW LITERATURE

Introduction – why and how

IN THIS ARTICLE, I will try to evaluate some recent trends in Hebrew literature to establish the tendencies represented by a group of writers on the left flank of Zionism when dealing both with Zionist identity and that of Palestine. This group has been chosen because of its high profile abroad, and within Israel and because its writings seem to be a poignant instance of the present cultural and political crisis of Zionism. It would be easy to quote at length from rabid, right-wing and racist publications by Gush Emunim or similar organisations, or even from established right-wing writers such as Alterman or Shamir. Instead, I have chosen to quote only those writers belonging to left-Zionism[1], the most progressive tendencies. It can safely be assumed that any racism and nationalism detected within this group will be even more evident within the Zionist mainstream. Since it is from this group that any shift in Zionist policy towards the Palestinians may emerge, it is extremely interesting to analyse the positions it represents. More will be said later about this choice.

Literature in Israel plays a central political and ideological role similar to that played by the electronic media in Britain or western Europe. While a full analysis of this phenomenon is beyond the scope of this article, some suggestions are made in one of the following sections. Literature is used here as an important litmus-paper of current shifts in Zionist thinking, and any lessons which may be learned from this analysis are not medium-specific.

This study attempts to relate the different aspects and current crisis of the identity construction within Zionism. The first chapter deals with the special role played by liteature within Zionism: the traditional positions taken by writers and, in the wider context of Zionist argumentation, the effect of regional and global political trends on Zionist writers, with particular reference to fascist developments in the 1930s. In the second chapter, the writer's self-image and its relationship to 'national' identity is examined. The third chapter examines the process of synthesizing a nation in Israel and the ideological material used in this construction. The last two chapters deal with the Palestinian image in recent Israeli writing and the identity crisis within Zionism. The concluding chapter attempts to connect these different strands together.

This article will look at a small but influential selection of recent Hebrew literature to examine the social, political and moral attitudes which form its ideological basis. Texts have been chosen for their social and political significance and raison d'etre rather than artistic merits. Examples include a relatively new and marginal literary genre – that of a writer/political activist setting out not so much to interview as to have rambling conversations with people belonging to the communities locked in mortal struggle in Palestine. This 'touring troubador' genre was reintroduced by Amos Oz in 1982, in a book called 'Po Vasham Be'Eretz Israel'[2]. This book is part of a wider Israeli phenomenon of a society speaking to itself through literature and poetry. While this may be true, to an extent, of most societies, it reaches an advanced stage of development in particular historical circumstances.

An historical perspective

THE PARTICULAR INTENSITY with which Hebrew and Arabic literature and poetry have taken up the conflict as their central theme, brings to mind other recent periods of great social and political tension in which literature played a similar role. An obvious example is that of pre-revolutionary Russia, the vast social landscape of which was painted with passionate detail by Tolstoy, Dostoyevsky, Chekhov and Gorky. Russian literature of the 19th century and since, is centrally placed as an influence on Hebrew literature. Many writers in pre-mandate Palestine came from Russia and wrote in Russian before writing in Hebrew. They had brought with them not only the rhythms of the motherland but a range of attitudes, subjects and themes specific to 19th century Russian literature. In that sense, Hebrew literature in Palestine was always of a polemic cast, a phenomenon not restricted to pre-revolutionary Russia but evident in many societies undergoing violent change, such as Weimar Germany or the USA during the Depression.

Thus, while Oz may be the current reactivator of the genre, the tendency itself has a long history. Not only are novels, poems and plays used a platforms for political argumentation as part of the political arsenal that reaches a wide and crucial audience, but writers consistently participate in the interminable and constant public debate on the nature of the Zionist project. The ideological battle fought over the direction to be taken by Zionism has been dominated from the start by literary figures in an abundance not seen elsewhere. It would be impossible (and unnecessary) to give here a full account of the role played by literati in the history of Zionism.

The obvious one to start with is Herzl, a journalist, mediocre playwright and novelist who attained fame through his books – *Altneuland* and *Der Judenstaat* – which describe, in different ways, the realisation of Zionist aspirations. The ideas expressed in those books were not new but had already been propounded a few years earlier, specifically in Leo Pinsker's book *Auto-emancipation*. Books discussing the options facing the Jews of Europe were not unusual; since Jewish communities spanned the globe, literature had been the paramount vehicle of dialogue within world Jewry. The debate fired by Herzl was joined by Jewish writers from various countries. Polemicists such as Achad Ha'am and Borochov and poets like Bialik joined the fray and the debate was brought to the public through newspapers, novels, pamphlets and poems. This was a formative period of the Zionist discourse, one in which politicians as such were missing, and was in effect a political debate held in the cultural arena. For a people that had survived longer than most and who cherished the Bible as a powerful combination of history, religion, culture, mores and a political programme for the future (not to mention a land-registry document), the choice of literary polemics to execute this crucial discourse on the movement's future directions was an obvious one.

Literature in Israel is the stage on which power struggles take shape, where opposing groupings within Zionism talk to each other, using the public arena as a testing ground for new tendencies. The Zionist right has never been short of literary proponents – from the poets Greenberg and Alterman, to novelists such as Agnon and Shamir. but amongst the voices of euphoric nationalism and neo-colonial jubiliation at the start of colonisation were voices of dissent and discord. After Achad Ha'am and his scruples, came Brenner who raised political and personal doubts about the direction of the Zionist project. These two were followed in the 1920s by a group of intellectuals led by Martin Buber, called *Brith Shalom* (Peace Pact). The group tried to set up a united front for peace in Palestine, but was less than successful in persuading substantial numbers of either Jews or Arabs to join. This was a period of gains for the Zionist right, with Jabotinsky, the leader of the Revisionist Zionist federation, attracting many young Zionists in Europe and Palestine. Jabotinsky, another Zionist writer-turned-politician, had been influenced by Mussolini during the early 1920s. Though he later disagreed bitterly with fascism and was one of its strongest opponents within Zionism, his organisation's youth movement resembled the *Hitler Jugend* and the armed motorcades of supporters clearly drew inspiration from the *Sturm Abteilung* in Germany. This accusation was continuously hurled at them by their opponents on the left flank of Zionism.

It is interesting to note, in passing, that the concept of state power and its crucial role within the future Zionist state, was developed by Jabotinsky in the historical novel *Samson*. The final message his Samson sends back to the Israelites consists of two words: 'Iron' and 'King'. (These two they are told to strive for, at any cost, so that they can become the lords of Canaan). His is a cry for 'normalcy', in a world where the norm has become the rule of naked power, racism and oppression. In this light, the liberation of the Jew is seen not as a freedom won from the socieyt of *goyim* but as freedom from the 'misguided' humanism preached and practiced by so many Jewish intellectuals in the diaspora. It is the rich tradition of Jewish radicalism, of the important role played by many Jews within the socialist and communist movements, which is being countered here. That tradition was the dominant voice of politicised Jews in East Europe before the holocaust, through organisations like the Bund, and various socialist and communist organisations. As a direct challenge to all they stand for, this tradition was, and still is, anathema to Zionist writers and has to be shown to be a futile and doomed stance, a miscalculation by the politically naive.

The retreat from 19th century radical and liberal traditions to a pre-historical, mythical and glorious past, had been the hallmark of fascist tendencies elsewhere – supplying an ideological justification for demands to establish new empires and a battle cry for the masses to follow. It continues to supply ammunition and argumentation for the current generation of fascists and racists in Israel who are closer in their thinking, political style and lexicon to Jabotinsky than to the Labour Movement.

Thus, the struggle for political control within Zionism in Palestine was not limited to brute force and armed provocation in the style developed in central Europe; like left-Zionism with its publication houses, the right enjoyed the full backing of the Revisionist publication machinery which included a journal called *Diary of a Jewish Fascist*, edited by another man of letters, Aba Achimeir. In the context of fascist victories in Europe, this group of ultra-right extremists was indicative of the general direction taken by Zionists during this period. It was inconceivable for *Brith Shalom* to succeed in such an atmosphere dominated by nationalist and neo-colonial sentiments. The decline of left-of-centre ideas and influence during the 1930s in Palestine has resurfaced in the 1980s with the coming to power of the right-wing block, and the formation of even more extreme, fascist parliamentary and extra-parliamentary blocks and parties which enjoy popular support, particularly amongst the Jewish youth.

A fuller account of the centrality and importance of literature and literary debate within mainstream Zionism during its formative period is available in Hebrew in publications too numerous to list here.

The 'macro political' context

THE RELATIONSHIP OF ZIONISM to wider trends is as true now as it was then. One has only to think of the rise of the right during the 1970s, although this may have been more dramatic in Israel than in some other societies. A look at the period of rising fascism in the 1920s in Europe, offers some important insights into the interdependence of similar political trends. This point is habitually denied by Zionists who prefer to describe themselves and their movement as totally unique. Comparisons of the colonisation process with any other, e.g. South Africa, enrages Zionist apologists who are adept at splitting methodological hairs like seasoned Talmudists. (While the differences between the two political situations are many and important, the failure to see the similarities is sheer blindness. It is no coincidence that both societies have grown closer to each other in many fields over the last decade).

Thus, a look at historical and political parallels, such as the rise of fascism in Europe, may provide conceptual keys to a number of ideological closed doors behind which the harmful creations of this tumultous period are still intact. It was during this period that terms such as *cruel Zionism* were coined to describe a dominant tendency within Zionism led by the undisputed strong-man of the Zionist establishment, Ben Gurion. The term evolved out of the priorities of building Zionism and its empire-in-the-making rather than paying attention to the millions of Jews living in Europe under the impending threat of extinction. It is especially illuminating to look at the 'poetic' terminology used by some 'liberal' Zionist leaders, such as Weizmann, to see how deep fascist ideology had struck. As early as 1937, Weizmann was using poignant language to describe the Jews of Europe and their projected future:

'The old ones will pass; they will bear their fate, or they will not. They were dust, economic and moral dust in a cruel world . . . Two millions, and perhaps less – *She'erit Hapleta* – only a branch will survive. They have to accept it. The rest they must leave to the future – to their youth.[3]

The reference to millions of human beings as 'human dust' cannot be conceived in isolation from the literary campaign by the Zionist right, politically and historically synchronised and related to the rise of European fascism. The ascendency of militant, empire-seeking nationalism has had a decisive dehumanizing effect on Zionism, through a complex system of links with the cultural centres around which this new growth has flourished. Not taking account of these links is tantamount to accepting the central Zionist myth of the uniquenes of Zionism, a movement not just denying the historical developments, but able to reverse some of them.

The 'cosmetic' alternative

THE DEBATE AROUND the central features of the Zionist utopia was held, from the start, between two unequal groupings. The first included those who, following Herzl's notions of the colonisation process in Palestine, and its links with and dependence on the empire of the day, set about achieving their goals in the shortest possible period. Despite important differences between right and left-wing Zionism about priorities and methods, both wings of mainstream Zionism form part of this first grouping and were in accord over the main tenets of political Zionism.

The second grouping was a motley crew – liberals, socialists, communists who found their way to Palestine as a result of European anti-semitism rather than as a result of ardent Zionism. This was not a tendency struggle between the dominant and an alternative – the alternative had by definition to exist outside Zionism and to offer not just an opposition to it but an alternative programme altogether. Such a group did not exist within the Jewish community in Palestine, at least not a group with any real cultural and political influence. Hence the debate was held between dominant, aggressive forms of Zionism and critics of such a tendency who, rather than disassociating themselves from it and fighting it outright, were reformers and not radicals or revolutionaries. Such criticism may be called 'cosmetic' as it is a disagreement about ways and means, not about goals.

An unusually clear and frank account of the relationship between the dominant tendency and its critics appears in Amos Oz's book, *Be'or Hatcheleth He'aza*.[4] Amos Oz is one of the few Israeli writers who are relatively well known abroad – his books have been translated into many languages and he is thought of as a left-wing activist and a supporter of Palestinian rights. In Israel he has been attacked by the right-wing groups numerous times, classified as an *ashafist* (Israeli jargon for PLO supporters from the Hebrew acronym *ashaf* for the PLO). His book is a collection of articles and public talks written during the 1970s. In it he says:

'Where the followers of the trendy school of thought are talking about "territories", the Greater Israel Movement is saying quite openly – "Eretz Israel". Where some smart Alecs are preaching: let's try to grab as much as the Goyish nations will allow, the Greater Israel people are saying: All is ours, the whole country and it should not be redivided. Where the nod and wink rule and where everyone uses synonyms in order to cover up, they are saying: colonize, Judaize, inherit.

These are necessary words. There is in them, amongst other things, a measure of neatness and trust. This movement was not born out of inferior elements; it comes out of the noble heritage of Jewry. I see it as a live branch, totally necessary to the main Zionist tree trunk. If we forget for a moment some specks of ugliness that have attached themselves to the movement (and which movement is clear of those?) then the movement of Greater Israel is founded on love, trust and visionary insight. I belong to a different and remote branch of the same tree, but even from a distance I can recognise the temperament, suffering, anger, heart-rendering wishes. Both them and me are partners of a kind, sharing a hostility towards those waiting to see which way the wind blows . . . '[5]

To fully appreciate those words, it may be useful to transpose them to other political realities. Would similar expressions be possible from a liberal or left-wing activist to describe links and connections to a tradition held in common with the extreme right? Brecht speaking about Nazism? Gramsci speaking about Fascism? Jackson eulogising about the Ku Klux Klan? A unique situation, indeed, for anyone purporting to be active on the left. But in the case of Oz and others like him in left-Zionist groups from the Labour party to Peace Now, sentiments connecting them to the extreme Jewish right are apparently firmer than any positive leanings they may have towards Palestinians, even those on the left of the political spectrum. This sense of belonging not to an internationalist left movement, but to a tradition created by reactionary forces and now dominated by the extreme right, may explain the images of Palestine and Palestinians they create. This innate racism is why the struggle of 'cosmetic reformers' of Zionism, while being the more sympathetic and acceptable aspect of a repressive system, can offer neither a real alternative nor an enduring resistance to the dominant.

The vacillation of this tendency on central issues, like the self-determination of the Palestinians or the colonial nature of the Zionist enterprise, limits their actions and proclamations to a corrective type, a rearguard cultural guerrilla activity. Such a position, by supplying a more acceptable and palatable face for both internal and external consumption, serves as an effective apologist for the excesses of Zionism. It also highlights the extent of the crisis in which Zionism has found itself 20 years after the 'miracle' of 1967.

The continued support of most such writers for Zionism seems to emerge not from a determined decision based on an evaluation of existing options, but rather a disregard for any political choices that might require a rethinking of communal and national identity. Such dissent as they voice arises out of a disenchantment with what their society has become, not from a political analysis. Concern for the lost dream of Zionist utopia, to find out 'where it all went wrong', assumes a pure and innocent dream that somehow became tainted. This romanticism has fired many Zionists whose need to see Palestine filled with Jews has made them blind to the existence of another nation there prior to their arrival. It is not the dream which is to blame, they argue, but only its realisation which did not measure up to the promised paradise. But the dream did not become tainted at all; rather, it had in it a fatal flaw, built into the very fibre of its being – the denial of the other. This denial operates on all levels – the ideological negation of a Palestinian people underlines and justifies the very material forms of denial developed by Israeli society.

When the existence of the other becomes visible and no longer possible to deny, further means have to be put forward. Immediately after the occupation in 1967, R. Weitz, a prominent member of the establishment and former head of the Colonization Department of the Jewish Agency, revealed that in his diary of 1947 he had written the following:

'Between ourselves it must be clear that there is no room for both people together in this country . . . We shall not achieve our goal of being an independent people, with the Arabs in this small country. The only solution is a Palestine, at least Western Palestine (West of the Jordan river) without Arabs . . . And there is no other way than to transfer the Arabs from here into the neighbouring countries, to transfer all of them: *Not one village, not one tribe, should be left* . . . Only after this transfer will the country be able to absorb the millions of our brethren. There is no other way out.'[6]

But it was Herzl, not Weitz, who invented the idea of a total transfer. His may be the first written reference to the idea of mass transfer as a political solution in Palestine:

'When we occupy the land, we shall bring immediate benefits to the state that receives us. We must expropriate gently the private property on the estates assigned to us.

We shall try to spirit the pennyless population across the border by procuring employment for it in the transit countries, while denying it any employment in our own country.

The property-owners will come to our side. Both the process of expropriation and the removal of the poor must be carried out discreetly and circumspectly.

Let the owners of immovable property believe that they are cheating us, selling us things for more than they are worth.

But we are not going to sell them anything back.'[7]

Interestingly, later the same day (12th June 1895), Herzl notes a task to be performed by the indigenous population before it is transferred to the 'transit countries':

'If we move into a region where there are wild animals to which the Jews are not accustomed – big snakes, etc. – I shall use the natives, prior to giving them employment in the transit countries, for the extermination of these animals. High premium for snake skins, etc, as well as their spawn.'[8]

That such thoughts were carefully edited and sanitised from published works and speeches, points to a systematic denial and rewriting of history, a reworking of the Zionist self. Herzl himself was meticulous in removing references to the indigenous population from his published material. Indeed, the silence on this point rings loudly in his other books. This effort still continues and signifies a censoring of political consciousness, forcing underground any evidence of embarrassing traits of Zionism during its formative years.

The solutions outlined above were necessary not because of shortage of space in Palestine, but because of a more crucial factor – the imagined nature and identity of the Jewish/Israeli self in Palestine.

Thus, while it is possible for left-Zionist writers to be critical of Zionism in practice, it seems more difficult, almost impossible, to question the theoretical and ideological basis of the whole enterprise. Criticising a mode of practice does not necessarily invalidate the theory behind it; finding basic faults with the theory invalidates the whole enterprise.

Other reasons for the infertile nature of the 'cosmetic alternative' concern the material and methods central to writers of that tendency, such as Yehoshua, Oz, Kenan, Kaniuk, Shabtai and Grossman, who use dreams and nightmares – namely, myth, fantasy and poetic liaison – to build their argument. As this is central to the analysis presented here, it will be dealt with in the section 'The Devil's Dark Fire'.

The great project – synthesizing the nation

AS A RESULT OF external and internal pressures during the 1930s, the fragile cultural and political dominance of left-Zionism comes to an early end. The new cultural activists of the ascending right are quick to pinpoint the internal contradictions permeating left-Zionism. To them, concepts such as social justice, class struggle and world revolution are simply anachronisms, symptoms of the 'diaspora mentality' and 'Jewish cosmopolitanism' which they wish to expunge. The proponents of this tendency were Jabotinsky and Ben Gurion. Though belonging to opposite poles within Zionism, they both understood their task not simply as political but as a cultural regenerative project aimed at synthesizing a new nation out of the broken bits of history, cultural tradition, geography, myth and religion of the Jewish diaspora. One of the best descriptions of this perspective comes from Oz, when talking about the pioneering period in one of his public talks:

'A world which is new fences, new saplings, a new and a bit artificial language when coming from the lips of the Shtetl people (until now we cry, laugh, count and have a bloody row in Yiddish) new buildings, new grass, a new syllabus, fresh paint everywhere. Even new lullabies and new "ancient legends" which were synthesized by eager writers from the Jewish National Fund for the new Israeli children, filling the new, experimental readers. Folk songs before the Folk existed. Folk song and dances that require the officially trained guides who, travelling up and down the country, are teaching the folk how to sing and dance properly!'[9]

The concept of the Zionist 'melting-pot' was to forge a manufactured identity from a set of unwanted ones – namely, that of the Ghetto Jew, an antisemitic stereotype embraced by Zionism and fought against until its physical extinction. The starting point for such a project was always the belief that the Jews were not a nation in the normal sense of the word. This has been pointed out not just by the critics of the Zionist project, but even by the father of political Zionism, Theodor Herzl:

' . . . But how will this phenomenon be perceived in the middle classes, where the "Jewish Question" (*Judenfrage*) is residing, as the Jews are a middle class nation?'[10]

and later, discussing the reasons for antisemitism:

'In the ghetto we have developed, quite strangely, into a middle class nation; having left it, we acted as terrible competition for the indigenous middle classes. Thus it was, that after the Emancipation, we found ourselves in bourgeois circles, having to face the double pressures, external and internal.'[11]

One does not have to agree with Herzl's peculiar reading of Jewish history in order to appreciate the point. The Ghetto Jew had to be expunged – this was agreed grounds between right and left Zionism from very early on. But what would replace it, what kind of 'New Jew' had to be constructed?

The 'New Jew' was not to be constructed in the abstract but would be forged on the battleground of Arab Palestine, a country yet to be wrenched away from the adversary, the indigenous Palestinian population. Hence, another negative determinant was added to the synthetic brew – that of the Arab, specifically the Palestinian Arab, as the 'other'. Between these two polarities of 'otherness' a space was made for the new identity. As pointed out by Childers[12], Said[13] and others, this traditional racist stance and function has a long history. The Arab as other has contributed to the identity forging of a number of European nations.

The new identity had to be European-based. It is clear from Herzl's diaries[14] that a new nation in the Middle East was to be a synthesis of the gaiety of Paris and Vienna, the efficiency of London and the military might of Berlin. The descriptions are too numerous to quote here.

The symbols chosen for the Zionist nation serve to make this point clearer. All were imported from other cultures[15] and appropriated as 'Israeli': the music of the national anthem came from the Czech nationalist musician, Smetana; most of the music used for nationalist songs came from Russian folk-songs; the term for a Palestinian-born Jew is the Arabic word *Sabar*, Hebraicised as *Sabra*, the native prickly pear grown as a hedge by Palestinian villagers. Different rationales were found to justify this project of producing a nation willy-nilly, with the help of science, technology and, not least, propaganda.

Thus the Zionist project was originally conceived less as a national liberation movement within the context of the rise of European nationalism, and more as the manufacturing of a nation from the cultural stock of spare-parts of mainly central-European Jewry. This would be achieved by colonizing Palestine, a Third World country of great interest to Europeans. The European nations that were to be counted on for support, and which have duly obliged, were to be lured by an image of a new nation that reflected their own biases. The 'New Jew' was to be created in the image of the model of European neo-colonialism. In this context, the role of the Palestinians in the brew was that of local spice, the proof of belonging to the sun-scorched plains of the Middle East, like the sabra plant. Certain aspects of Israeli architecture reveal such a tendency to take over local cultural elements and motifs which are then adapted to suit the coloniser. The arch, dome and enclosed courtyard are all elements of Palestinian Arab architecture, although their true origin is sanitised by being referred to as 'regional' or 'Middle-Eastern'. Thus the very existence, history and creativity of the victim supplies ammunition to the oppressor and Zionism can argue that, despite the mainly European components of its identity, there are sufficient 'regional' and 'Middle-Eastern' features to make it a true inhabitant of the khamsin-swept plains of Palestine.

This obsession with synthesizing a nation at all costs and in a short period of time, may be the underlining reason for the centrality of literature within the Zionist project. Much literary effort is devoted to debating aspects of Jewish, Israeli and Zionist identity. How else could that identity be defined and examined?

At this point, it might be useful to examine the viewpoint of the literary proponents of left-Zionism to establish the similarities and differences from the official line, and most importantly, their positions, hopes, aspirations and fears.

'The Devil's Dark Fire' - a look in the mirror

THE FIRE OF THE TITLE is the one lit by one of Israel's foremost writers, Amos Oz, in his book *Be'or Hatcheleth He'aza*. [16] In it we discover Oz's conception of his and other writers' role within Israeli society - that of 'tribal witchdoctor' responsible for raising the 'Devil's dark fire . . . ', of excorcising the ghosts and shadows of the national past. Analysing the macabre motif evident in Moshe Dayan's speeches (' . . . the man sitting in the garden of his villa, surrounded by sarcopagi . . . the smell of death emanating from every single one of his political speeches . . . '), Oz defines the difference between political leaders and writers like himself, thus:

'It may well be that in Dayan we lost an authentic poet of the Israeli experience of those who spent their lives in wars and the funerary interludes between them. But I do not wish poets by the helm and dashboard of power. The emotional twilight, the Devil's dark fire, I myself know a little; and not from a distance. Those infected by it, should sit and write. By the control panels and the brakes I prefer to see not a visionary with figurative speech, but a sane pilot, enlightened, accurate and cool. No "divine voices", no "intuitive types".' [17]

His analysis of Dayan's linguistic devices is indeed fascinating but even more fascinating is Oz's perception of his own role, mandate and realm of operation. What he allows himself, he denies the politician, in a country where politics is so deeply affected by millennia-old texts, legends and mythical/political ghosts! Is this division of labour between the 'cool pilot' and the 'tribal witchdoctor' anything but wishful thinking?

The problem with this artificial separation has been pointed out by N. Calderon in an article published in 1979. [18] Calderon points out that Oz appropriates for the witchdoctor all areas of meaning, leaving the politician the mere technical function of an automatic pilot. This separation between 'meaning' and 'action' or between 'form' and 'content' does not merit the effort of serious theoretical refutation here. Such a view of politics, myth and ideology is either naive or, more likely, insincere. For Oz the writer, politics and political action are not only technical and bureaucratic, but also meaningless. In comparison to the 'Devil's dark fire', politics pales into grey insignificance and is simply a diversion from the deep, full world of the poetic ruptures denied to so many of us . . .

Were Oz a mere 'witchdoctor', his views would be of little consequence, part of Israel's post-colonial cultural neurosis. But Oz does not stick to his own rules. The fact that he is involved in the political wrangling on the left flank of Zionism changes all this. [19] While denying the dark fire to the politicians, he allows himself pilot's seat, functioning now as the driving instructor, now as the seer and prophet with foresight, analysis and judgement. The contradictory position taken by Oz is not just his own but applies to the tendency of which he is a proponent. In this political camp, the unavoidable contradictions are not faced with a view to arriving at a position to be taken and followed. Instead, the contradiction itself becomes a closed regenerative loop, a promising poetic spinning-wheel of self-pity and navel gazing. Pacing around in a circle of one's own making becomes the inspiration for the tunes being hummed, Pooh-style, so as not to lose heart while travelling down the political and historical spiral of 'there is no alternative'. The shallowness of this position is not lost on Oz himself, always the perceptive onlooker:

'Yes, I know: We had no alternative. Our backs to the wall. To die – or take the mount. A new country and a new leaf. I know; I only try to explain, maybe to apologise, to tell you why it is so difficult here to create a narrative with some depth and which is, like all good stories, a tale of witchcraft, of raising devils and ghosts from their rest.

It may be that we need to give up, to do our best and wait a century or two, until some literature of the calibre of the writers at the beginning of the century may be written here . . . ' [20]

The self-pity of the powerful, of those 'forced' against their will into despicable situations, has an extremely hollow ring. Nonetheless, this specific ghost of 'There Is No Alternative' needs a witchdoctor to raise it from uneasy rest; and who better than Oz, with his gentle irony?

To say this is not to denigrate the sincere efforts of Oz and others on the Zionist left, on behalf of the Palestinians and against the atrocities carried out by the state in their name. These efforts, however, amount to little more than an ameliorating factor in Israeli politics and cultural discourse unless the root cause of the problem is tackled. There is little doubt that Oz, and a number of other Israeli writers, is emminently suited to the task of facing up to the heritage of Zionism and its harvest of doom. Were they equal to the task, they would have a captive audience in Israeli progressive circles. This inability to face the past and present in order to guarantee a humane future, is a result of failing to systematically analyse Zionism and its characteristics. By accepting ideological claims and rejecting empirical evidence, these writers seem to be trapped in a cultural neurosis. The process of socio-analysis has not yet started; the patient is still dominated by the super-ego and in disavowing the nature of the political id, thereby denies the subconscious elements of colonialism.

Here we may turn our attention to the problem plaguing Oz's argument at a deeper level. If one accepts his above description of the synthesizing process and its artificiality, with what is one left? What constitutes for him the 'real' human experience? Where are his ghosts hidden? In which area of the Israeli experience are the devils buried, the black fires waiting to be rekindled?

It is no surprise that the devils and ghosts reside within the most concrete Israel experience – that of fighting, killing and dying, the daily soiree with death he so graphically points to when discussing Dayan. In other words, the great synthesizers have failed in their efforts to put the nation together, Frankenstein-fashion, from the dead bits of the past. Like Mary Shelley's count, what they needed was some higher form of energy to fuse it all. And they found this higher form of energy in a continuous and unending ritual, holy war.

This is not a conspiracy; the state of war is there for very real, material reasons. But it serves as a socio-political binding agent more efficient than the cultural efforts described above. Oz's people, his nation in the making, were *not* put together by cultural efforts. The nation became what it is because of the one real experience that binds it – the tribal camaraderie of warriors. This happened because of politics and not despite it. Indeed, a witchdoctor comes in handy in the context of battle and death, of a war without respite to the bitter end.

Palestine – the 'other' defining Zionist self-image

LIKE A NUMBER of other left-Zionist writers, Oz is not content in the role filled for many years by Alterman, the confidante and apologist of Ben Gurion, the poet laureate of the Zionist court. Such crude support for a system – which, after all, cannot be described along the 'David versus Goliath' model, at least not with Israel playing David – is beyond the pale. The system is too despicable for them to identify with, though most of their political positions are identical to official ones. So, while differing temperamentally and emotionally from right-wing Zionists, these writers nonetheless accept the tenets of Zionist propaganda apparently unquestioningly. One is defining oneself by defining the other and otherness. Oz again:

'The Al-Fatah organisation started its activities in the mid-60's because the maddest extremists amongst our enemies could not stand the relative calm during those years – The massacre of the sportsmen in Munich was designed to drag Israel and the Arab states into a total war . . . '[21]

While Oz is quick to criticise this type of 'analysis' when used by others, he falls into the same trap himself. Thus the dominant organisation in the PLO is a creation of the 'maddest extremists' and the massacre in Munich achieves the proportions of a potential Armageddon.

This may well be a result of the constant pressure on such writers in Israel to prove their patriotic credentials. In another book, he reaches even higher; while describing his first visit to the editorial offices of the Jerusalem Palestinian paper, *Al-Fajr*, he says:

'Behind the Dawn (*Al-Fajr*) stands the fortune of the mysterious Paul Ajlouni. Behind Ajlouni stands, so they say, the PLO, the mighty resources of Libya and Saudi Arabia and Iraq, the power of the Islamic bloc, the resources of the Soviet alliance, the masses of the Third World. Behind them stand the phalanxes, the mouthpieces of the simplistic New Left and of the reactionaries of the old right, as well as humanitarian do-good liberalism aching for symmetry and light.'[22]

No 19th century antisemite would fail to identify the inspiration of this description, namely, the great masterpiece of racism – 'The Protocols of the Elders of Zion'. Even the crudest propaganda coming out of Israel had never put it as clearly. This latter-day racism seems to jump out of the author despite his caution elsewhere, in the only chapter in the same book which deals with Palestinians directly. On entering the editorial office of *Al-Fajr*, Oz does not fail to note:

'The atmosphere . . . is similar, perhaps, to that in the office of a

Hebrew-language journal or a Yiddish newspaper in Eastern Europe before the fall: poverty and enthusiasm, lofty rhetoric and irritating prosaic hardships, poetry and politics.

I count five medium-sized rooms, slightly shabby, furnished with simple wooden desks, peeling-painted chairs . . . ' [23]

Like the racist meeting a Jew and seeing not a human being but a representative of the plots and machinations of World Jewry, so Oz rejects all evidence of senses and logic, even evidence he himself has provided, in favour of the 'Elders of Palestine' plot. Obviously, the *Al-Fajr* offices with their shabby desks are a mere camouflage, a front for the powers of darkness of the conglomerate Palestinians/Soviets/Third World/New Left/Old Right/Humanists. How impressive!

This brings us back to the starting point: while writers like Oz are critical of some government policies *vis-à-vis* the Palestinians on humanistic grounds, most of them accept the official version of the history of the conflict. Behind such lines is hidden not just simple racism, but a more far-reaching distortion of perceived realities. In Israel, a term has been coined for this popular abberation of experience – *ha'olam kulo negdenu* or 'the whole world is against us'. This 'common-sense' notion, popularised by ministers and media, is more surprising when detected in the higher echelons of left-Zionist culture; but there it is, unmistakably. The description of the enemy above, hiding behind the shabby desks of *Al-Fajr* and waiting to pounce on poor little Zionism, is as sad as it is ridiculous. Notably absent 'friends' are the West and assorted military dictatorships of a sympathetic nature, such as Chile and South Africa.

It would be wrong to reject Oz's notions as being particular or specific to him. Many left-Zionist writers express similar views, but a difference may be drawn between those who look at Palestinians as the 'other', and writers who venture into the minefield of trying to talk to and understand the 'other'. While Oz, Yehoshua and others, belong to the first category, some of the new generation of writers belong to the second, more risky, variety. Two such writers are Sammy Michael and David Grossman, who try to understand and describe the Palestinian position as a valid one, even using it as the basis for their critique of Israeli society.

In his recent novel, Michael chose a young Palestinian woman, Houda, as his protagonist; the narrative tells of her love for a Russian Jew, a new immigrant called Alex. The description of Houda's family and their tribulations is sensitive if not politically inspiring. A window is opened for the Hebrew reader, through which the Palestinian is seen as a person with history, memories, wishes, fears and hopes. This is not the 'Arab' in

Yehoshua's writing, an anaemic and passive figment of the Israeli imagination, a servile creature. The people described by Michael are full human beings; this is quite understandable – Michael, an Iraqi Jew, was active in the communist underground movement in Iraq before fleeing the country. He speaks Arabic, knows and respects the culture and history of the Arab peoples; this gives his characters an authentic touch, a degree of intimacy unusual in Hebrew literature when dealing with the Palestinian man or woman. Indeed, in his novel it is the Israeli and not the Palestinian who plays the role of 'other'.

One peculiarity in this novel is interesting to note in connection to the identity question. Houda, the young Palestinian woman, is most attracted to the poems of the famous Hebrew poet, Yehuda Amichai. For her birthday, she gets a book of his poems from her Jewish office colleagues, who know about her great admiration for Amichai. Throughout the novel, she finds solace and strength by reading his poems:

'I opened Amichai's book and read several times a couple of lines:
And my door is ajar
like a grave of the resurrected.'[24]

While Houda's knowledge of Amichai's poetry is not surprising in a country where Palestinians are not allowed to study their own poets at school and are taught Hebrew poetry instead, the absence of any Arab or Palestinian cultural reference weakens the character and makes it more palatable to the Israeli reader. A Palestinian who reads and loves Amichai – surely this must be the 'Good Arab' stereotype in operation here, as in many other instances in recent Hebrew literature. The Arab who knows and loves Hebrew poetry has now become almost a stock character. Another example is Nai'm, a young garage worker in Yehoshua's novel, *The Lover*[25]. Na'im brings to the garage a book of poetry by Bialik, the 'national poet'. On a number of occasions he manages to surprise Jews by his knowledge of Hebrew poetry:

'She looked at him in astonishment, whispering to me, "What's this? Can he read Hebrew or is he just pretending?"
"He knows Hebrew very well ... he's been to school ... he knows poems by Bialik by heart ... "'[26]

This proficiency of Palestinians in Hebrew poetry, at the same time lacking any knowledge or interest in Arab poetry and culture, says more about the writers than any real character they may try to describe. The attitude is one of the 'dog-playing-piano' description; a full analysis of this peculiar trait of modern Hebrew writing about the Palestinians, is beyond the scope of this article but is definitely necessary.

A different Palestinian emerges from Grossman's writing. Grossman is younger than the other writers mentioned but, like Michael, knows Arabic and Arab culture is not alien to him. Both in his novel *The Goat's Smile*[27] and in his book of conversations with Palestinians and Israelis, *Yellow Wind*[28], an unusual perspective for Hebrew literature is presented to the reader. The old Arab woman he meets in the village reminds him of his grandmother, he realises with a certain embarrassment; he treats all the Palestinians he meets like human beings, but not quite as equals or comrades. An invisible line, a line of ideology, history, material reality, still separates him from his Palestinian subjects. Such a line does not separate him from Israeli Jews, however, even when he disagrees violently with them. The language he uses to describe his arrival at Ofra, a Gush-Emunim settlement, reveals a soft spot:

'For the careful outsider, coming from afar, a surprise is awaited at Ofra. On a Friday afternoon it is soft and green, fenceless and open, its people hearty, simple and kind, and quickly, very quickly, even the careful outsider is lured by the festive feeling of Sabbath here; and with surprise one discovers in oneself a soft wish to wholly integrate, to become part of this, to shed one's armour, to be worthy of this kindness, the nostalgic palpitations of candlelight at the end of a rocky road between the villages Ein-Yabroud and Silouad.'[29]

The choice of adjectives, the elevated, almost poetic prose, is unusual in this book of harsh sentiments; it reminds one of the analogy made by Oz and quoted above – the two different branches belonging to the same tree. One thing becomes clear from the description of Ofra's people – Grossman considers them as equals even when disagreeing with them. He feels close to their milieu, he identifies with many of their signs and signifiers. The last sentence reveals his surprise – surprise not so much with the place and its atmosphere, but because it is located where it is – identifying sameness in the heart of otherness or Jewish candlelight in the heart of darkness . . .

The same cannot be said about Grossman's relationship to the Palestinians he meets. He may (and does) sympathise with them, feel their pain and anger which he conveys efficiently; nonetheless, they are forever others, foreign, different and remote.

Hence it can be seen that even for 'progressive' Hebrew writers, the Arab and specifically, the Palestinian, connotes not only 'otherness', but represents that entity of otherness particular to Judaism, that of the *goy*. This may be one of the reasons why the term 'Arab' replaces 'Palestinian' both in daily speech and in literature. The particularity of 'Palestinian' makes it difficult to read it as the total 'other', a role filled very well by 'Arab', a word relating to hundreds of millions in the region.

The writers of this left tendency seem to see the Palestinian as a subject, a victim, one being subjected to the Israei rule and will, a subject devoid of autonomy. It may be that the Palestinian for them serves at the outline to what they see as their own identity, autonomy, independence and power. To see and describe the Palestinian as a free agent, a person of complexity, coherence, internal contradictions, options for action from which to choose and a historical context in which to operate – that still remains to be done by some future Hebrew writer.

In this connection, it would be unjust not to mention a few notable exceptions. The most obvious one is a recent Hebrew novel by a Palestinian writer, Anton Shammas[30], in which exactly the task outlined above is undertaken, with great power, intellectual and political integrity and important artistic/aesthetic achievements. It is less than surprising that it takes a Palestinian like Shammas to do that – the more surprising aspect is his choice of Hebrew as the vehicle for his discourse – a complicated political and cultural choice directed at the Israeli public. Thus, Shammas manages to problematise the issue of identity for the Hebrew reader, as the Israelis described in his book are not just 'others', the Palestinians not just subjects or victims. As I have dealt with this novel at some length in a recent article, it may be inappropriate to repeat here arguments made elsewhere.

The other, more significant exception, is a novel by Hemda Alon[31], dealing with the relationship of a Palestinian academic and an Israeli woman student in Jerusalem of the early 1960s. It is significant that the fullest, most progressive description of a Palestinian in Hebrew literature has been written by a woman, while all the quotes from many male writers used here connote otherness. The candid descriptions of Israeli racism are quite unusual for the period in which the novel was published. In an internal monologue, while separated from her secret lover by her family and the Jewish holidays, she muses:

'My brother Gideon, Colonel Bar-On. What common language can you find between you? For him you are the enemy. His whole life is devoted to fighting you, undoing your schemes, preparing to kill you before you manage to kill him. How can he stretch his hand out towards you, in a gesture of peace? My father. Moderate, calculating, objective. ''I have many acquaintances amongst the Arabs'' he tends to insert early in the conversation. ''But, believe you me, with the best will in the world, it is impossible . . . '' and mother concludes the argument, cuts him short, decisively, ''I *hate* them, I – hate them.'' Once, during one of the seasonal charwoman-crises, which every working woman encounters, a friend suggested an Arab charwoman, enumerating her qualities. ''No!'' said mother. ''I will not bring an Arab home. I hate them.'' That's it. This is my family. This is my world. I may not love them, but I belong to them. This evening it was proven again. Ali, my dearest love, the distance between us is so much more than the geographical space between Jerusalem and Haifa.'[32]

Family, friends and the secret service all join in the effort to separate the lovers once their secret is discovered. Ronny, the young student, relents and gives in to the pressures. In a letter she receives from Ali who is writing from jail while awaiting trial for alleged security offences, she reads:

'My future is no longer in my hands. I am detained here, in Nazareth, until the trial that will take place in six months. I expect to be imprisoned; they say, at least a couple of years. After that, I obviously will not be able to continue my scientific work, the only career I can consider. It so turned out, that in my homeland there is no place for me. The only chance I may get is a permit, after some time has passed, to leave and settle abroad. It is not an ideal solution, but there is no other way.

In England, if I am lucky, my research may be completed. I will continue my doctorate work; In contact with one college or another, I will join the long, anonymous line of dry and lonesome dons working through fog and drizzle on worthy subjects, interesting no one but themselves. I will not bloom in England, will be neither successful nor happy. I know it well, without illusions. But there is no choice.'[33]

Hence, when inspecting the normative features of the Palestinian stereotype in Hebrew literature, exceptions aside, one finds totally contradictory elements. The Palestinian is seen as a mixture of similarity and difference, a conditioning presence for the Zionist onlooker. Could those dualities of 'murderer' and 'extremist' on the one hand, and a poor journalist with a shabby desk on the other, connote anything but a negative relief, outlining Israeli identity for Oz and his ilk? The Israeli is someone who is not extreme, not a murderer, someone who does not reside in a shabby office where the paint peels off the walls. Once we start analysing these images of the Palestinian from his perspective, an interesting function of Zionist literature is revealed. How clear are those writers about their own identity? Can they define it without the use of the Palestinian as background, as contrast? Are they aware that they are using this particular other in contradictory roles – as the all-powerful goy from the diaspora and as the stereotypical colonial native?

These questions are of central importance in trying to determine the potential of future developments. If, as seems to be the case, the main fountainhead of Zionist identity is the difference it marks from the Palestinian Arab, if the conflict seems to supply the main reservoir of meaning for Israeli existence, then how is it possible even to dream about coexistence? As long as identity is read as the racist distance from 'otherness', no political settlement can either take place or have any serious chance of success, as it would by definition mean the loss of hard-earned identity. The next section deals with the forces contending for the last word on Zionist identity.

The identity crisis

A CRISIS OF IDENTITY is not new in Israel, yet the current one is quantitatively different from any other. In a country that refused for years to play football in the Asian League, claiming itself part of Europe, the concept is loaded with the most powerful political explosive.

That Zionist identity is not a resolved matter is expressed by Amos Oz in a talk he gave to settlers at Ofra, a right-wing settlement:

'I have stated many times that Zionism is not a first name but a surname, a family name, and this family is divided, feuding over the question of a "master plan" for the enterprise: How shall we live here? Shall we aspire to build the kingdom of David and Solomon? Shall we construct a Marxist paradise here? A Western society, a social-democratic welfare state? Or shall we create a model of the petit bourgeoisie diluted with a little *yiddishkeit*?' [34]

This debate within Zionism is as old as the movement itself. In it a number of models compete for dominance. The basic one has been developed by Herzl himself – one could call it the 'colonial dependency' model. While Herzl fancied himself as a Jewish emperor with a court filled with the new nobility[35], in his actions he was much more realistic. His modus operandi for Zionism was based on getting the whole territory from the imperial power under a 'charter', thus enjoying that power's protection. His many pilgrimages to as many potentates in Europe and Turkey were all planned to yield the charter over Palestine and win it in one swoop. But the more meaningful part of this strategy was rooted in mid-European identity. Reading his diaries and books, one is struck by this utopian obsession with building the model European society outside Europe – a bizzare mixture of some of the most reactionary and the most progressive elements of European history, overlaid with Viennese waltzes. By definition, it constituted a totally dismissive, ill-informed and racist position relative to the indigenous population, which is either absent from any considerations or is busy being thankful to its Euro-saviours for bringing the delights of the Vienna comic-opera to the Middle East. Total dependency on the host empire is a requirement pivotal to the scheme. The role portrayed is obviously of a *colon*, a client-state, an agency and a branch of 'civilisation'. One of the clearest descriptions of it is by Herzl's deputy, Nordau:

'Our aspirations point to Palestine as a compass points to the north. Therefore we must orient ourselves towards those powers under whose influence it happens to be.'[36]

Herzl himself describes it graphically in *Der Judenstaat*:

'If His Majesty the Sultan were to give us Palestine, we could in return undertake the complete management of the finances of Turkey. We would form there a part of a wall of defence of Europe in Asia, an outpost of civilisation against barbarism. We would, as a neutral state, remain in contact with all Europe, which would have to guarantee our existence.'[37]

While this description sounds like a caricature, it is not only an accurate description of Herzl's strategy but of an influential and dominant trend within recent Zionism. The shift of allegiances from Britain to France, then to the USA, followed the global power shifts in the Middle East, and resembles Herzl trotting from Bismarck to Abdul Hamid, to Plehve, then back to the Kaiser again. Behind the niceties of rationale is hidden a simple formula – Zionism is only able to control Palestine under the aegis of an imperial/neo-colonial power; it will support and seek the support of the dominant power, according to changing situations. Though many Zionists have criticised Herzl for holding this position, some notable critics did not hesitate to apply the very same policy.

But such a policy is problematic, even when it yields the hoped-for results. Being the agents of a foreign power raises certain problems not only with the indigenous population, but with the *colon* itself. It is likely to hit the population exactly where it hurts – its identity. Hence, though the political model of action has been accepted and applied by Zionism, it fell short on the need to supply a coherent identity structure.

The second model on which identity was constructed within Zionism, is the 'utopian autonomy' model, based on mixing Jewish heritage with Western humanism. Its adherents preferred to leave politics out of the discussion altogether, concentrating on ideology/culture. Achad Ha'am is followed by Borochov in suggesting some Jewish autonomy in Palestine, which somehow does not infringe on the Palestinians, mainly by not discussing them and their rights as problematic. Having thus solved the problem of the Palestinians by elimination, they are then able to concentrate on the makings of the Jewish identity in Palestine – a subject dear to their hearts. The writers quoted and mentioned above belong in the main to that tendency. Amos Oz again, in his talk at Ofra:

'In any event, we have no intention of breaking up this "marriage" between the Jewish heritage and the European humanist experience for the sake of some "purist" return to the sources . . . Most of those who have experienced this humanism will not abandon it – Nobody will force us to choose – because we will refuse to make such a choice – between our Judaism and our humanism. For us they are one and the same . . . We have assimilated that meeting, internalised it to such a degree . . . that my identity has already become a combination of the Jewish and humanist elements.'[38]

If for Herzl, in his naivete, identity is seen as unproblematic, not so for the writers of 'utopian autonomy'. What will be the materials from which this Jewishness is to be built? Whose Jewishness will win?

When it comes to Jewishness, there are, of course, other contenders for the identity project – the clergy. It may be true to say that there were two elements affecting the lack of development in Judaism throughout the centuries – the Jewish religious establishment and anti-semitism. Between them, these two have managed to contain Europe's Jewry as an (almost) unchanging entity.

With the clergy as an undeniable partner to the forging of this new identity, the atheistic tendency within Zionism lost the battle even before it started. 'Who is a Jew?' is a query that could not arise in a similar form in most other countries but only in theocratic states in the region. Yet, this question has been central to Zionist debates for decades, obscuring in its fervour the real issues of importance linking Israelis and Palestinians. As Israel is actually called 'a Jewish state' in its declaration of independence, it is hardly surprising that this concept will give rise to ferocious arguments.

Bearing in mind the extremely varied ethnic, cultural and linguistic myriad thrown into the Zionist 'melting pot', there were obvious struggles for the right to establish this or that version of Judaism as the official one.

This brings us to the third and last main model of identity construction, rather more 'simple' than the first two. It is a combination of the ultra-religious and ultra-nationalistic, the perspective of Gush Emunim and related organisations. This model is the most recent of the three, an ascending force that has emerged in the last decade like a phoenix from the ashes, boosted by the rise of the right to power and dominance. Like its counterparts in the region, this form of Jewish religious fundamentalism is introspective and self-sufficient; it is a root-seeking formula. So, part of the new identity is a rejection of universally heralded values as 'unJewish'. After all, the Torah does not mention democracy, so it must be a goyish invention. While talking to the settlers in Tekoa, an ultra-right settlement south of Bethlehem, Amos Oz reports one of the women saying:

'Weapons aren't what win a war! Men win wars! Faith wins! God almighty wins! The world has to realise that. In the Six-Day War, and the Yom-Kippur War, too, we should never have stopped. We should have gone on, brought them to total surrender! Smashed their capital cities! Who cares what the goyim were yelling?'[39]

When Oz asks about the Palestinians (the 'Arabs') – 'should they live under our sovereignty and do the dirty work for us?' the same woman (Harriet, from Queens, New York), says:

'Why not? . . . Isn't that the way it is in the Bible? Weren't there hewers of wood and carriers of water? For murderers that's a very light punishment! it's mercy!'

And is there no point in trying to compromise?

'With the goyim? Whenever we gave in to them we had troubles.

That's the way it was in the Bible. King Saul lost his whole kingdom because he took pity on Amalek. The goyim are bound to be against us. It's their nature. Sometimes it's because of their religion, sometimes it's out of ideology, sometimes out of anti-semitism, but actually it's all God's will. God hardens Pharaoh's heart and then He destroys him. It's them or us.'[40]

And another man, Amiel, explains:

'Wondrous are the ways of the Lord. Slowly but surely those who oppose us will understand their errors. Western culture is not for us, even though there is a lot we should adopt from it. The only path for the people of Israel is the path of the bible . . .
. . . It's all American import, from Vietnam, all this left-wing stuff. It's a fashion. It's passé in America – pretty soon it'll be passé here, too. It's all imitation, alien to the Jewish spirit.'[41]

From this cursory description, it can be seen that the conceptual location of left-Zionist writers, somewhere between neo-colonials and Jewish Ayatollas, is not an enviable one – to criticise and be criticised but without being able to offer a fresh and alternative identity. The complexity of their offering, a product of the enlightenment, is difficult to market in contemporary Israeli society.

None of the tendencies described ever rules without opposition. The development is movement from one specific mix of these tendencies towards another, due to a complex tendency struggle. Needless to say, a large degree of super-imposition exists between the tendencies. Thus, the recent move towads a stronger position enjoyed by the religious right-wing has not reduced dependency on the USA, for example.

An important additional factor related to the 'identity models' is the struggle of the Oriental Jewish community to reestablish its own identity. This was forcibly repressed by the European Jewish majority in Israel during the 50s when large numbers of Jews from the Maghreb countries started arriving in Israel. This struggle for identity cuts across the other Zionist trends developed and dominated by intellectuals of European origin. A recent novel devoted to the early days of this spec-ific struggle is Yehoshua Kenaz's *Heart Murmur*[42]. In it he tells the story of a group of army trainees during their basic training in 1955. The group is made up of European (Ashkenazi) and Oriental Jews, the latter be-ing mostly recent arrivals. To the Ashkenazis, the arrival of the new-comers is a catastrope, a disaster for Zionism. The 'proper' Israelis, like the kibbuznik Alon, describe them:

' "The army" said Alon, "that's our only hope. Only in the army can they be educated, converted into proper Israelis, until they become like us. They do not know any part of this country outside their transit camps, know nothing of its history, its beauty, its culture. When they are brought to the new settlements in Lachish, they refuse to get off the lorries. They are not ready for this life of work and fields and agriculture. So how can they like our songs? The army has to reeducate them into it. At least the youth, as the old ones are hopeless, nothing will ever come out of them; The Desert Generation." ' [43]

And elsewhere in the same novel, Alon proposes the 'new life' to one of his colleagues:

' . . . there are now places in the Negev, in Lachish, all sorts of places, there are new immigrants' settlements. That is where you should have gone. There you can start to live a healthy, new life, not the way you lived abroad"
"Life abroad was great" said Rachamim, "it was excellent! You know nothing about it. You Sabras think that here in Israel it is the best." ' [44]

But the clearest expression of this position is later provided by Alon towards the end of the novel, shortly before he commits suicide:

' "It all goes wrong here," said Alon, "everything we had in this country. What a great people lived here before. And the things they did. Now it is all reversing. Soon nothing will remain of it. Even our Hebrew will not survive. In a few years children will not understand the Hebrew of the Bible. People will not be able to read Alterman and Yizhar. They will speak a new, ugly language. And the Arabs are already preparing for the next round; huge arsenals are hoarded. Who is going to stand up and be counted? The underworld? All that was built, all the blood shed here, the suffering and the diseases and the hunger, so that a new people can be built, a new land, all this for nothing? This madness, egoism and the underworld will pulverise it all? Why are the Arabs collecting all these arms? Their work will be done by these . . .
. . . the whole Arab society is shot through because of these drugs. Everyone know that. Now they bring it here. And the country is full of new, weak and desperate people that cannot adopt our way of life – of labour and fighting . . . I don't mind their laughter; I say what I believe

in, what frightens me, what is important to me. Weeds have to be pulled out, everywhere you see them. Otherwise they take over, strangling everything. Our heroes shed their blood in covert operations, while those continue with their diseases brought from the diaspora. They want to turn this into a new diaspora. We should not let them! Can't you see?'' '[45]

This monologue is complementary to another monologue of reported speech in Oz's book:

' ''My parents came from North Africa; all right – from Morocco. So what? They had their dignity, didn't they? Their own values? Their faith? Me, I am not a religious man. I travel on the Sabbath. But my parents – why did you make fun of their beliefs? Why did they have to be disinfected with Lysol at the Haifa port? . . . The Mapainiks just wiped out everything that was imprinted on a person. As if it was all nonsense. And then they put what they wanted into him. From that ideology of theirs. Human dust, supposedly. Ben Gurion himself called us 'human dust''.'[46]

This struggle is only starting, the struggle between the colonising fathers and their labour imported exactly because the indigenous population could not, at the time, be used for this purpose – it had to be expelled and dispossessed, unhinged off the land. That the imported labour consisted of people from the Arab countries is a bitter twist of irony in Zionist history. That meant their 'Arabness' had to be expunged, they had to be cleansed of it, to be 'Israelised' (or really, Europeanised). In order to fit into the dream they had to change their identity, lose their culture, their language and oral traditions – their history[47]. History is written by the winners . . .

Postscript: mid-life crisis

THIS BRINGS US to the main point of argument: never before has Zionism controlled so much territory, been so strong militarily, enjoyed such unswerving support of its policies from its friends and paymasters. This is paralleled by an overall reduction in the military capabilities of the Palestinians. On the face of it, Zionism has 'never had it so good', and yet . . .

The crisis hastened and sharpened by the *intifada* in the West Bank and Gaza is now well established. I call it a mid-life crisis because it is at the point of maximum strength that the long decline starts. It is at that point that the empire feels strong enough to both openly repress its adversaries and look at their situation for the 'first time', with the naiveté of the powerful. It is the time of checking oneself in the mirror of the other, a time for doubts, cracks and fissures to appear. It is the beginning of the end.

The Zionist self is now being defined by the Palestinian 'other' like a contour defining the form; hence no sympathy and closeness is possible between the Zionist writers of right and left alike, and the Palestinian – either as person, as culture, language, national aspirations, class or gender – the Palestinian is, and continues to be, the great 'other'. When one realises how deep this gap now is, even deeper than it was in 1948, when S. Yizhar was writing, it becomes clear how little the Israeli consensus has moved in forty years towards an accommodation. Accommodation must start with acceptance of the enemy as human, similar to oneself, and the state of conflict as a temporary aberration in the order of things. But instead of growing accommodation, the grim prophecies of S. Yizhar in his story *Khirbet Khizeh*[48] seem to have come true. In this short story, Yizhar recounts the destruction of a peaceful Arab village, the arbitrary killing by the Israeli 'Defence Forces' of many inhabitants and the forced explusion of the rest, all this without a single provocation. After the horrors of the day are over, the commanding officer notes the storyteller's reticence and, finding out that he disagrees with the atrocities which he took part in perpetrating, the officer tells him:

' "You, listen to me here!" said Moishe and his eyes searched for mine, "to Khirbet whatsitsname, will come the new immigrants, you hear, they will take this land and till it, it will be great!" of course and what? This is it! How come I did not foresee this. Our Khirbet Khizeh. Problems of accommodation and establishment on the ground! And we will accommodate and establish, Hurrah, Hurrah: a cooperative shop will be opened, a kindergarten and school, maybe even a synagogue. And there will be political parties. A lot of debates, discussions about everything, they will plough the fields and sow and reap and grow big. Hurrah to Hebrew Khizeh! Who would ever believe, realise that there once was here some Khirbet Khizeh, one we expelled and inherited. We came, shot, burnt, blew up, pushed off and displaced and expelled them to their diaspora.

What in hell are we doing here?'[49]

What current writer in Israel can equal the frankness expressed in S. Yizhar's lines, shocking after all these years, because their message is still not heeded? The comparison to Yizhar seems to suggest that in the battle between his Judaism and humanism, humanism always won. Not a claim that can be made by the current generation of Zionist apologists, who use humanism as a cultural figleaf to obscure their Zionist pudenda.

But the central methodological problem with the theories of reforming Zionism and Israeli society, so that coexistence may be possible, is the absence of understanding of the identity crisis. As this identity is so pivotal to Israeli existence, as so much of it revolves exactly around the difference and struggle with the great 'other' – how can any change be tackled, before the eradication of the Zionist self? As the military, economical, cultural and class struggle against the Palestinians is filling the Israeli image with every ounce of meaning that it holds – how can it be abandoned? What will replace it? After all, this is not a purely national struggle between oppressor and oppressed, it is a total struggle between opposing stereotypes, a struggle to the bitter end. In that way, the oppressed Palestinian may have become the condition for the continuation of Zionism, a necessary ingredient of a complex formula, part of the heart of the matter – of modern Zionist identity. This aspect and root cause of the struggle in Palestine is one that the Zionist right understands very well, and is more open about than the left. Since the beginning of the *intifada*, the transfer of the Palestinians is openly discussed as a viable political option for the near future. I will quote here only one example of this latter-day Zionism, difficult to differentiate from Herzl's ideas on the same topic, in connection with the crucial issue of identity. The quote is from a report about General Ze'evi, an ex-arms dealer, currently heading the Tel Aviv Museum:

'Ze'evi brushes off such accusations angrily. Removing Arabs from Eretz-Yisrael (greater Israel), he argues, is part of the ideological basis of Zionism. He opposes forced explusions, but believes instead in creating what he calls a "negative magnet" that will induce Palestinians to pack their bags and leave.

"If the transfer idea is immoral," Ze'evi said recently, "then Zionism itself is immoral. All the settlement that has been carried out in the last 100 years was based on the transfer of Arabs." . . .

. . . Ze'evi represents what seems to be a powerful new force in Israeli politics. According to a recent poll, 49 per cent of the Jewish adults believe that the "transfer" of Palestinians from the West Bank and Gaza "would allow the democratic and Jewish nature of Israeli society to be maintained." . . .

. . . "A transfer will take place in Eretz-Yisrael," he predicts, "because two peoples cannot live in one country. The question is, who will be transferred, the Jews or the Arabs?"[50]

Hence, the right is stating quite openly that because of national identity, it will be necessary to rid the country of its indigenous population. In comparison with such positivist clarity, the left-Zionist arguments seem weak and disorganised, more hypocritical than Ze'evi's openness.

The failure of left-Zionist writers is one of not noting their own position, of accepting their vantage point as transparent and constant. Though they disagree with the oppression in many cases, the only Palestinian they see and describe is the oppressed Palestinian, the subject dependent and lacking autonomy of action, passive.

The most that is offered by the new generation and its writers is a painful recognition that the Palestinian refuses to satisfy the Zionist dream and dematerialise. In these circumstances, they agree to talk, to negotiate, even to argue on-behalf-of, charity-fashion. What they are not prepared for, at least not yet, is to drop the mask of otherness and exchange their coloniser-oppressor identity – a total transformation of the self. This metamorphosis, without which no real change is possible – is continuously and emphatically denied. Life side-by-side, maybe; human and national rights, maybe; togetherness, solidarity, brotherhood – No!. At least, not yet.

Notes

1 When using terms like 'left-Zionism' or 'right-wing Zionism' one should always be aware that these carry different meanings to the ones we assume in Europe. As Zionism is based, in the main, on the need to expunge class struggle within it, to form a unity which is supposedly beyond class barriers, the terms 'left' and 'right' are approximations of 'liberal' or 'humanist' on the one hand, and 'conservative' on the other. These terms do not apply to social divisions within Israeli society but rather to the different modes of looking at the Palestinian entity. Hence, it is usual to find extreme right tendencies within the Labour Alliance. Conversely, the right-wing party Herut has been reacting to (and exploiting) the anger of the majority of Oriental Jews directed against their oppression by successive Labour (left-Zionist) governments. It will be important to note the different groups who support both blocs: the left was traditionally supported by the main beneficiaries of its policies, the kibbutz movement and sectors of the skilled working class and the middle class. Begin and his party have traditionally scored very well in the

oriental Jewish community, made of farmers, the petty-bourgeoisie and blue-collar workers.

2 Oz, Amos; *Po Vasham Be'Eretz Israel*, Tel Aviv, 1977, Published in English as *In the Land of Israel*, Fontana, London, 1983. Quotes are from the English edition.

3 Weizmann, Chaim; in 'Dr Weizmann's Political Address – 20th Zionist Congress', quoted in *New Judea*, London August 1937, p.215.

4 Oz, Amos: *Be'or Hatcheleth He'aza* ('Under This Blazing Light'), Tel Aviv, 1977; All quotes translated by H.B.

5 Ibid, p.116

6 Weitz, R; in *Davar*, Hebrew newspaper, Sept. 29th, 1967.

7 Herzl, Theodor; *The Complete Diaries of Theodor Herzl*, The Herzl Press and Thomas Yoseloff, London, 1960, p.88.

8 Ibid, p.98.

I found it necessary to quote at length here, as these paragraphs from the Herzl diaries are themselves an example of suppression and denial. These same ideas about the indigenous population are totally missing from the published works. Though they appear in the Hebrew edition of the diaries, they are missing from most English editions, like numerous other quotes relating to the Arabs of Palestine. It is interesting to note that in his introduction, the editor of one of the most important editions, Marvin Lowenthal, points out that the German edition of the diaries is incomplete, mentioning as one of the reasons for cuts –

' . . . political observations of equal embarrassment'. When describing his own rationale for editing the text even further, he notes:

' . . . the omissions mainly deal with the financial endeavors and intramural politics of the Zionist movement, which would have comparatively feeble interest for the general reader.'

One may be forgiven for wondering whether this central quote was excluded because of its 'feeble interest for the general reader'. (From – Lowenthal, Marvin; in a prefatory note to Herzl, Theodor; *The Diaries*, The Dial Press, New York 1956, page vi).

9 Oz, Amos; Ibid, p.24.

10 Herzl, Theodor; *Der Judenstaat* ('The Jewish State'), Leipzig und Wien, 1896, p.13. All quotes translated by H.B.

11 Ibid, p.25.

12 Childers, Erskine; *Common Sense About the Arab World*, London, 1956.

13 Said, Edward; *Orientalism*, Routledge and Kegan Paul, London, 1978.

14 Herzl, Theodor; *The Complete Diaries of Theodor Herzl*, The Herzl Press and Thomas Yoseloff, London, 1960. This edition is far preferable, as it includes many allusions edited elsewhere.

15 In pointing this out, I am indebted to Dr M. Machover, who first drew my attention to this form of synthesizing within Zionist history.

16 Oz, Amos; Ibid.

17 Ibid, p.29.

18 Calderon, Nissim; *Be'heksher Politi* ('In a political context'), Tel Aviv, 1980.

19 Oz, Amos; *Mi'mordoth Halvanon* ('The Slopes of Lebanon'), Am Oved, Tel Aviv, 1987, pp.83-86.

See his reaction to the accusations by the left, after he signed an open letter, together with three other writers, calling for a national unity government, including the Labour Party and the Likud.

20 Oz, Amos; *Be'or Hatcheleth He'aza*, p.24.
21 Oz, Amos; *In the Land of Israel*, Flamingo, London 1983; p.157.
22 Ibid.
23 Ibid, p.164.
24 Michael, Sammy; *Khatsotsra Ba'Wadi* ('A Trumpet in the Wadi'); Am Oved, Tel Aviv 1987, p.56. Quote translated by H.B.
25 Yehoshua, Avraham Buli; *The Lover*, Doubleday, New York 1978.
26 Ibid, p.201.
27 Grossman, David; *Khi'yuch Ha'gdi* ('The Goat's Smile'); Tel Aviv, 1986.
28 Grossman, David; *Hazman Hatsahov* ('Yellow Wind'); Tel Aviv, 1987. Quote translated by H.B.
29 Ibid, p.31.
30 Shammas, Anton; *Arabesquoth* ('Arabesques'); Tel Aviv, 1986.
31 Alon, Hemda; *Zar Lo Yavoh* ('No Trespassing'); Hakibbutz Hameuchad, Tel Aviv, 1967; All quotes translated by H.B.
32 Ibid, p.146.
33 Ibid, p.279.
34 Oz, Amos; Ibid p.128.
35 Herzl, Theodor; Ibid p.132.
36 Nordau, Max
37 Herzl, Theodor, *Der Judenstaat*, p.29.
38 Oz, Amos; Ibid p.138.
39 Ibid, p.60.
40 Ibid, p.61.
41 Ibid, p.69.
42 Kenaz, Yehoshua; *Hitganvuth Yekhidim* ('Heart Murmur'); Am Oved, Tel Aviv 1986; Quotes translated by H.B.
43 Ibid, p.95.
44 Ibid, p.244.
45 Ibid, p.555.
46 Oz, Amos; Ibid, p.34.
47 There are, of course, a few other important sub-tendencies dealing with the issue of identity in Israel – I have tried to outline only the main, influential ones. One should mention here the Canaanites, a group of Israeli intellectuals in the 50s and 60s, who tried to invent an Israeli nationality based on pre-Jewish civilisations in Palestine. They described themselves as 'pagan' and opposed religious oppression. This approach is interesting, inasmuch as it tries to deny many millenia of history by making it irrelevant, by annuling its results. The group always remained small and obscure, a kind of literary club.
48 Yizhar, Smilanski; *Shiv'ah Sipurim* ('Seven stories'); Tel Aviv 1971; Quote translated by H.B.
49 Ibid, p.86.
50 Black, Ian; in *the Guardian*, 6th September 1988, London.

Rosemary Sayigh

PALESTINIAN WOMEN: TRIPLE BURDEN, SINGLE STRUGGLE

Before the Uprooting

THAT THIRD WORLD national liberation movements have borne within themselves important feminist elements is becoming recognised as our knowledge of early Third World feminism expands. Jayawardena's valuable study of the interaction between nationalism and feminism in 11 Asian countries demonstrates both the complexity of this relationship, and the falsity of the notion that feminism is a recent Western import without indigenous roots.[1] Third World women have thrown themselves into national struggles with an energy that derives ultimately from their social oppression, and in doing so have often expressed their own critiques and aspirations. National movements have formed both a liberating and constraining framework for change in women's lives, as stages of state and economy formation call them into new kinds of political action and labour. As Jayawardena notes, however, the constraints of family on women have proved less yielding. While family structures and ideologies have been affected by modernising programmes, the effects on women have been contradictory rather than liberating. Because of the family's implication in the assertion of cultural authenticity, it has seldom been submitted to the level of critique raised against the world economic or local class systems.[2]

The aim of this paper is to examine the involvement of Palestinian women in national struggle, as a case that shows in particularly striking fashion the expression and repression of feminist consciousness in different historical phases of a protracted and difficult struggle. It is a kind of feminism that has seldom aspired to explicit or organised form, yet has contributed a continuous and distinctive 'charge' to the national movement. Although the pre-1948 period affords many examples of this 'latent feminism', the main focus of this paper will be on the post-1967 Palestinian Resistance Movement (PRM). It is here that we can view most clearly the different kinds of contradiction that affect women: between the PRM's mobilisation programmes and its dependence on families for recruits, support and *sumud* (steadfastness); between progressive and conservative currents within the PRM; and between the PRM's generally progressive and secular stance, and its more conservative, more sectarian Arab environment. It is here too that questions arise about what kind of society Palestinians will build and what role and image women will have in it. The harshness of the struggle deprives these questions of immediacy, yet they are no longer dismissed as heretical or irrelevant. Behind the current stage, characterised by the emergence of a corps of professional political women, stretches 70 years of collective and individual effort, a rich history that can be introduced here only briefly.

Looking back at the beginnings of their movement, Palestinian women emphasize its 'organic unity' with the broader national movement.[3] While we cannot doubt that the national crisis was the major precipitating factor for the women's movement, the 'organic unity' idea is somewhat distorting: first, it represses questions about the real relationship between the national and the women's movement and second, it represses consideration of other generative factors. Several signs indicate that reality was more complex. For example, the early emergence of women's political groups, coeval with the main national movement, suggests that the national crisis acted *directly* on women rather than through the mediation of men's organisations.[4] The vigour and creativity of women's first political actions have no counterpart in the national movement as a whole,[5] and no contemporary model of Arab women being drawn into political action by male kin or by well-established liberation movements can account for it. It becomes intelligible, however, in the context of women's agitation in neighbouring countries, particularly Egypt, Syria, Turkey, and Iran, countries with which urban Palestinians had contacts, and to a burgeoning feminist literature.[6] The development of schooling for girls in urban areas since the turn of the century[7] played a role in producing women self-confident enough to organise, speak in public, and address the Mandate Authorities. The fact that peasant women were among the casualties of street demonstrations early in the Mandate directs our attention to 19th century peasant uprisings – against Ottoman taxes, against the first Zionist settlers – in which women certainly took part.

Very little is known about the relations between the national leadership and the leading pre-1948 national women's grouping, the Arab Women's Association (AWA). [8] Later writers have pointed out that the AWA was directed by women of the upper class, most of whom were related to the leaders of national movement. [9] This view is correct as far as the Jerusalem-based central Executive Committee was concerned and though there is no systematic study of the social origins of all AWA members, it is probable that most came from upper and middle urban strata since only such women had the education background and social freedom to organise. But some of the most active and persistent AWA organisers were not from *'ayan* families. Further, the view that they only acted within the limits of their class origins obscures the originality of some of their actions, such as hiding escaped prisoners, attending trials, writing for the nationalist press, and taking part in demonstrations. Some also defied convention by remaining unmarried or by marrying across religious boundaries. That the AWA failed to incorporate rural and poor urban women and that it remained entangled in cliques and rivalries cannot easily be disconnected from a social structure and culture that still today enter into political formations and may have contributed something both to the tenacity of resistance as well as to its sometimes 'backward' character.

More seriously, the view of the AWA as tied to the national leadership by family and class obscures the question of possible dissociation or even conflict. Did the AWA simply carry out actions handed down to it by the national leadership? Further research is needed on this point, but there are several contrary indications. The historian A.W. Kayyali hints that women, along with students and intellectuals, formed a 'vanguard' within the national movement, pressing the leadership to take more militant action; for example, they were prominent in calling for the General Strike in April 1936. [10] Further, whereas the national movement increasingly divided into parties and factions, the AWA, according to surviving members, did not reflect these divisions. This remaining 'above' partisan politics cannot be reduced to the simple fact that women at that time did not join political parties, but may rather be attributable to a conscious decision to uphold national unity. AWA women may also have undertaken communicating and mediating functions between conflicting factions well established in Arab culture. [11]

While the AWA's programme of action was clearly of an 'auxiliary' nature, it seems to have been adopted spontaneously from women's own concepts of their political role rather than passed on to them by the leadership of the national movement. [12] Another point to be noted is that the AWA was self-financing – indeed one of its tasks was to raise money for the national cause. Thus in several important respects, the AWA was more autonomous than the later General Union of Palestinian Women (GUPW).

The expression of feminism in the earliest stage of the Palestinian women's movement was proudly Arab nationalist. One can find no better example than Mogannam's *The Arab Woman and the Palestine Problem*. Here feminism and Arab nationalism are perfectly harmonised through the evocation of an Arab Golden Age, when women played a prominent part in political, religious, and cultural activity. Writing for an English audience, Mogannam proclaims her faith in the restoration of this past under the aegis of the Arab kings and British justice – a political error that deeply divides the founding mothers of the AWA from women who grew up after 1948. Invaluable as a source on pioneering social, educational and political work of women, Mogannam's account stops short in 1932, and we must search elsewhere for answers to questions about the history of the AWA in the last years of the Mandate. Dissatisfaction with its leadership and methods is suggested by the fact that younger women began to seek other frameworks of action: syndicates, underground parties, military cells. We see here a dialectic between conventional and radical forms of women's nationalism which is still at work today. Every escalation in national crisis forces the most nationalist women into less conventional, more militant, more 'feminist' forms of action.

One issue we know to have caused conflict within AWA ranks is that of clothing. Some members wanted to express their emancipation by wearing 'modern' clothing, others strongly opposed any lapse that could damage the AWA in the eyes of the masses. [13] This emotive issue crystallizes a more profound divergence between conservative and progressive tendencies within the women's movement. It is perhaps to this incipient conflict that we can attribute the strongly phrased anti-feminism expressed by AWA leaders. This discourse employs the terms the 'woman issue' or 'women's rights' explicitly to subordinate them to the national struggle. Sometimes these are treated almost as a heresy, a subversive ideology originating from 'outside'; speaking of an aborted attempt to form a feminist group in Jerusalem in the 40s, an AWA leader presented it as British-inspired. [14] Other examples: 'Usually when there are women's demands they come from women outside the struggle–if they were in the struggle they would have reached their demands';[15] 'The women's rights issue could have come from Egypt–Palestinian women always saw the national issue as a priority';[16] and, most succinctly, 'Women's education yes, women's rights no'.[17] Yet as the rest of this paper shows, the contradiction between mobilising women for national struggle and ignoring the sociocultural constraints that bind them to limited kinds of action has become sharper with time.

Women and the post-1967 Resistance Movement

SOON AFTER THE UPROOTING, one of the historic leaders of the AWA, Sadij Nassar, opened a new branch in Damascus; this was closed down by the Syrian government in 1956. Another historic leader, Zuleikha Shihabi, was refused permission by the Jordanian government to attend a conference of the Leage of Arab Women's Unions in 1953, unless she went as a Jordanian delegate. These two episodes illustrate the political environment out of which the post-1948 Palestinian national and women's movements were reborn.

However crushing the effects of the erasure of Palestine from the political map, and the dispersion of some 65% of its people, national struggle continued through the years of 'burial' from 1948 to 1964, and though still hardly researched, women's part in it has several interesting features. Briefly: i) women were foremost in relief work, individually as well as through old and new social associations;[18] ii) some entered banned political parties (the various communist parties, the Arab Nationalist Movement, the PPS, the Ba'th), and took part in anti-American, anti-Arab regime demonstrations;[19] iii) a few women were closely involved in the setting up of the PLO[20]; iv) a substantial number of younger women entered professional work (eg in public health, university teaching, literature, journalism), establishing claims to competence and creativity; v) the majority of women, mothers struggling to bring up families in difficult circumstances, transmitted Palestinianism to their children in ways as effective as they were spontaneous. Women's alienation in the *ghourba*[21] was more complex than men's, since they bore the humiliation of their menfolk and anxiety for their children's futures as well as their own loss.[22] Their kinship ties and the collective context of their domestic labour were disrupted; their mobility was restricted; some were forced into heavy manual work or the humiliation of domestic labour; and young girls suffered from witnessing the oppression of their parents. [23] Thus when the PRM emerged with its call for armed struggle and return, it was greeted with joy and enthusiasm by women of all social classes and generations. Support took many forms: joining the PRM, training in arms, knitting jerseys for the *feda'yeen*, teaching camp children to paint, volunteering in Red Crescent hospitals, writing poems, singing songs . . . It was an explosion of specifically women's nationalism, pent up by two decades of mourning and anger.

The rest of this paper examines the evolving slogans and structures through which the PRM has harnessed this wellspring of female energy, and the effects of its programmes on women's role and on the family sphere. It will also consider the PRM as a framework for working on the 'woman issue'-defining it, linking it to national struggle, developing consciousness and programmes. But it must be noted that these questions cannot be treated in isolation from the total situation of the Resistance Movement. The role of women in Third World liberation movements has often been seen to rest on the ideology of their leaderships (based on class background, level and place of education, political orientation). But the question of the mobilisation of Palestinian women cannot be viewed simply in terms of ideology, whether of the 'collective leadership' or of any sector of the PRM. Rather it must be viewed through an interacting system of constraints: those imposed by the Arab environment (laws, controls, socio-cultural atmosphere); those arising from the geographical and political dispersion of the Palestinian people, with its effects on the structure and internal relations of the PRM; and those imposed by a history marked by abrupt and radical changes-major reversals (1948, 1967, 1970, 1982), uprisings (1936, 1968/9, 1987/8), internal splits (1974, 1983)-all equally unpredictable and disruptive. Within such a context, the 'woman issue' could not but be eclipsed by the national crisis, its development interrupted, uneven and subject to local conditions.

Two types of limitation in this paper's approach to women and the PRM must be noted at the outset. First, political: it should not be read as a comprehensive view of all parts of the PRM but as part of work in progress. [24] Second, regional: in relation to women, the dispersion can be divided into two zones-a zone of confrontation (the Occupied Territories, Lebanon), where daily crisis precipitates broad sectors of women into the political arena; and a rearline zone (Jordan, Syria, the Gulf, etc), where repression and stability give rise to a more conservative social atmosphere, and a more ritualistic nationalism. It is with the zone of confrontation that this paper is concerned.

The ideological framework

AT FIRST VIEW, what is striking about the PRM's stands towards the 'woman issue' is their generality and nondevelopment. From the PRM's emergence until now, one basic slogan – that women make up half society, that they must have a role in the national struggle – has formed a pole, a lowest common denominator on which all groups and all women can agree. There are certainly some differences between the resistance groups: the Marxist groups in general and the PFLP in particular have given importance to women's liberation, and have occasionally come out with 'advanced positions' or condemnations of existing practices. But such differences have never given rise to sharp or sustained debate within the PRM, nor to bids for women's support. In general, women do not join a particular group because of its stand on women – what counts for them as much as for men is its position on the issue of the hour. Nor does it seem that when women leave a group, they do so out of dissatisfaction with its position on or treatment of women. [25] Thus although discussion of the 'woman issue' has been continuous within the PRM – it has its ritualistic celebrations, for example on International Woman's Day, and in some milieus it has received more sustained, more serious treatment – yet even for leftist women it remains a minor theme, never debated with the passion aroused by national or party issues.

Careful examination of the period 1970 to 1982 in Lebanon would be valuable in raising concrete instances of the way structures for mobilising women contradicted, through their conflictual nature, any collective development of ideology by organised women. [26] This was a period exceptionally rich in women's initiatives, some of which have proved to be among the PRM's most lasting legacies, [27] but many others were short-lived, competitive, and reactive to crisis rather than following a plan of longterm development. This created an atmosphere of chaos and recrimination that played its part in aborting ideological development. Yet in spite of all this, there were moments of a collective feminist consciousness among organised women. Perhaps the most striking instance is a study, undertaken soon after the expulsion from Jordan, into women militants' experiences inside the revolution. Published by the GUPW in spite of internal opposition, this study expresses criticism of the PRM's failure to link armed struggle to social change, or campaign to change attitudes to women. [28] Echoes of these criticisms appeared from time to time in marginal PRM media, but they never became the basis for a collective campaign.

It is worth noting too that the GUPW had its own, slightly more feminist version of the universal PRM slogan, ie that women's liberation will be reached through their participation in national struggle. However limited, this version opened the way for discussion of obstacles to women's participation; and in fact such discussion continued throughout the PRM's Lebanon period, and goes on today. To inaugurate the GUPW's 3rd General Assembly in 1980, this slogan was given a twist in a more feminist direction towards a greater participation of women in struggle. The implicit criticism did not escape Chairman Arafat who is reported to have objected that women were already doing more than could be expected. Though such signs of revolt may seem minimal to an outsider's eye, they are interesting because, throughout this period, the GUPW was subordinated to a Fateh-dominated PLO in which Fateh women cadres were dominant. In spite of this, there were several instances of friction between the GUPW and the Fateh/PLO leadership, notably in 1974 over the issue of the 'West Bank state'.[29] Towards the end of the period, there was a collective GUPW campaign to have its Chairwoman, 'Issam Abdul Hadi, taken into the PLO Executive Committee.

Though Fateh contained leftist as well as rightist currents, all those in leading positions, women as well as men, were conservative. The atmosphere inside Fateh on the 'woman issue' is conveyed by a junior cadre who described the reaction of male comrades to women who brought this up: 'Have you come here to liberate Palestine or women?'[30] Younger Fateh women, many of whom had been militants in Jordan, and who were generally more progressive on the 'woman issue', were too divided among themselves to bring pressure on their leadership.

The conserative trend within Fateh was strengthened by the growth of Muslim fundamentalism throughout the 70s, and by the Islamic Revolution in Iran. Symptomatic of this connection is the publication in 1977 of a position paper by a leading Fateh intellectual, categorising the woman issue as a 'secondary contradiction', and calling on Palestinian women to face the Israeli enemy with their babies in their arms, as women had done throughout Muslim history.[31] Although the article challenged the foundation of women's organising, and aroused the anger of organised women, they did not respond. Involvement in practical tasks and in resistance group competition, the difficulty of reaching a collective position, change of ideological climate: all these factors weighed against their taking up the challenge.

Both major leftist groups, the PFLP and DFLP, have put forward more progressive positions on women, placing the goals of class and gender liberation on the same level of value as national liberation, yet, through a Marxist theory of stages, postponing dealing with the 'woman issue' until after national independence and the building of a socialist society. This view does not label the women issue as 'secondary' – on the contrary, it endorses women's liberation – but it subordinates it through time. Like Fateh, these groups point to national struggle as the only road for women's emancipation, and emphasize that each woman must wage her own struggle with society without waiting for general campaigns of social change.[32] The Marxist groups also underline the necessity for women to engage in productive labour. Women are thus harnessed to political, social and economic struggle without any commitment to gender democracy in a future state. If both these parties have succeeded in recruiting a substantial corps of women members it is less because of advanced slogans than because of an atmosphere that values women as political workers, encourages their projects, and does not put obstacles in the way of work on the 'woman issue'. It has been the basic principle of DFLP policy towards this issue that slogans should not be 'ultra-leftist' or too far ahead of mass thinking. Ideological development is important, but it must be subordinated to practical and political work among the masses, and to the requirements of each specific stage of struggle. In the current stage, ideological development around a certain number of issues is seen as fruitful and necessary:

'Women's issues should be discussed now because the mobilisation of women has revealed many social obstacles . . . and we have to combat those who say, Do not bring up anything specific about women's issues until the national struggle is victorious . . . Organised women have the duty to build for a better future, one which will guarantee all human rights.'[33]

Structures of mobilisation

Structures through which women are mobilised are also ideological statements; and those that emerged with the PRM concretized the idea of 'organic unity' between the national and the women's movement. On the one hand, a plurality of groups continues to characterise Palestinian women's organising;[34] but on the other, there has been a definite trend towards inter-coordination and closer ties with PRM parties. Four significant forms will be focused on: the General Union of Palestinian Women (GUPW); the resistance groups; mass Women's Organisations affiliated to resistance groups; and Women's Work Committees in the Occupied Territories.

i) ***The GUPW***: Part of the structure of the PLO, the GUPW is funded and supervised by the PLO's office of Mass Unions. Like the other mass unions, the GUPW's own structure is highly centralised, designed to achieve two types of unification: laterally, through branches spread across the diaspora; and vertically, from the national Executive Committee down through country and provincial levels to the local base committees. Such centralism has a certain symbolic unifying power, but it has proved cumbersome and ill-adapted to dealing with the problem of reaching the 'ordinary' women it is supposed to mobilise.

Though nominally elected by its General Assembly, the GUPW's leading Executive Committee has up to now reflected the system predominant throughout the PLO, which guaranteed the representation on all committees of all groups in the PLO's central Executive Committee, with Fateh predominant. The most active and influential women were all members or delegates of specific resistance groups, thus turning the GUPW into an arena of inter-group conflict; this in turn partially nullified the goal of unification as well as damaging the GUPW's image at the mass level. Except in crises, PRM women cadres working in the camps competed with each other; GUPW projects were generally neglected in favour of resistance group projects.

Examination of the work programme of the GUPW reveals three broad categories of activity: i) those closely linked to informational and diplomatic struggle – attending conferences, receiving visiting delegations, issuing statements supporting national positions; ii) social concerns arising from traditional concepts of women's maternal, nurturing role – relief, visiting the wounded, caring for orphans and martyrs' families, running camp kindergartens; iii) developmental work among the women of the camps – adult literacy, vocational training, income-generating projects, health education. It was this third category that was most neglected. Programmes at the camp level were rudimentary, and frequently suspended for lack of personnel. Leading GUPW women rarely visited the camps, especially those distant from Beirut headquarters.

Several projects that were formally adopted and that could have been useful in creating a common circuit of consciousness between women – for example, a regular publication, and a library and document collection – were never put into effect. During this period of the GUPW's history, both structural and ideological obstacles impeded its development, while after 1982 it was further divided and weakened by the split within Fateh. It remains however a vehicle capable of playing a more dynamic role at a later stage.

ii) *The Resistance groups*: Second in point of time, the PRM has become the dominant framework of women's mobilisation. By now, all three leading groups (Fateh, PFLP, DFLP)[35] have a substantial number of longterm women cadres in leading positions. In the early 70s, joining a mixed political group was still a difficult step mainly confined to educated urban women; but after the Lebanese Civil War (1975/6), membership spread to the camps, marking a significant break both with the past and with other Arab women.

While it is nationalism that propels women to join PRM parties, this step also expresses an inexplicit feminism. Whereas an earlier generation of women had claimed *a* role in struggle, women who joined the PRM claim an *equal* role with men. This claim took its most extreme form right at the beginning of PRM action in Jordan, when some women insisted on taking military training, and volunteered for operations inside Israel. Change in PRM strategy after 1970 deflected women away from military into other forms of action,[36] yet every attack on the camps has brought women into defence. Fighting and martyrdom remained a persistent aspiration, exemplified by Dallal Mughrabi[37] and this young struggle front cadre who defended Chatila camp in 1985:

'I decided to stay with our comrades in the base because I believe women's role in this arena is important. She shouldn't just sweep and cook, she should fight side by side with her comrade fighters to defend the camp . . . If I had been martyred it would have achieved something big for the Palestinian cause. People would say, A girl was martyred! It would prove our role and encourage other girls.'[38]

What role and function have the resistance groups assigned women members? To some extent women's roles are gender-specific, but there has been no clear 'zoning' of women even after the formation of women's bureaux and sections. Women are found fairly evenly distributed across all sections except the military, though most are concentrated in the social sector, in information, administration and finance (women are often found entrusted with money and stores), and certain kinds of political work. Women form a major channel of communication between PRM headquarters and families in the camps. Absent from high level intergroup meetings and contacts with Lebanese parties, women cadres help build mass support for their group's 'line'. Their concentration in the social sector is based in their traditional nurturing role, but at the same time this is work with a political importance, since social projects and institutions in the camps are ways of attracting clienteles and political support. Women are also concentrated in clerical and service work (cooking, cleaning) although such jobs are often kept for widows and members' dependents.

The formation of women's bureaux by some of the groups has not led to segregation since they do not group all women members, but only those directed to work in the GUPW or mass women's organisations. Up to now there seems to have been no move towards all women members of a resistance group meeting together or raising common issues.

In terms of status, women are less represented at leadership levels than men, but the central committees of PFLP, DFLP, and PSF all have women members. As for Fateh, while there is one woman on *its* Revolutionary Council, women cadres have on the whole less influence than certain women outside the party, whose power is based on seniority, control of institutions and personal connections.

Although organised women sometimes express a sense of common situation with women in other groups, their sense of organisational belonging is too strong to allow gender solidarity scope to develop. Many factors explain this loyalty; recency of membership, pride in being part of a 'vanguard', the chance given them to work, training, travel and *'asabiyya* (group solidarity). Many camp cadres have grown up inside their organisation, graduating from scout to student section to full membership. Longterm members, those who joined in the early 70s, by now have considerable experience and status, and are treated with respect by male comrades. If there are complaints, they are aimed at the PRM as a whole rather than the leaders or men of a woman's own organisation. This example is unusual:

'Men still treat a woman, however high she reaches, as a weaker member, not basic, secondary – even though she sometimes works more than a man, in mass work, in struggle work, she comes and goes. But after all this, they still look at her with a limited perception . . . In the Marxist groups, there is an advanced outlook on women, but there is a fluctuation in leaders and comrades in their dealings with them. The responsible may have correct principles, but it depends on his mood, and in the end it's he who is the stronger.'[39]

Another set of factors besides their dispersion between PRM organisations acts to reduce women's collective weight in the PRM as a whole. These derive from the female life-cycle and obligations, which in turn are influenced by class. As will be discussed later, the PRM has had many effects on women's life-cycle, particularly in drawing out the pre-marriage stage and filling it with activities. Yet marriage remains a universal expectation. Thus women's organisational membership is stamped with a transitory quality, even though many cadres remain unmarried, or marry without dropping their work. Depending on social background, pressures on women to give up active membership after marriage are strong: in the camps these take the form of large families, harsh conditions of domestic labour, often the necessity to take salaried employment (however, women in camps can depend on kin for childcare). Women from bourgeois strata, though likely to have smaller families and more time, may yield to the pressure of the 'perfect housewife' model. Thus while women form a substantial minority of the membership of the three main resistance groups (if one discounts their military 'wings'), the majority do not stay long enough to form a permanent body capable of pressing women's issues on the leadership. At the same time, senior women cadres, as a heroic 'vanguard' enjoying respect and responsibility, may lose touch with the problems of the mass of women. It is for this reason that the formation of mass women's organisations is promising.

iii) *Mass Women's Organisations*: This type of framework evolved during the 70s in Lebanon specifically among women who want to be active but without joining a political party. The first Democratic Women's Organisation (DWO) was launched in 1978 by the DFLP after several years of mass work and careful preparation. [40] Others now exist in several parts of the dispersion. DWOs are built from the base upwards, beginning with local committees set up in streets, camp quarters and work locations. These local committees elect leading committees representing a larger region, and elections continue until they reach an administrative body at the country level (Syria, Lebanon, etc). The administrative bodies decide their activities on the basis of the needs of the community, independently of the DFLP's Central Committee and of each other. By beginning at the base and encouraging working women and housewives to get involved, DWOs are structured to avoid the GUPW's failure to activate its local committees, while its decentralisation and relative autonomy allow activities to be chosen by women members, in response to their sense of local needs and conditions.

DWO programmes include day-care centres for working women, typing and language courses, adult literacy and cultural events. In Jordan, Syria and the Occupied Territories, women's magazines are published and distributed. DWOs also mobilise women to respond to local crises, for example agitating for the release of prisoners or missing persons, defending and rebuilding the camps.

What kind of woman would join a Democratic Women's Organisation? 'She should have a basically progressive attitude to the national struggle, support the PLO, and the Palestinian state. But she doesn't have to be committed to the programme of the DFLP.'[41] Such specifications suit 'ordinary' women, those who have strong nationalist feelings, but who do not want to become identified with a political party, or do fulltime political work. Thus they should open the way for capable women without high educational levels to rise to positions of responsibility: 'There are several women in the leadership of the DWOs who were never members of the DFLP but who stood out because of their activities and patriotism.'[42]

Though linked to the DFLP through its women's bureau (which started them up, and continues to form a part of their membership), DWOs appear more autonomous than the women's 'wings' of many Middle Eastern parties. They offer women's bureau cadres a field of activity relatively free of party and male control; and at the same time, they provide an appropriate vehicle for 'ordinary' women to acquire organising experience, and help to build a politicised woman 'mass' around the vanguard minority.

iv) *The women's movement in the Occupied Territories*: The situation here differs radically from that in the neighbouring Arab countries. Since 1967, neither the GUPW or PRM have been able to work in the Occupied Territories except clandestinely. Here women have been to a large extent self-mobilised, responding in different ways to Israeli repression, the absence of a national authority, and the inadequacy of all public services. Among their responses has been the building of autonomous associations to carry out social, productive and cultural work. In a valuable paper on the development of the women's movement in the West Bank,[43] Giacaman notes how women's charitable associations filled the gap in public services under British and Jordanian rule, a function that continued after Israeli occupation in 1967. By 1976, there were more than 38 such associations in the West Bank alone, offering basic health care, nurseries, orphanages, relief and income-generating projects for needy families, and constituting practically the only institutional obstacle to the Israeli destruction of Palestinian social structure and culture. Giacaman's paper describes how, as the full extent of the Israeli occupation's destructive intentions became clear, women began to search for new frameworks and methods. Founded before the Occupation, both *In'ash al-'Usra* of Al-Bireh and the Arab Women's Union of Bethlehem set up projects aimed at helping women to earn money rather than remain aid recipients, as in the past. But both these projects remained urban-based, directed by urban women, incorporating women of other classes as clients rather than full members. What was needed, younger women felt, was 'a mass organisation directed towards the radical solution of the women's and the national problem.'[44] From their discussions emerged the first Women's Work Committee (WWC) in Ramallah in 1978. Others followed.[45] One of the first actions of the first WWC was to carry out a study of women workers in Ramallah factories.[46]

The WWCs differ from the earlier charitable associations in structure and ideology. Without formal membership or offices, they are less susceptible to Israeli or Jordanian control. They are de-centralised, allowing maximum self-direction to local village, camp and work-place committees, so that their activities are chosen on a basis of local needs rather than decided by an urban-based governing committee. They have recruited members among all sectors of women with the aim of building a mass women's movement, thus trying to go beyond the class limitations of the associations. While the older movement is guided by the 'perspective of charity or steadfastness' the WWCs aim at mobilising women in 'both the women's and the national struggle.'[47]

Those who launched the first WWC are described by Giacaman as 'active, well-educated and young bourgeois women', some of whom were 'politically committed', others 'nationalistic and socially aware'.[48] Already radical, their work among rural women had a 'feminizing' effect on them, as one of the most interesting passages in their paper relates:

'The organizers were shocked by the realization that, with existing conditions of women's lives, particularly in the villages and among the poor urban dwellers, it was impossible for them to effectively mobilise women in the national struggle. Illiteracy, overwork, poverty, economic dependence, the limited interests of women that result from all this and the general low social status were crucial stumbling blocks. It was precisely this realization of the Palestinian women's condition that precipitated the awareness for the need of women to *organise around their own problems, and for the need to adopt specific programmes aimed at the improvement of women's lot.*' (my italics – R.S.)[49]

Such an explicit feminism could hardly have been expressed within the structures of the PRM. Emerging directly from involvement in the lives of poor women, without the mediation of party goals or interests, it is a statement that clearly articulates women's issues to national struggle, and proposes autonomous action now. It points to a difference between the West Bank, where Israeli occupation has pushed the different sections of the women's movement into closer cooperation, and the diaspora situation, where women's consciousness has been stamped by PRM hegemony as well as by its internal divisions, both encouraged by diaspora conditions.

The Resistance Movement and the family sphere

I MENTIONED EARLIER the charges raised by a 'feminist tendency' within the GUPW that the resistance movement had not done enough to change social attitudes to women; and in the section on ideology, I suggested some reasons for stagnation in this sphere. This brings us to the PRM's major dilemma in relation to the family: on the one hand, the need for radical social change to expand mass mobilisation; on the other, the equally strongly felt need to preserve the cultural patrimony, of which the family and women's role in reproducing it are core elements. But the dilemma extends beyond ideology. The importance of the family was reinforced by the Uprooting: as a matrix of identity, a source of emotional support, and a vehicle of material survival. Further, all sectors of the PRM depend on families for recruits and support, especially in camps which form the only equivalent of a 'liberated zone'. These considerations have played a role in inhibiting any approach to family values that might cause negative reactions. In addition, there is a problem of the dependence of the rightwing of the PRM on Saudi Arabia and other conservative Arab governments, while some of the leftist groups have been made cautious by fear of attack from the right, and of alienating the masses. [50] Another consideration that may enter the picture is the difficulty of detaching the family issue from religion. [51] The over-riding importance attached to Muslim-Christian unity since the beginning of the Palestinian national struggle tends to repress any issue likely to arouse sectarian reactions.

Yet pragmatic developments set in motion by PRM institution-building in Lebanon have created a very different situation on the ground. At this level, inter-group competition has had some positive effects, through expanding activities for women at a speed that a unified, centralised movement would have been unable to achieve. Mass mobilisation has opened up a range of non-domestic roles for women – militant, martyr, party cadre or supporter, worker, committee member – which did not exist before. [52] Even though, up to 1982, only a minority of camp girls and women had been recruited into membership of PRM parties, resistance projects inside camps had transformed social space in a way that has emancipating effects for women. Whereas in the early 70s camps were divided into two clearly demarcated zones – homes and PRM offices – by 1982 the PRM's programmes of family support (scout and youth sect-ions, recreation clubs, clinics, workshops, training cycles) had penetrat-ed the family sphere, creating an intermediate zone where party and fam-ily intermingle. In this zone, which is politically charged without being formally structured and which no one organisation controls, women move and act and take responsibility.

The difficulty faced by the PRM in mobilising *binat* (young unmarried women) has already been referred to. Ethnographic studies tell us that a central feature of the Palestinian peasant family system was the marriage of girls before they reached social maturity. [53] This tradition was preserv-ed with only slight modifications after the Uprooting. Right up to the civil war, camp mothers who willingly went out to work kept their un-married daughters at home; it was attacks on the camps that loosened such constraints. [54] The struggle of PRM women cadres to mobilise *binat* into routine activities outside crisis was thus an arduous one, demanding patience, tact, understanding of custom and self-control. Camp girls also played their part by waging struggles with their families and by guarding themselves from gossip and scandal. Through offering *binat* other activities besides party membership, through guaranteeing their protection in its milieus, and through the respect earned by its women cadres, the PRM radically changed the phasing of the female life-cycle, first, by drawing out the period between puberty and marriage; [55] sec-ond, by filling this period with activities of varied kinds, all of which con-tribute to the formation of an independent personality and create a 'space' at a difficult phase in women's lives, when an intense nationalism is often felt as they confront the constraints of their future as women. Even if this period of activism is terminated by marriage (an institution whose sanctity and implications for women the PRM has never challeng-ed), yet its existence enhances womens position *vis-à-vis* family and future husband.

As men and women encounter each other in the intermediate zone be-tween party and family, parentally-arranged marriage is eroded in favour of consensual marriages often brokered by resistance groups. The criter-ia on which spouses are chosen shift from family background and financ-ial position towards compatibility and personal qualities (patriotism, courage, outlook, etc). Women are more likely to marry a party comrade and to put conditions concerning life after marriage (or refuse conditions put by men), and are thus more likely to continue study, work or political

activities. Such processes also modify relations between parental and fil-
ial households, with ties remaining warm and close, but losing their former authoritarianism. Young married women become freer to make decisions, for example about work or family size, through discussion with
their husbands, instead of being submitted to pressure from their husband's family to bear more children, or give up working.

However reticent the PRM has remained towards the family, it inter-
venes continuously and at many points, though in ways too diffuse to allow the term 'family policy'. In an earlier period the PRM often put
pressure on families to allow their daughters to marry *feda'yeen*, and in
cases in which a bridegroom came from outside Lebanon, his organisation would stand in place of his family as negotiator and guarantor. The
more respected PRM cadres in camps are often sought as arbitrators in
family problems and conflicts. Another way that the PRM affects the
family sphere is through family allowances: the DFLP, for example, dis-
courages polygamy by limiting allowances to one wife; Fateh on the other
hand pays for up to four wives.[56] In the DFLP, and perhaps in other
parties, there has been informal party intervention to prevent conflict or
divorce between spouses who are members. Pressure may be put on a
male comrade who does not allow his wife to work, ill-treats her, or gives
her so little help at home that she cannot carry out her party responsibilities. Though Peteet's observation that the involvement of women in the
PRM has not changed the domestic division of labour between men and
women is true in general,[57] this picture is beginning to change in the case
of marriages between party members. Here we can detect the emergence
of a new type of family, characterised by more egalitarian relations between husband and wife, and between parents and children.

Criticism of the PRM for failing to raise the question of change in family law have been raised from time to time,[58] but such voices are few.
Most consider that it is impossible to make laws without a state, and still
too early to discuss this matter. It is worth noting, however, that the
PFLP drafted a code of family regulations to be observed by its members. Because of the slight differences between Muslim and Christian
family practice referred to earlier, it would be difficult to draw up re-
forms that do not lean towads the western (Christian) nuclear family
model (for example by banning polygamy, or making divorce rights more
equal). Without research on family problems, there is no objective basis
for reform campaigns; forums are needed where women feel free to raise
such problems.

It is when we come to camp mothers and housewives that we find least
evidence of change. In another paper,[59] I have discussed this question in

terms of the class and culture gap that separated the first women cadres from camp women, as well as the overriding concern of the former with formal organisation and with gaining recruits. Camp mothers had their own strong traditions of political struggle and showed their readiness to serve the revolution in their accustomed ways;[60] but in the early 70s, most of them were illiterate, with large families. Though this never prevented them from demonstrating or defending the camps, it did make it difficult to involve them in routine activities. Camp mothers were also opposed to divisions within the PRM which they knew from experience would lead to conflict and endangering their sons. The developmental projects that would have served the housewife sector were, as we saw before, the most neglected part of the GUPW and PRM programmes. Mothers benefitted from many of the family activities carried on by the PRM in camps; kindergartens and youth clubs lightened childrearing labour; mother and child clinics increased the chances of safe pregnancy and delivery. Housewives were helped as widows and recipients of social aid, and as martyrs' mothers they received special status and respect; but rarely were they the direct targets of programmes as women.

This question of course cannot be isolated from broader political and cultural factors. On the one hand, the difficulty of the national struggle and the heavy human losses it has entailed bring out the importance of women's fertility. Consciousness of child-bearing as a form of struggle is very widespread among camp women and has not required PRM campaigns to deepen it.[61] It is their voluntary assumption of the 'demographic struggle' that makes the terms used by some PRM leaders such as the 'fertile womb' less fascist than they would otherwise be.[62]

On the other hand, the critical importance of *sumud* in the Palestinian struggle, necessitated by setbacks and loss, calls up culturally implanted images of women's ideal nature, as exemplifiers of patience, self-denial and 'giving'. Camp mothers have assumed these qualities, aiding the process through which their domestic role has been transformed into a form of political struggle, a women's *jihad*. By giving sons to the resistance and by stoically bearing their loss, mothers locate themselves at the heart of the national struggle. It is to these traditional aspects of the social construction of womanhood that we can attribute the slightness of PRM programmes for women. As a West Bank woman once told me. 'Women are the unknown soldiers of the national struggle.'

However, heroically living up to cultural expectations is only one part of camp women's behaviour and it would be distorting to over-emphasize this at the expense of their capacity for self-assertion and claiming their rights. It is on this equally strong, though culturally unendorsed tradition that we can place hope for the development of women's issues within the PRM.

Conclusion: thinking about women's issues

THIS PAPER HAS TRIED to present the historical, ideological and structural settings within which Palestinian women have thought about and acted on their situation. Such a review suggests that the protracted, difficult nature of the national struggle has contradictory effects for women, engaging large numbers of them in many forms of activism, but also suppressing the 'woman issue' and postponing its discussion to a still far-off stage. The PRM has set up structures that mobilise women and help legitimise their activism; yet its reluctance to undertake campaigns of socio-cultural change has put the burden of this struggle on women themselves. Nationalist women have thus been forced to assume the role of agents of social change, through struggle with their families and activities outside the home; yet at the same time they continue to carry the obligations imposed by woman's traditional image: sexual self-censorship, marriage, fertility, housewifely competence. Meanwhile the most active, most experienced women are dispersed in different PRM parties and are actively involved in building support for their policies on national issues. Such conditions do not easily give rise to collective discussion of or action on women's issues. Yet at the same time they do not completely negate them. The intractability of the national struggle also gives more time for women to gain organising skills. It brings large numbers of women into the political arena and creates a 'field' of action for PRM women cadres, one in which they meet at close quarters the socio-cultural obstacles that limit other women's participation. The definition of women's issues in this context becomes not so much permissable as necessary:

'In each stage of our struggle we must do everything we can to allow the greatest number of women to participate in struggle. There are many issues and traditions that we have to face directly. We can't just say, No, this is part of our tradition, we must stop at this point.'[63]

The conditions for further work on women's issues – defining, raising and setting up programmes directed towards them – now appear to exist in certain sectors of the resistance movement and in the Occupied Territories. We would not expect instant agreement on what women's issues are, nor on which are priorities. In the West Bank it seems that women are ready to 'organise around their own problems', whereas within the PRM context, women's issues are much more closely linked to national and community needs. DWOs focus on *social* issues:

' . . . not women's issues in the sense that a feminist would use the term, but important matters that affect women, such as lack of water, prisoners, the destruction of camps. Other issues that DWOs are said to be taking up are: the rights of working women, childcare centres, and campaigns against young age of girls at marriage. These are seen as justified because "they are not women's slogans only but are in the service of our whole society." ' [64]

An obvious danger of linking definitions of women's issues so tightly to the national struggle is, to paraphrase Giacaman, that if Palestinian aspirations to nationhood are fulfilled, women may lose the incentive and justification for organisation. One should expect that after such a long and bitter struggle, there will be a reaction that will de-mobilise many women. However, there are good reasons why such a reaction should not last and should not lead to a by now familiar pattern of an official women's union tied to state or ruling party, repression of human rights and a re-domestication of women. Palestinian women have been organising for 70 years, and have fully shared with men in constructing a 'public sphere' through which Palestinian peoplehood is expressed today. It is not inconceivable that there should be attempts to dislodge them, but the wide reach of women's mobilisation guarantees resistance:

'It's not a few elitist individuals experimenting, we have a broad base of women. When we have to deal with a new challenge, these women will be up to it.' [65]

Notes

1 K. Jayawardena, *Feminism and Nationalism in the Third World* (London: Zed Books Ltd., 1986)
2 'The women's movement in many countries of Asia achieved political and legal equality with men at the juridical level, but failed to make any impression on women's subordination within the patriarchal structure of family and society.' Jayawardena, op cit, p24.
3 See as examples two PLO booklets: *The Struggle of Palestinian Women* (Beirut: Palestine Research Centre, 1975); and *The Women's Role in the Palestine National*

Struggle (Beirut: Department of Information, nd).

4 Political women's groups appeared in Jerusalem in 1919 and 1921; in Nablus in 1921; in Haifa in 1928. These local unions joined in the national Arab Women's Association launched in 1929. See M. Mogannam, *The Arab Woman and the Palestine Problem* (London: Joseph, 1937) p62; also L. Jammal *Contributions by Palestinian Women to the National Struggle for Liberation* (Washington: Middle East Public Relations, 1985) pp12-16. According to Mogannam, Jaffa women organised even earlier, before World War 1.

5 When Allenby visited Jerusalem in 1932, the AWA organised a dramatic protest demonstration, in which a Christian member spoke from the pulpit of the Mosque of Omar, and a Muslim member from the Church of the Holy Sepulchre. The AWA was also the first national institution to publicize the plight of the *fellahin*. (Mogannam p97 seq; p83).

6 See Jayawardena, op cit, chapters on Egypt, Turkey and Iran. She notes: 'The proliferation of women's journals and of women who wrote on various issues was striking: prior to 1914 there were 15 Arabic women's magazines, many of which were edited by Syrian Christian women.' (p52) Mogannam, op cit, has a section on women's movements in Syria and Lebanon, pp63-6.

7 Mogannam, op cit, p249-257.

8 Ibid, p69, gives a detailed account of the Arab Women's Congress held in Jerusalem in October 1929, which formed an Executive Committee, and branches in urban centres throughout Palestine. Named at this stage the Arab Women's Association, it later on became a member of the League of Arab Women's Unions, and changed its name to Palestine Arab Women's Union.

9 Eg K. Abu Ali, *Muqaddima hawl waqi' al-mar' a al-filastiniyya wa tajribatuha fi al-thawra* (Beirut: GUPW, 1975); and R. Gaicaman, *Palestinian Women and Development in the Occupied West Bank* (Birzeit University, mimeo, 26pp, nd).

10 A.W. Kayyali, *Palestine, A Modern History* (London: Croom Helm, nd); see especially pp171-3 and p192. In a footnote on p185, Kayyali cites a report by the British High Commissioner after a visit from a delegation of women, that 'they displayed more courage and determination than their notable menfolk.'

11 See L. Sweet, 'The women of 'Ain ad-Dayr', *Anthropological Quarterly*, vol 40, 1967.

12 The range of women's actions is remarkable: demonstrations, meeting with Mandate officials, statements and memoranda, fund-raising, support for martyrs' families, visiting prisoners, and setting up girls' schools, clinics and orphanages. See Mogannam pp55-63, and Jammal pp12-20. For a comprehensive list of women's organisations with dates and aims, see Y. Haddad, 'Palestinian Women' in K. Nakhleh and E. Zureik eds, *The Sociology of the Palestinians*, (London: Croom Helm, 1980) p167.

13 Ruqeyya Huri, AWA leader, discusses this question in R. Sayigh, 'Femmes palestiniennes: une histoire en quête d'historiens' in *Revue d'Etudes Palestiniennes* no 23, printemps 1987.

14 Meeting with Zuleikha Shihabi, Jerusalem, May 1980.

15 Interview with Ruqeyya Huri, Beirut, January 1981.

16 Interview with Natiel Mogannam, Washington, August 1985.

17 Inverview with Wadi'a Khartabil, Beirut, March 1982.

18 See Jammal pp21-24. Giacaman lists 38 women's associations in the West Bank alone, several of which date from this period. For a portrait of an individual woman 'helper' see E. Said, *After the Last Sky* (London: Faber and Faber, 1986).

19 Abu Ali, op cit, cites the anti-Baghdad pact demonstration in Amman in which a Palestinian woman member of the Communist Party, Raja' Abu Ammasheh, was killed. See also Leila Khaled's autobiography, *My People Shall Live* (London: Hodder and Stoughton, 1973).

20 See R. Sayigh 'Femmes palestiniennes . . . '

21 *Ghourba* is not just exile, but gives the sense of being among strangers.

22 Women in camps queued for UNRWA rations and worked in manual and domestic labour to save their husbands from humiliation.

23 For descriptions from this period, see J. Peteet in R. Sayigh and J. Peteet 'Between Two Fires: Palestinian Women in Lebanon', R. Ridd and H. Callaway eds, *Caught Up in Conflict* (Basingstoke: Macmillan Education, 1986) pp111-2.

24 The main sources are: i) interviews with organised women in Lebanon before and after 1982; ii) on-going fieldwork in Chatila camp. I am particularly indebted to V.N., member of the DFLP since 1973, with whom I had two long interviews in January 1988.

25 Women's membership in resistance groups shows some interesting differences from men's. Women may drop out of political activity but usually remain in the network of their organisation. I know of no cases of switching from one to another. Men seldom leave the PRM to return to civilian life, but they often move from one organisation to another.

26 For a more detailed discussion of this question, see R. Sayigh, 'Palestinian Women and Politics in Lebanon', paper for the symposium on 'Women and Arab Society, Old Boundaries, New Frontiers,' Georgetown University, Washington DC, April 1986. (in publication)

27 Several Palestinian social institutions in Lebanon were launched and directed by women: *In'ash al-Mukhayem* (1968); the Ghassan Kanafani Cultural Association; Najdeh Assocation. *Beit Atfal al-Sumud*, orginally set up by the GUPW as a home for Tel al-Za'ter orphans, is now an autonomous institution with a range of social care activities.

28 Abu Ali, op cit. A summary is given in R. Sayigh in 'Women in Struggle' *Third World Quarterly* vol 5 no 4, Oct 1983.

29 Early in 1974 the Fateh/PLO leadership adopted the goal of a state in any part of Palestine that could be liberated. The GUPW rebelled against this position, and as a result were 'frozen' for six months.

30 Interview with J.H. (Fateh) May 1982.

31 N. Shafiq, 'Maudo'at hawl nidal al-mar'a', *Shu'oon Filastiniyya* no 62, 1977.

32 See 'PFLP marks Womens Day', PFLP Bulletin no 61, April 1982, for Habash's position. Habash often addresses the 'woman issue' in his speeches, as well as in a booklet, *Hawl taharrur al-mar'a*, Beirut, nd.

33 Interview with V.N. (DFLP), January 1988.

34 Pluralism is expressed in the number of autonomous social associations; also in the existence in Israel of women's political groups, such as the Democratic Women's League, which do not come under the PLO umbrella.

35 Few other resistance groups have a corps of women members, except for the small Marxist Palestine Struggle Front. When other groups need a woman representative on a committee, they tend to recruit members' wives.

36 There was no sudden decision to withdraw women from 'military work'; light arms training continued in Lebanon, PFLP hijackings continued for a while, and some attempts were made to form a women's battalion. But the PRM leadership gradually stopped giving support.

37 Dallal Mughrabi was a Sabra girl who managed to remain in a Fateh fighting unit after women's participation was discouraged. She was killed leading a sea-borne attack against Israel in March 1978.

38 Interview with 'Samar' (PSF), October 1986.

39 Interview with J.H. (PSF), March 1986.

40 In 1985, the PFLP launched a mass women's organisation in Damascus. The following year a sister WO was founded in the USA.

41 Interview with V.N. (DFLP), January 1988.

42 Ibid.

43 Giacaman, op cit. As its title indicates, Giacaman's study is limited to the West Bank. For voices of women in Gaza and information on organising there, see P. Cossali and C. Robson, *Stateless in Gaza* (London: Zed Books, 1986).

44 Giacaman, op cit, p15.

45 Other Women's Work Committees have been formed, and all are now said to be associated with resistance groups. Information given here only covers the first WWC.

46 Lajnet al-amal al-nissa'i, *Hawla awda' al-mar'a al-filastiniyya fi al-manatiq al-muhtalla: dirasa maydaniyya*, Ramallah-al-Bireh, 1980.

47 Giacaman, op cit, p19.

48 Ibid, p16.

49 Ibid, p21.

50 A resident of Chatila told me of an incident in the early '70s when women in an office of a leftist group were observed 'in a state of undress'. Immediately all camp families withdraw their daughers from PRM activities. V.N. reported another (or possibly another version of the same) incident, saying that a woman's carelessness or showing off had given rise to a gossip campaign against the DFLP.

51 Differences between Muslim and Christian family practice tend to become accentuated in conditions of 'modernisation'. In Palestine, there was a tradition of symbiosis. In some Christian families women were veiled out of respect for Muslim neighbours. See T. Canaan, 'Unwritten Laws Affecting the Arab Woman of Palestine' *Journal of the Palestine Oriental Society* vol 11, 1931.

52 See R. Sayigh and J. Peteet, op cit. This section owes much to Peteet's fieldwork. See her *Women and National Politics: The Palestinian Case*. 1985. PhD dissertation. Wayne State Unversity, Michigan; also 'Women and National Politics in the Middle East' in B. Berberoglu ed. *The Middle East in Crisis: Class Struggles, the National Question, the State and the Revolution* (forthcoming 1988 from Zed Books).

53 The best source is H. Granqvist, *Marriage Conditions in a Palestinian Village* (Helsinki: Societas Scientarium Fennica, vol 1 1931, vol 2 1935).

54 This quotation from a Tel al-Za'ter girl is illuminating; 'During the battle for the camp I worked in the clinic and the bakery along with many other young women. Before that most girls weren't allowed to work in the resistance clinics . . . But after the battle of Tel al-Za'ter, no mother would prevent her daughter from going out. On the contrary, she would tell her to go out and work to help her people.' In Sayigh and Peteet, op cit, p113.

55 Other factors also contributed: educations subsidies, rising employment, demands for educated brides, etc.

56 Polygamy rates among Palestinians are low. But cases arose when PRM cadres came to Lebanon from other areas, sometimes leaving a wife behind, and taking a second wife in Lebanon.

57 See the interview with a Fateh cadre, Jihan Helou, in *PFLP Bulletin* no 61, April 1982, p32.

58 See Peteet, op cit.

59 R. Sayigh, 'Palestinian Women and Politics in Lebanon'

60 For a good description of such a woman in Chatila, see Mahjoub Omar, 'Les gens et le siège', *Revue d'Etudes Palestiniennes* no 7, printemps 1983, pp98-9.

61 See I. Bendt and J. Downing, *We Shall Return: Women of Palestine* (London: Zed Press, 1980). There is a particularly good discussion between women about family size in the chapter 'Having Only Two Children Ought to be Forbidden'.

62 Nevertheless this terminology has been fiercely criticised in *al-Hadaf* (PFLP): 'Why do some of the leaders . . . continue to use the most backward feudal language, such as "the woman procreator", or "the Palestinian womb" or the "fertile wombs"?' Quoted by N. Abdo-Zubi, *Family, Women and Social Change in the Middle East* (Toronto: Canadian Scholars Press, 1987), p46.

63 Interview with V.N. (DFLP), January 1988.

64 Ibid.

65 Ibid.

PALESTINIAN WOMEN IN THE OCCUPIED TERRITORIES

An Interview with Laila al-Hamdani

*Q. Perhaps we could start by talking about the role of women in the Palestinian national movement in the occupied territories, and especially about their role in the **intifada**.*

A. On the more general point, I will be very brief. Women have been involved in the national struggle since the beginning of the 'Palestine problem'. They have been active since as early as the 1920s, although until the revolution of 1936, this was confined to urban women who had the opportunity to receive education or who were related in some way to men active in political life, the elite. Rural women did not participate in political life because rural men also did not. In the uprisings of 1921, 1923, 1929 and 1933, women had little opportunity to take part with rural men. The 1936-1939 revolt was the first time that Palestinian women actually went into the mountains smuggling arms or carrying food or water into battlefields. Although the role of women was rather traditionalist in this form, my research has shown that there were women who took up arms just like the men. Women carried the economic burden during the period when the men were in the mountains. It is estimated that some 10,000 men took part in the revolution, out of a total population of less than one million. The economic burden that this entailed has often been ignored.

At this time, urban women were organising strikes, providing aid to prisoners' families, holding conferences and issuing leaflets which were noticeably more radical than those of male organisations. This was because the men still hoped to be able to persuade the British to renounce their support for Zionism and had not developed a full critique of the mandate system as a whole. With the exile of 1948, women in different areas played different roles which were mainly economic, unlike in the rest of the Arab world where women were more integrated into the national struggle. This point is often ignored. This does not mean that Palestinian women lacked consciousness, but with the creation of 650,000 Palestinian refugees and the economic burden this brought, Palestinian women began going out to work, selling vegetables, cleaning houses – a step towards the proletarianisation of peasant women. Economic life for the refugee women was transformed and this change played a role in developing women's independence and consciousness in a political, rather than feminist sense.

In the territories occupied in 1967, women were involved in organising before the occupation but, like the men, they tended to favour the wider Arab ideologies like Baathism and Pan-Arabism. Being under backward Jordanian rule did not help West Bank women to advance politically. In this period women in the West Bank were generally confined to working in charitable organisations and other traditional female roles. After '67, active women gravitated towards the various PLO factions which put no particular emphasis on women's organisations. Most Palestinian women say 'Let's solve our national struggle first and then talk about our situation as women'. Rightly or wrongly, this has been the state of play for the last 21 years. This said, women have played a role within the organisations, which is important for them as women. People like Rosemary Sayegh have tended to ignore that for an Arab woman to be in a political organisation necessarily means breaking down barriers, being more self aware than women who are not involved in politics. If I might generalise, in conventional society it is possible for man to know about Marxism and to be heavily politically involved but to still confine his wife or his daughter to the house. For a woman to be politicised, she must have fought and she cannot retreat because traditional society will no longer accept her. The only path open to her is to become more revolutionary. This is not because Palestinian women are better than men but because they have no choice.

Q. Are you talking only about urban women now?

A. No. Between 1948 and 1967, it was urban women who worked in charitable societies while rural women worked on the land and in the house. This said, rural women are more economically independent and have more say in the household because they share in production. They do not wear the veil and are more open in their relations with men. From 1967, more rural women became involved. When I was in prison in 1975, almost half the women there were rural. Now rural women are in the majority.

This brings us to the *intifada* and to the fact that most tasks are being carried out by women.

Q. Let me interrupt for a moment. What proportion of women were involved with the PLO before the **intifada***?*

A. The best I can say is that it was a growing number.

Q. But are we talking about the PLO as a mass movement or as a small organisation with mass support?

A. Until the *intifada*, thousands of people were enrolled within the PLO, with even greater support outside the organisation. Now, a large percentage of politically active men and women are involved with PLO organisations. Support for the PLO in rural and urban areas, in the 1948 and the 1967 territories, is massive.

To return to the *intifada*, the long history of women's involvement and growth in consciousness has not developed into feminism but has produced an increasingly active female role. Without the women, it is debatable whether the *intifada* would have continued for the last ten months. Women's involvement in the *intifada* is on two levels: mass participation and the organisational level. The women's organisations which have developed over the past 20 years are now geared towards organising for the *intifada*. The popular committees, for example, are dominated by women. They are active in the medical relief committees which gather information about people's blood groups and pass the information on to the hospitals. The health committees supervise sanitation to prevent epidemics and check the water in the wells because the Israelis are cutting off supplies of piped water. Women form the majority in the education committees which organise alternative studies in houses to substitute for the schools which the Israelis have closed down. The aid committees go to areas which are under curfew or siege and distribute food, money and moral support. The Israelis have difficulty in dealing with these committees because they involve women, not only those who are involved in political groups or women's organisations but also other women.

Q. Does this mean that sexual segregation has been broken down during the **intifada***?*

A. Yes, and this is even clearer on the mass level. In towns, villages and refugee camps, women guard their neighbourhoods with knives and clubs, staying awake for three or four nights at a time. Women are at the front of demonstrations, many of which are comprised only of women. Women who are not in the popular committees nonetheless play a role in social organisation. One woman told me how she and her friends make sure that no-one goes hungry during a curfew, even if it means clambering from roof to roof. Women are not telling their children to stay indoors but are saying: 'Don't forget to take an onion with you' to counteract the teargas.

A neighbour of ours has four children, the oldest five years old. A year ago she would tell her children to play inside because she is a teacher and, in her view, children are not supposed to play in the streets. Now she goes out with a camera to photograph her children playing at making roadblocks! This may not sound like much but it is important because it shows she is proud of her children associating with the *intifada* and also because it is dangerous to take photographs – if the Israelis saw them, they might arrest her husband or beat the children. There are many examples, like all the houses which open their doors to shelter boys or men who need to hide. Women are protecting men from being arrested or shot. A woman in Toubas was shot dead shielding a boy with her own body. This was the second time she had stood between someone and Israeli bullets. I interviewed a woman who intervened when troops were about to shoot a young man. 'Is he your son?' they asked her. She said, 'No.' 'Is he your husband?' 'No.' 'Is he your brother?' 'No'. 'So why do you want me to shoot you instead of him?' She did not need to answer. Women are moving away from being family oriented towards a more nationalist orientation. Another woman went to picket a prison and was asked which prisoner was her son. She replied that all the children of Palestine were hers. Perhaps it is premature to discuss the impact of the *intifada* on the role of women, but Palestinian women in the occupied territories are practising feminism, not discussing it. It will be very difficult for men to say to the women, 'Now go back home!' Many women can say, 'But I have done so much more than you.' This is all the more true with so many men having been detained. Women are active in every field, there is no sexual division.

Q. Do you mean that women do everything but men's roles are still defined?

A. Yes, that's right. Women are accepting the double burden of providing aid and relief, and going onto the streets.

Q. Are we talking about the development of a whole new life style or is it just women who were previously politicised who are active in the committees? Has family life in general changed?

A. A large number of men of the occupied territories are oppressed (as migrant workers) in Israel, humiliated, treated like dogs. When they get home they often take their wounded pride out on their wives and children. With the *intifada*, men have begun to regain their pride and things are changing on two levels; firstly, they are less humiliated and bitter and secondly, their wives are not sitting at home waiting perhaps to be beaten up. While the husband has been working, she may have been at a demonstration or gathering stones or involved in some other action.

When I was last in Palestine, I went out on a massive demonstration and there I met my brother and my sister-in-law. She had left her child at home so she could come on the demonstration. She felt she could not stay at home and simply watch. My mother was dying to go to the demonstration but had to stay and look after the baby.

Q. So the older women are taking on that burden.

A. Not necessarily. That's not the end of the story. My sister-in-law later returned to the house to release my mother. If my mother had not been around, my sister-in-law would have gone to the demonstration with the baby. But my father has never been politicised and he tried to justify to us why he had not gone on the demonstration, by saying that his leg hurt and so on. He has never felt the need to do this before but – and this is the point – my father felt ashamed.

Q. Presumably this sort of social pressure is similar to that which operates against people who have been collaborating with the Israelis.

A. Yes, although, of course, my father was never a collaborator.

Q. So there has been a shift in the power relationship between men and women.

A. Yes, but it is not explicit. My mother does not say to my father, 'Go to the demonstration.' But neither does my father say to her, 'Don't go'. He cannot, because everyone is on the streets.

Q. What about child care? Are women dividing it amongst themselves?

A. Yes.

Q. Is this done along generational lines?

A. Well, certainly older women who cannot go onto the streets play a larger role and that seems natural enough. At the same time, I have seen elderly women take to the streets.

Q. Do religious norms play a role in the relationship between men and women in the **intifada***?*

A. I have to admit that people have seemed more religious since the *intifada* began but this has not prevented even those women who are veiled from going on demonstrations alongside men. Let me just say this much about Islam in Palestine. In the 50s and 60s, the Palestinians turned to different political groups, the Baathists, the Nasserites. They all proved to be failures. So people have turned back to religion. In a Muslim society it is easier to turn to Islam than to Marxism. The Iranian revolution encouraged this.

Q. Has this affected women's organisations?

A. No, it hasn't. There are some veiled women in the political organisations, but in general they are involved with religious organisations, not the PLO groups. But let me say something else. Women are actually feeling that they are stronger than men. For example, an Israeli patrol stopped in front of our house and took away a man's identity card, saying they would return it if he removed a Palestinian flag that was flying from a high position. Suddenly, five women arrive on the scene, march down the street and say, 'Did you give them your ID card, you fool?' 'Yes', he says. They push him away, follow the patrol and bring back his card. These were not educated women from the elite, but simple women.

Q. Is this true of the Gaza Strip as well as the West Bank or are there differences?

A. Both are occupied, both have settlements and both are oppressed. What makes Gaza a more difficult situation is the higher population density, the more extreme poverty and lack of access to the bridges [into Jordan]. Educational standards are also lower, most schools being UNRWA schools. These factors have made the Gaza Strip a more fertile breeding ground for religion, so many Gazan women are religious and wear the veil. But often this religiosity is combined with a fighting spirit that makes many of the women there really tough. But I do not want to separate the religious groups from the framework of national struggle. 'Islamic Jihad' is part of the PLO inasmuch as it is one of the five groups in the leadership of the uprising. It is working within the nationalist movement and cannot have a purely religious platform.

I want to conclude by stressing a couple of points. Firstly, the involvement of women in the national struggle has affected the position of women in the social strata and in the family. The process has been slow but that has made it stronger and it will not collapse when we have our country. Women will not be pushed back as they were in Algeria. Feminism has been a process which has developed without discussion within the community of Palestinian women. I cannot really talk much about the future but I think there will be more women's organisations. I also think we will have more women playing a prominent role in the national struggle and in our liberated country. Secondly, I believe that the *intifada* would not have continued this long without the participation of women, be they women who see their children gunned down, women who work in the popular committees or women who go out into the streets.

Khamsin

A publication forum of revolutionary socialists of the Middle East.

Editorial Group: Haim Bresheeth, Hagit Borer, Ben Cashdan, Alain Hertzmann, Moshe Machover, Sonia al-Nimr, Haim Scortariu, Toby Shelley, Nira Yuval-Davis.

Articles and editorial correspondence: send to *Khamsin*, BM Khamsin, London WC1N 3XX, UK. Authors are asked to send in two copies of their typescript, typed on A4 sheets (297mm × 210mm) with broad margins and not more than thirty lines per page, accompanied (if possible) by a copy on computer disk.

Previous publications in this series:
- *1-4* published in French by Maspero, out of print.
- *5* **Oriental Jewry**.
- *6* **Women in the Arab World**, small number available to subscribers.
- *7* **Communist Parties of the Middle East**.
- *8* **Politics of Religion in the Middle East**.
- *9* **Politics of Religion/Capitalism in Egypt**.
- *10* **Israel and its War in Lebanon**.
- *11* **Modern Turkey: Development and Crisis**.
- *12* **The Gulf War/Arab Nationalism and the Palestinian Struggle**.
- *13* **Women in the Middle East**.

☐ **Previous publications** are available from bookshops or direct from *Khamsin*.

☐ **Bookshop orders** and sales enquiries to Zed Books, 57 Caledonian Road, London N1, UK. Telephone 01-837 4014/0384.

Khamsin Bulletin
Khamsin now publishes a bi-monthly bulletin incorporating topical material such as analysis and comment on current events in the Middle East, book reviews, documents, and ongoing discussions of socialist perspectives. Readers contributions are welcome.

☐ **Bulletin subscription** rate per six issues: UK £5, overseas £6.50 (surface mail). For overseas airmail rates please enquire. Available direct from *Khamsin*, BM Khamsin, London WC1N 3XX.